THE SHAAR PRESS

THE JUDAICA IMPRINT
FOR THOUGHTFUL PEOPLE

Inside
Thei

THE
SHAAR
PRESS

RABBI NACHMAN SELTZER

Homes

**A young man's warm
and personal encounters
with the world
of Torah greatness**

Meet over 20 Torah personalities up close

Published by **SHAAR PRESS**
Distributed by MESORAH PUBLICATIONS, LTD.
4401 Second Avenue / Brooklyn, N.Y 11232 / (718) 921-9000

Distributed in Israel by SIFRIATI / A. GITLER
Moshav Magshimim / Israel

Distributed in Europe by LEHMANNS
Unit E, Viking Business Park, Rolling Mill Road / Jarrow, Tyne and Wear, NE32 3DP/ England

Distributed in Australia and New Zealand by GOLDS WORLD OF JUDAICA
3-13 William Street / Balaclava, Melbourne 3183 / Victoria Australia

Distributed in South Africa by KOLLEL BOOKSHOP
Northfield Centre / 17 Northfield Avenue / Glenhazel 2192, Johannesburg, South Africa

ISBN 10: 1-4226-1544-8 / ISBN 13: 978-1-4226-1544-7

Printed in the United States of America by Noble Book Press Corp.
Custom bound by Sefercraft, Inc. / 4401 Second Avenue / Brooklyn N.Y. 11232

To the holy leaders

of the past generation —

those who still lead us today

and those who have passed on —

for holding the torch

and showing us the way.

Contents

The First Introduction

by Rabbi Nachman Seltzer

There are many *tzaddikim* living in Eretz Yisrael in general and in the city of Yerushalayim in particular. Many of them have become famous for their *berachos*, *tzidkus*, and exalted way of life. Others have managed to slip beneath the radar, successfully avoiding the limelight and endless crowds.

It's difficult to imagine that in a day and age when the media is so very pervasive and invasive that there could possibly be people of such precious greatness still remaining relatively unknown to the outside world. Yet this is the reality. Yes, there are many *tzaddikim* who are known to all and visited by hundreds and thousands of people on a weekly basis. There are other men of stature, however, who have opted to remain anonymous, immersed solely in their world of Torah and *yiras Shamayim*. *Tzaddikim* like Rav Yitzchok Nosson Kupershtok, *zt"l*, and Rav Zundel Kroizer, *zt"l*, who, while during their lifetimes were familiar to the citizens of Meah Shearim as human angels, were content to live out their days in the web of tiny streets and alleyways of the enclaves of Batei Ungarin and Batei Broide. And there were, and still are, many more people like them. Together, these men of greatness, both known and unknown, make up an unofficial "sacred society." Having attended the same yeshivos and studied at the tables of the same scholars, they were childhood friends and in many cases related to one another through marriage.

This book gives us a vivid look at these men, as seen through an "insider's" eyes. It tells us about Rav Chaim Kanievsky, *shlita*, and his Rebbetzin, *a"h*, and Rav Sraya Diblitzky, *shlita*. We'll read about Rav Asher Arieli, *shlita*, and Rav Dovid Barkin, *zt"l*. We will draw closer to the glowing fire of *tzaddikim* like Rav Refael Levin, *zt"l*, and Rav Yitzchok Zilber, *zt"l*.

How does one get to encounter greatness, both revealed and hidden, in a truly personal way? How does a person become part and parcel of these lives? How does he build a relationship with men like Rav Nachman Dubinki, *zt"l*, Rav Mordechai Aharon Scheinberger, *shlita*, and even Rav Mordechai Gifter, *zt"l* (who lived in America)?

For the answer to those questions, you can refer to an old friend of mine, Reb Binyomin. He is a man who possesses a rare ability, an uncanny knack of meeting a *tzaddik* and developing a relationship with him. Reb Binyomin has written *sefarim* in conjunction with Rav Chaim Kanievsky and was asked by the Kupershtok family to eulogize Rav Yitzchok Nosson Kupershtok at his *levayah*. Much of the royalty of the Torah world calls him affectionately by his first name. The stories and anecdotes related here are taken from his encounters with these men of distinction.

When Reb Binyomin meets a *tzaddik*, he doesn't look at him from the perspective of "What can I get from this person?" On the contrary, Reb Binyomin asks himself, *What can I do for the tzaddik I have just met?*

Sometimes (but not always) he manages to find something he can do. At other times, their relationship develops through different means. But somehow, this young man consistently connects to the *gedolim* that he meets. There is a unique element within him that binds his *neshamah* to that of the *tzaddikim* he so respects. In essence, this trait is the secret of his success and his close connection to so many of the "sacred society": both members hidden and known. He is beloved by them and vice versa.

With many of the society's members having passed away, or having grown very old, he feels the time has arrived to share the stories, special traits, and *hanhagos* of a generation of *tzaddikim* who are nothing short of legendary: stories that he personally witnessed.

It has been an honor to work together with my dear friend Reb Binyomin on this project. May the *Ribbono shel Olam* continue to set his footsteps in the right direction, as Reb Binyomin continues leading his fellow members of *Klal Yisrael* into the most precious doorways of the nation.

The Second Introduction

by Reb Binyomin

Throughout this book, the reader will come across stories about *emunas chachamim*, the power of will, and *hashgachah pratis*. The truth is that I view *hashgachah pratis* as having led to the writing of this book in the first place.

As the reader will see, *Inside Their Homes* is a compilation of stories that took place over a 20-year period. Often while bringing others to meet *gedolim*, I have shared some of these stories in order to provide a sense of whom they were about to meet and what to expect or not to expect.

Almost inevitably the reaction was "That's unbelievable! You must write a book," or something of that sort. Yet it never actually occurred to me to put anything in writing; I'm not a writer after all, and who has time for such a thing? I was warned that over the years precious incidents would be forgotten, but even that didn't give me the motivation to sit down and write. I had also been approached by several authors over the years, but I never felt any ambition to work on such a project.

One day I overheard a conversation between my wife and a client of hers: an intelligent and well-read woman who was praising the writing skills of one Rabbi Nachman Seltzer. At that time I hadn't known that Rabbi Seltzer is the best-selling author of many Jewish literary classics, since I do not read English books in general and find myself busy enough with the thousands of *sefarim* that I own. I had been a classmate and friend of his back in the second and third grade in Torah Vodaath elementary school, but we had not crossed paths in the more than 20 years since then. I was happy to hear about his success, but thought no further of the matter.

By this time, both of us were busy raising families in Ramat Beit Shemesh, and it was only a question of time before we would bump into each other. After several minutes of conversation and catching up, it became clear that between all the personal experiences and stories that I have to tell and Rabbi Seltzer's literary success, there was a reason for this reunion. Yet our collaboration didn't happen then.

At the time of our original encounter, I was working on a *sefer* with Rav Chaim Kanievsky, and that was my top priority, to the exclusion of everything else. I told my old friend that I would consider the matter, but I always found myself busy with other things... and suddenly three years had gone by since that meeting and nothing had happened. We bumped into each other a few more times, shared a quick hello, but never discussed the book idea again.

◆ ◆ ◆

One Friday afternoon I was thinking about my conversation with Rabbi Seltzer, and it occurred to me: *Who knows if my whole relationship with him so many years before was arranged in Shamayim only to pave the way for us to get back together years later to produce a very unique book that could provide all manner of chizuk for the Torah world?*

The following Sunday I attended a wedding where I "happened" to meet Rabbi Seltzer on the dance floor. He reminded me of our previous book-related conversation. Incredible! On Friday I had been thinking about this for no apparent reason, and here it was, a mere two days later, and he had brought it up! Ten minutes later we were outside, and the idea of the book had become a reality. I could not help feeling that this was a clear sign from Heaven that the time was ripe to finally collaborate on this book.

And, indeed, within days we were meeting once a week to work on the book full force.

The majority of the stories in this book were experienced by myself firsthand. Rabbi Seltzer did a great job adding background and flavor to the manuscript. The facts in every story were carefully preserved and are as accurate as my memory was able to recall. Small, unimportant details and names were sometimes changed in order to protect the privacy of people involved. (Names that have been changed are marked with an asterisk.)

Even though many people involved with this book asked me to use my full name, after a lot of thought I chose not to include my family name. One of the many lessons I have learned from the *gedolim* I have merited to meet is to avoid standing out, to stay out of the spotlight and not look for publicity, and though I feel my encounters with *gedolim* are important to share, my identity is not vital, and I prefer to keep out of the limelight this way.

One vital disclaimer: If a *bachur* reading this book thinks he's going to start running around to *gedolim* all the time, he should know that none of the relationships described in this book came about at the expense of my regular *sedarim* in yeshivah. None of them. Either they took place during *bein hazemanim*, *bein hasedarim*, on Shabbos, or on *motza'ei Shabbos*, — so they didn't detract from my learning in yeshivah. My determination not to sacrifice any part of my normal learning obligations made developing connections with the *gedolim* much more difficult for me. But it was worth it. Well worth it.

It is my fervent hope that this book will be *mechazeik* people in many different ways and that the numerous lessons to be gleaned from the beautiful *tzaddikim* whose stories grace these pages will inspire the readers.

Enjoy your reading.

Encounters with

Rav Mordechai Gifter זצ"ל

Rav Dovid Barkin זצ"ל

Rav Gifter and Reb Binyomin sharing a special moment

The quintessential American gadol, Rav Mordechai Gifter, was an anomaly in the yeshivah world. Whereas the majority of America's roshei yeshivah in his day were European born, here was a man who had been raised on baseball, apple pie, and the creature comforts of America. And yet a gadol emerged who would delight the Torah world with his razor-sharp insights into both people and learning, while educating hundreds of talmidim in the methodology that the cream of the European yeshivos had to offer.

Rav Mordechai Gifter will forever be remembered as the legendary Rosh Yeshivah of Telshe.

Rav Mordechai Gifter and Rav Dovid Barkin

Part A

I had recently arrived in Eretz Yisrael, and navigating Yerushalayim's narrow streets was still a new experience for me. As I walked from the *beis medrash* to my apartment, I reflected on the road that had led me to Eretz Yisrael and the incredible people I had met along the way. One such individual was HaRav Mordechai Gifter. The city of Yerushalayim receded into the distance as my mind and memory took me back a few years, to the unique world of Telshe...

◆ ◆ ◆

I had been learning in Rav Shmuel Miller's yeshivah, Beis Yisrael, when my *chavrusa* decided that it was time for me to move on. He convinced me to consider the world-famous Telshe Yeshivah in Cleveland as an alternative. The idea excited me, especially considering the fact that my grandfather was an alumnus of the original European Telshe. It seemed only natural to me that I continue *shteiging* in such an environment.

When word got around that I was thinking of learning in Telshe, there were many naysayers who attempted to change my mind. "Many *bachurim* who go to Telshe without a *chevrah* don't end up lasting there," they warned me.

"It's an extremely challenging regimen," others said in ominous tones that conveyed the feeling that I was not up to the fight.

This was going to be a tough call. At Rav Shmuel Miller's yeshivah I was considered one of the top *bachurim:* a *chavrusa* of the *Rosh Yeshivah, gabbai* of the *beis medrash,* and the one in charge of the library. I had been assigned many roles and tasks and was carrying them out with alacrity, authority, and complete trust from the administration.

But it wasn't only that. Rav Shmuel's student body was a small one: about 20 or 30 students plus a *kollel* of young married men who sincerely cared about the *bachurim.* It was a very personal kind of place, and I had made great strides in my learning there. Telshe was exactly the opposite.

It was no wonder that the idea of moving on to Telshe was met with firm opposition by almost everyone I knew in the yeshivah and beyond. Only one *yungerman,* Reb Yinun Ben Mashiach, who himself had learned in Telshe and to whom I will forever be grateful for insisting that I give Telshe a chance, felt that it was the right place for me, but his voice was almost drowned out by the sea of opposition.

Telshe had the well-deserved reputation of being one of the most prominent yeshivos in the United States. It was a citadel of Torah thought, a bulwark, a fortress — but along with its exalted status came a certain rigid, super-*litvish* approach in its dealings with the students. In a battle between emotion and logic, Telshe chose logic hands down. It was as analytical an institution as was possible to be and proudly so. No one was going to coddle you at this yeshivah. The approach and curriculum were designed in such as way as to make a student take a good, long, honest look at himself and decide whether he wanted to work harder than he had ever worked before.

With a student body of over 200 serious and diligent students, I was warned that I wouldn't find my place and would be forced to return to Brooklyn in shame. The level of learning was extremely high, and almost all the students had entered as part of a group. There was a *chevrah* from Toronto, another from Monsey...while I was coming as a loner, without the moral support needed to survive in such a high-pressure environment. In my current yeshivah, I had access to Rav Shmuel Miller (the son of Rav Avigdor Miller, *zt"l*) any time I wanted and was able to talk in learning with him for an hour at a time. In Telshe, I was told, I would be one of hundreds and just another face in the crowd. Still, I had heard so much about Rav Dovid Barkin, who would be my rebbi in Telshe, and I wasn't about to chicken out just because I wasn't part of a group.

Rav Dovid was a truly gifted individual. A brilliant thinker, he towered over mere mortals in his approach to Torah study and life in general. He had been a student of Rav Shach, *zt"l*, Rav Shmuel Rozovsky, *zt"l*, Rav Gifter, *zt"l*, and Rav Pesach Stein, *zt"l*, and he was widely respected by all who knew him. Just thinking that I might spend a year or two learning in the company of such a person excited me. And so, despite all the dire warnings I had been given and despite the fact that almost no one believed that my moving to Telshe was a good idea, I followed my heart to Cleveland, and the world-famous Telshe Yeshivah.

◆ ◆ ◆

Driving to Telshe Yeshivah from New York is a trip of close to eight hours and 500 miles of tedious driving, either via Route 76 or Route 80. While Route 80 is a toll-free road, Route 76 costs about $30 for the privilege and is usually peppered with blue-and-red flashing lights for those intrepid souls who feel the need to speed. Both routes leave much to be desired in the scenery department. In a nutshell, there is nothing to see along the way.

The original campus of the Telshe Yeshivah had been 50 acres in size. It is no longer that large, since parts of the campus have been sold to the state of Ohio for the construction of a highway. Nonetheless, it still hosts a very large, scenic campus, with 10 houses for the yeshivah staff and a pleasant park. There are quite a few buildings on campus for the administration, the *mesivta*, the high school, the gym (which was considered state of the art back in those days), the dorm, the dining room, and Telshe's crown jewel: the *beis medrash*. There are also playing fields for baseball and other sports for those so inclined and plenty of deer and other assorted wildlife that feel completely comfortable strolling through the grounds at any given time of the day or night.

This was Telshe, a prominent institution and mainstay of the American yeshivah world.

◆ ◆ ◆

My arrival at the yeshivah can be categorized by a feeling of true loneliness. I had been told that I would be just another face in the crowd, and it was true. If I had fondly imagined that my grandfather's having studied in Telshe would serve as some sort of icebreaker with the *roshei yeshivah*, who no doubt recalled learning with him back in their youth, I found, in fact, that I was going to have to prove myself based on my own merits.

I had taken an entrance exam to the yeshivah during the previous semester and had concluded, perhaps naïvely, that since I had been accepted a few months earlier, I could show up for the following semester. Upon my arrival, however, I was asked by the administration why I had come, since I had been accepted for the previous semester and not this one. For a short while, I wasn't even sure whether I was going to be allowed to remain, let alone granted the opportunity to make a name for myself.

Telshe was packed with *bachurim* who sat and learned for hours at a time with true *hasmadah*. They sat together and spoke in learning with one another and enjoyed the beauty of friendships and the unspoken power that comes from being a part of something greater than oneself. I, on the other hand, was on my own. There were a few other *bachurim* who had been accepted to Telshe at the same time, and we formed a group that hung out together sort of by default and basically spent all our free time discussing how tough Telshe was and how we were getting out of there just as soon as we were able.

◆ ◆ ◆

There were 45 boys in Rav Dovid Barkin's *shiur*. Rav Dovid would enter the classroom a moment before *shiur* was to begin, his face shining with a purity and radiance I had rarely encountered anywhere before. It was almost as if an earthly angel had swept into our midst to deliver a segment of celestial Torah. He possessed a rare ability to give over the Torah in a fluid, almost endless stream. He was able to present his thoughts with lucid clarity for an hour at a time — there were no interruptions allowed — while the *bachurim* sat and took notes the entire time.

With the conclusion of the *shiur*, he'd rise and was already striding out of the room while we'd remain with four to five pages of notes to review. Ten to 15 boys would be on their feet instantaneously, chasing after Rav Dovid to try and gain an additional moment of clarification. The time frame they had was the amount of time it took for him to walk from the *shiur* room to his office. Once he reached the door, he said good-bye, entered his room, and that was the last we saw of him until *shiur* the next day. No one was allowed to disturb Rav Dovid in his private room, and the only time that he was considered approachable was on his way to and from his home to the yeshivah. As soon as anyone caught a glimpse of Rav Dovid, he would be immediately surrounded by boys clamoring for his attention.

It was extremely difficult to develop a close relationship with Rav Dovid. The Telshe boys viewed him as positively angelic and awe inspiring, and he simply didn't have time to waste. Few on the planet could keep up with the type of learning regimen that

Rav Dovid Barkin (right), visiting Rav Dovid Cohen,
rosh yeshivah of Chevron, in his *succah*

he imposed on himself. There was no question that Rav Dovid
Barkin was one of the most diligent people of his generation.

Later on the yeshivah instituted a change, where Rav Dovid
came to the *beis medrash* for about half an hour during second
seder and was available to answer questions from the *talmidim*.
But here, too, there was always a line of at least 10 boys ahead
of you, and unless you were truly focused on your goal, most
bachurim resigned themselves to the fact that they were never
going to develop a close relationship with Rav Dovid.

Needless to say, this did not bode well for my adjusting to
this very different yeshivah. I missed Rav Shmuel Miller and his
insightful words of wisdom, I missed my friends in yeshivah, and
I missed the warmth and camaraderie of the *avreichim* in the *kollel*. I had gone to Cleveland against virtually everyone's advice
and single-handedly placed myself in a position where I seemed
to have no chance of success. I was floundering — drowning in

an ocean of anonymity — and it didn't seem like I would ever be granted the opportunity to make my mark in the famous halls of Telshe Yeshivah.

◆ ◆ ◆

After hanging around with the other boys who weren't part of any group, and spending a lot of time complaining and bemoaning the unsatisfying situation that we found ourselves in, I came to a realization. While each of the other boys found his own way of dealing with the stress — this one through music, that one through reading — I had no way of alleviating the negative feelings I was experiencing on a regular basis.

I did not dare complain to my parents or Rav Shmuel Miller, because they had been against my leaving Brooklyn and transferring to Telshe in the first place — and their fears had been proven correct. Even my grandfather, who was a Telsher, had been against my decision. I didn't even have the moral satisfaction of being able to complain, since in all honesty everything happening to me was all my fault.

Nobody else. All me.

Every day was a war. I'd wake up in the morning, look around, stare out the window at the Cleveland skyline, and think, *I can't believe that I'm still here!*

One day I had an epiphany. I suddenly understood with startling clarity that my Telshe experience could go one of two ways. I realized that the rest of the loners were on their way out (and, in fact, by the end of the year every one of them was gone). We were learning *maseches Yevamos* in the yeshivah, and I said to myself, *Either I go the way of these other guys, in which case I might as well give up now, or I throw myself into my learning in a way that I never did before. Maybe by completely immersing myself in Torah… maybe that will help me achieve a modicum of satisfaction and happiness with the yeshivah and where I am in life.*

I thought things over and decided to give it a truly honest shot. I was going to learn harder and with more dedication then I'd ever done before and see where it took me.

I wasted no time in carrying out my decision. I found a *bachur* who had come to Telshe at the same time as I had and asked him if he was willing to try the learning experiment of his life. He thought it over and agreed to give it a chance.

The idea I was bringing to the table was a simple one. We were going to begin our *seder* after the yeshivah's daily regimen was finished and learn until we dropped. Literally. I was young and idealistic, and I recalled the Rambam's statement *"Ein adam koneh Torah ela balailah"* — that a person can only truly acquire Torah learning during the nighttime hours.

There are times in life when we reach a crossroads. This was one of those times. I knew that the other boys in my group felt I had abandoned them, thinking that I had picked a *derech* that made it seem as if I were better than they were, but I also knew that this was my only chance to make it work. I finally understood that I had been granted an opportunity that I didn't want to miss. Thus began one of the most challenging periods of my life.

My new *chavrusa* and I threw ourselves into the learning. It wasn't long before I began to enjoy the heady feeling of success.

◆ ◆ ◆

One night, after we'd been learning for a few hours, my *chavrusa* started feeling very tired, and he told me that he wanted to wrap things up. He left the yeshivah building at about 2 o'clock in the morning, while I remained, thinking that I could still give it another hour. The dormitory was located about a block away from the main study hall, but it meant walking through the Telshe campus, which was dark, freezing cold, and a somewhat scary place for a stroll in the middle of the night.

Cleveland is a far cry from New York City, and the campus was busy with nighttime prowlers: all sorts of animals who called the campus home. Raccoons were spotted frequently, and if you think they're just a bunch of cute little animals with rings around their eyes, you are mistaken, because they can get vicious. Someone once spotted a wolf roaming the grounds as well, and if there was a downside to our learning schedule, having to return to the dorm through the lonely campus paths was it.

I decided that I was not up to returning to the dorm and instead elected to remain in the *beis medrash*, where I'd learn until I collapsed. I fell asleep around 4 in the morning, nodding over my Gemara, drifting off, until I finally lay down on the hard bench and fell into a deep, contented slumber. It had been a long, long day and I was exhausted.

Suddenly I heard banging. I had never been in a war zone in my life, but in my dreams it sounded like I had strayed into the middle of a fierce battle. Bombs were falling all around me! It was terrifying, and I woke up, my heart racing with terror and anxiety.

I sat up on the bench and, rubbing my eyes, caught sight of a huge man standing not two feet away, towering over my inert form, staring at me with what looked like murder in his eyes. When he opened his mouth, no words emerged; instead, there was a series of grunts that instilled a primal fear in me that I can't even describe.

Besides the grunts and the half words, he made shooing motions with his hands, communicating to me as best he could, that he wanted me out of his way, the sooner the better!

It took me a minute to realize that I wasn't in danger, after all: the man obviously worked as the yeshivah's nighttime custodian and was there to clean the *beis medrash* for the coming day. The "bombing" and "gunfire" sounds that I'd heard in my sleep, and which had led me to wake up thinking that World War III had come to Telshe, were caused by his lifting the rows of *shtender*s and smashing them down on the benches with a terrific clatter. There was a rhythm to his actions and a reason for his behavior, but I was clearly in his way, and I knew that I needed to vacate the premises immediately.

Without a word, I rose and sought shelter in the nearest place of refuge I could find. He scared me and I needed to hide. Without thinking too deeply into it — remember, I was still half asleep — I picked myself up and ran for my life…into the nearby office and private sanctuary of the universally acclaimed Telshe *Rosh Yeshivah*, Rav Mordechai Gifter.

◆ ◆ ◆

During my years at Telshe, Rav Gifter was already reaching the end of his long and successful tenure as *Rosh Yeshivah*. He suffered from serious ailments that impaired his quality of life. And yet he came to the yeshivah for hours every day, where he learned to the best of his still formidable capabilities.

The room that I'd chosen for my refuge was where Rav Gifter donned his tefillin and prepared himself for davening with the yeshivah. His *sefarim* lined the walls, and his unique personality permeated the tiny room's atmosphere. Although certain people had permission to use it, it was unheard of for a regular *bachur* to just waltz into this private room and use it for his personal needs. Still, this was an emergency, and as I said, I had just woken up and still wasn't thinking clearly. All I knew was that I had to escape from the ferocious gaze of the hulking man with bulging muscles who looked capable of eating me for breakfast.

Luckily the door was unlocked. Rav Gifter's chair had been left in position at the desk, awaiting its occupant like a soldier on parade. As I mentioned, there were other *rebbeim* who used the room as well, so sitting in the chair didn't seem to me to be the ultimate chutzpah. Still, I would never have done such a thing had I not so feared the man in the *beis medrash*.

I sat down at Rav Gifter's desk, removed his personal Gemara from the nearby shelf, placed it squarely in the center of his desk, turned on the heater to comfort me a little, and began to learn. And, of course, within a few minutes my eyes began to close of their own accord, and I found myself nodding off over Rav Gifter's Gemara. Finally, my head dropped completely onto the well-used pages. Beyond a shadow of a doubt, here was one *bachur* who was out for the night.

◆ ◆ ◆

The next morning, the door to the office opened at 6:30 on the dot. Rav Mordechai Gifter and his Rebbetzin stood there framed by the doorway. She had arrived with him, as she did every morning, to assist him in donning his tefillin. Rav Gifter walked into the room and saw a sight he had probably never seen before in all his years in Telshe. A *bachur* was fast asleep in his chair, at his desk, head comfortably pillowed on the *Rosh Yeshivah's* personal Gemara!

There's something you have to understand. Rav Gifter was a man who inspired awe in people. To be honest, I'm not sure who I was more afraid of: the fearsome creature who had woken me up in the *beis medrash* or the formidable *Rosh Yeshivah* of Telshe, who was famous for speaking his mind and for not suffering fools lightly. Rav Gifter possessed a razor-sharp wit, brilliant intellect, and powerful acumen. It wasn't only the *bachurim* who trembled before him. Even older *roshei yeshivah* stood at attention when in his presence, like officers before a wizened general. As always, he commanded the yeshivah's respect and was a pillar of the Telshe community.

And so, when the door suddenly opened and the sound of Rav Gifter and his Rebbetzin entering the room woke me, I almost jumped out of my skin. Here was the legendary Rav Mordechai Gifter, *Rosh Yeshivah* of Telshe, inheritor of the mantle of the European *derech haTorah,* catching me at *his* desk, over *his* Gemara, in *his* chair.

I had never dreamed of still being there when he arrived, having assured myself that I'd be awake and long gone by the time he put in an appearance. But my exhaustion had gotten the better of me, and now here I was, completely taken by surprise at his arrival, my heart beating rapidly with fright at how arrogant my behavior must seem to him. The fear I felt at that moment made my earlier terror in the *beis medrash* seem to fade into insignificance.

I had overstepped my bounds. There were no excuses for my behavior. How was Rav Gifter going to react?

To be perfectly honest, two very incongruous thoughts entered my mind at that moment, seemingly at the same time. I was reminded of the fairy tale of Goldilocks waking up surrounded by the bears looking down at her, sleeping in the bed that was "just right." I was also reminded of King Achashveirosh storming back into his palace from the royal gardens only to find Haman on Queen Esther's couch, and Achashveirosh's never-to-be-forgotten fearsome outcry: "Will you vanquish the queen with me in the house?!"

Those were the thoughts vying for attention in my mind when I saw Rav Mordechai Gifter standing in the doorway staring at me. I silently prayed that he not be too harsh on me, deserving of harshness though I might be.

◆ ◆ ◆

Certain things that happen in a person's life, certain memories, remain with you forever. The next moment was one of those. Rav Gifter looked at me, the *bachur* who had just lifted his head off the *Rosh Yeshivah's* very own Gemara, and he recognized the confusion and fright of someone who had just woken up and was discombobulated and alarmed. He gave me a big smile and said, in a loud and comforting voice, "Nothing to worry about, pal. Keep up the good work!"

Rav Gifter and his *talmid*,
Reb Binyomin

There was such love and goodwill in those words. His chair, someone else's chair, it made no difference. The main thing was that a *bachur* had been learning with such diligence that he'd fallen asleep over a Gemara, and that made Rav Gifter as happy as a person could be.

At that moment, there was a fundamental shift in my appreciation of Rav Gifter and who he really was. The fear I had felt when standing before him suddenly disappeared as if it had never been, replaced with an understanding and awareness of the true happiness his Torah learning afforded him.

This chance encounter would also lead to our developing a relationship. I had grown up in a home where people went out of their way to develop relationships with their *rebbeim* and with *gedolim* in general. My father was a close *talmid* of Rav Moshe Feinstein, *zt"l*. Not only that, but as a child, my father used to accompany his father, my grandfather, as he'd walk Rav Yaakov Kamenetsky, *zt"l*, home from shul. My grandfather had been a *ben bayis* at the home of the Rogatchover Gaon back in Europe. To me it was an obvious thing, that a rebbi was there to get close to. Now it was my turn to try and get close to Rav Gifter.

◆ ◆ ◆

After this first encounter with Rav Gifter, I started seriously considering how to begin developing a relationship with him. He was one of the most respected *roshei yeshivah* in the United States, and although he was ailing, there was still so much to learn from such a great man. I asked around and was informed that it was possible to approach him and tell him a nice piece of Torah, and I decided that this could be a way through the door.

One day I mustered my courage and asked Rav Gifter for permission to share with him a Torah thought. What followed was not the reaction I had been fondly expecting. At the party that the yeshivah made for me before I left Telshe, Reb Moshe Dovid Shwekey, one of the *chashuve* members of the Telshe *kollel*, had this to say about the incident:

"I still remember the first time Binyomin approached Rav Gifter. We didn't know who this *bachur* was, yet we said to ourselves, 'This boy knows how to get his way.'"

For my first attempt at speaking in learning with Rav Gifter, I had chosen to share a brief idea I had seen in the *Da'as Zekeinim MiBa'alei HaTosafos*. The *Chumash* uses the words "*V'el habakar ratz*

Avraham — Avraham ran to the cattle." *Da'as Zekeinim* points out that the letters of the word *bakar*, "cattle," are the same as those of *kever*, "burial place," which implies that Avraham ran after one of his livestock all the way to Me'aras HaMachpeilah, and that's when he discovered the most sought-after cemetery in Jewish history.

I hadn't yet managed to tell Rav Gifter that the author of this thought was the *Da'as Zekeinim*, having begun with the *vort*'s clever play on words, when Rav Gifter interrupted me loudly by saying, "*Dos gefelt mir nisht* — I do not like it!"

This was one of our first conversations, and when he shouted at me, I jumped back in sudden fright and started to run away. Rav Chaim Nussbaum, one of Rav Gifter's closest *talmidim*, witnessed the interchange and called me over.

"Tell me, Binyomin," he questioned me gently, "what did you tell the *Rosh Yeshivah* that got him so upset?"

"I started telling him this *vort* that I saw, and he got upset and didn't let me finish."

"Where's the *vort* from?"

"It's a *Da'as Zekeinim*."

"Did you tell Rav Gifter who you were quoting?"

"I didn't get there. He cut me off right away."

"Go back to the *Rosh Yeshivah* right now and tell him that you were quoting a *Da'as Zekeinim*!"

If Rav Chaim Nussbaum was insisting with such force that I go back, I figured that he knew what he was talking about. Mustering my courage for a second time, I returned to Rav Gifter.

"Rebbe," I said, "the *vort* that I started telling the *Rosh Yeshivah*" — he nodded at me — "I saw it in the *Da'as Zekeinim MiBa'alei HaTosafos*."

His attitude changed instantly. "If that's the case," he said enthusiastically in Yiddish, "you should always merit to repeat such precious Torah thoughts."

I learned an important lesson that day. Nothing changed besides Rav Gifter's newfound knowledge of the author's identity, but that made all the difference. Even if the idea seemed simple on the surface, once he'd heard that a *Rishon* had said it, he treated it with complete respect. I never forgot the moment I learned just how important it is to verify the origin of an idea. And that when it comes to Torah, you can't just say whatever you want; it needs to have a solid basis and backing.

It was only a few words on his part, but sometimes that's all it takes.

◆　◆　◆

Once I realized that Rav Gifter was approachable, I began going to his house to share with him the Torah thoughts of Rav Avigdor Miller, *zt"l*, whom he liked very much. After I'd been coming for a while, the Rebbetzin mentioned to me that the doctors felt it would be beneficial for the *Rosh Yeshivah* to have more stimulation, and would I consider becoming his *chavrusa* during second *seder*?

To me it wasn't even a question. It was a rare honor, and I jumped at the opportunity. We ended up learning together over a fairly lengthy period of time, though the subject matter didn't remain the same. We studied *Minchas Chinuch* for a while, then Gemara for a few months. To me it made no difference what we were learning as long as I was granted the chance to sit and study with such an acclaimed master. His incredible *bekius* was something amazing to witness.

One afternoon we learned the majority of *Perek HaKoneis* in *maseches Bava Kamma* from start to finish — the Gemara with *Rashi* and *Tosafos*. Rav Gifter read — he always read and I always listened — the words of the Gemara rolling off his tongue with the ease and familiarity of two friends who have known each other for decades. We went through every *Rashi*, every *Tosafos*, his voice rising as he read the questions with the proper nuance and tune, his body language clearly at home within the complexities of the *sugya*.

Daf after *daf*, *sugya* after *sugya*, he read with clarity and understanding and a sureness that spoke of a lifetime of toil in Torah.

At some point, Rav Gifter decided that we should begin learning together during *mussar seder*. *Mussar* was studied in the last forty minutes of second *seder*, and it was followed by supper, when the Rebbetzin would arrive to pick him up and escort him home. The end of *mussar seder* was heralded by the resounding clatter of 200 *bachurim* pushing their *shtender*s to the side and leaving the study hall en masse for the dining room. Rav Gifter never looked at his watch to see when it was time to stop; he merely concluded our *seder* when everyone else began exiting the room.

One afternoon, the shadows had grown long outside the brightly lit study hall, and it was already dark outside as second *seder* began to draw to a close. Rav Gifter, however, didn't seem to notice when the boys stood up with a massive force of movement and began leaving the room. The *beis medrash* was empty five minutes later, with everyone already in the dining room, but still Rav Gifter carried on learning, without giving any indication that he was planning on stopping any time in the near future.

The Rebbetzin, who was standing outside the *beis medrash* waiting for him to finish up for the day, soon came to the realization that she might need to intervene and convince Rav Gifter to finish. *Seder* was over, after all. The room was empty. It was only the two of us now sitting up front in the massive Telshe *beis medrash*, Rav Gifter's voice chanting the timeless words of Rabbeinu Yonah with profound emotion.

In the manner of a true Telshe Rebbetzin, Rebbetzin Gifter entered the *beis medrash* and walked through the rows of benches until she reached the front of the room. "Reb Mordche," she addressed her husband, "*der bachur darf essen*. The *bachur* has to eat."

Rav Gifter continued to chant.

Later on, I would explain to the Rebbetzin what exactly had transpired in the empty Telshe *beis medrash*, and why her husband hadn't been able to pull himself away from the words of Rabbeinu Yonah. As we sat there, Rav Gifter had repeated the section we were learning over and over again. He had tears running down his face as he read the words. You could see that he felt a personal connection to the words, as if they applied directly to him. He read and reread the paragraph, again and again, and every so often he'd exclaim, "*Ah, azelecheh goldene verter fun de heiliger Rabbbeinu Yonah!* — Ah, what golden words from the holy Rabbeinu Yonah!"

I sat there, stunned into silence, watching him as he wept.

In that piece, Rabbeinu Yonah discusses how important it is to repent of one's sins while still young and still strong. "Because," he says, "Hashem attaches much greater meaning to repentance when a person is still young enough to enjoy the pleasures of this world. Once a person is elderly, and his body doesn't work the same way anymore," concludes Rabbeinu Yonah, "his repentance, though vital and important, is not cherished by Hashem with the same love and happiness."

As Rav Gifter read those words — words describing a day that would come when a person's body no longer carried out his will, when the body had grown weary and fatigued — I could see that he felt that Rabbeinu Yonah was describing his situation

In Rav Gifter's house, at a *siyum Mishnayos* that I made
with his grandson and other children

in life. Rabbeinu Yonah was speaking to him, and he couldn't stop himself from repeating the paragraph over and over. He was totally focused on the words, with an intense concentration that couldn't be broken. He didn't realize that the boys had risen and left the room for supper, and he didn't pay attention to the Rebbetzin when she tried to tell him it was time to go. He was utterly immersed in the golden words of Rabbeinu Yonah to the exclusion of everything else.

I would say that he read the paragraph about four or five times out loud, with the tears sliding down his face. It was a poignant and emotional experience for me, as I watched one of the *gedolei hador* applying Rabbeinu Yonah's words to himself with such sincerity. The memory of that night in the Telshe *beis medrash* left an incredible imprint, marking itself with indelible ink across my psyche. If I close my eyes right now and concentrate just a little bit, I can see him sitting there, see the teardrops running down his cheeks, and hear his voice repeating the holy words over and over until they burned a hole in my soul.

Some people learn *mussar*. Others internalize *mussar*. With Rav Gifter, there was nothing superficial about anything he did. It was honest and real, and I knew that every word he read was branded on his heart. When we finally finished learning, and Rav Gifter closed the *sefer*, the Gifters invited me home with them for supper, since I had missed the meal provided by the yeshivah. Eating supper with the *Rosh Yeshivah* was the perfect end to a perfect day.

Rav Gifter had taught me so much. Being with him had shown me firsthand what diligence was, and how the material and ideas that a person focuses on during his youth remain with him until the end of his life. Rav Gifter had demonstrated to me through his actions that holiness is there for the taking, that this world is a gift to take advantage of and that laziness is no excuse.

Rav Mordechai Gifter and Rav Dovid Barkin

Part B

The road that eventually led me to Bnei Brak and into the home and life of Rav Chaim Kanievsky, *shlita*, and so many other great men, passed through the *beis medrash* of Telshe, where Rav Dovid Barkin taught us Torah "like an angel of Hashem," as the Gemara says. By the time I left Telshe, I had become one of Rav Dovid's closest *talmidim*, but there were many steps along the way.

He would come to yeshivah in the morning and, except for the time when he gave *shiur*, sit and learn undisturbed the entire day and leave at 11 o'clock at night. On *erev Shabbos*, Rav Dovid would arrive in the middle of Friday-morning *seder* dressed in his Shabbos finery, having already made his Shabbos preparations. He would go straight to his room and learn there uninterrupted until Shabbos commenced.

His room was looked at by one and all as the *kodesh hako-dashim*, the "holy of holies" of Telshe. His face was infused with a brilliant Torah light, and his entire personality was suffused with the Torah that he studied from morning till night. We all knew that he'd been one of Rav Shach's closest students in Ponevezh and that almost all the letters that Rav Shach had penned on *chinuch* had been addressed to him.

Rav Shach possessed a certain *kuntres* that he had written during some of his most difficult wartime experiences. The *kuntres* was very dear to him, and he wouldn't lend it to anyone — anyone, that is, besides Rav Dovid Barkin. Rav Shach loved Rav Dovid. It was that simple.

One of the stories people used to tell was how, on one of Rav Dovid's visits to Ponevezh, Rav Shach rose from his spot near the front of the cavernous room, headed straight toward his *talmid*, and kissed him in front of the entire *beis medrash*. When Rav Shach was later asked by those close to him how he allowed himself to kiss someone in the *beis medrash* when that is clearly forbidden by halachah, Rav Shach explained that this halachic ruling didn't apply to Rav Dovid Barkin, because he was a walking, breathing *sefer Torah*!

One of my reasons for coming to Telshe was for the immense privilege of learning under the tutelage of Rav Dovid, whose clarity and grasp of the Gemara was legendary. My goal had been to develop a personal connection with him. It had been thwarted until now by the sheer volume of students and Rav Dovid's seclusion, and I was extremely frustrated. But, as we all know, when you want something enough, all you have to do is your *hishtadlus*. After that, allow Hashem to run His world.

◆ ◆ ◆

As in every yeshivah, the boys in Telshe were a mix of personality types and temperaments. Some were quiet and shy, while others were outgoing and popular. Some were ignored by the student body, while others enjoyed a reputation for their sharp minds, possession of vast amounts of Torah, or extreme diligence.

Every yeshivah has its *masmidim* — the boys who burn the midnight oil — and Telshe was no exception.

After a few months of being basically overlooked, I suddenly found myself something of a sensation. Our newfound *seder*-till-you-drop at night turned my *chavrusa* and me into the biggest *masmidim* of the yeshivah by default, since no one else kept those kind of hours. I don't know who it was, but at some point someone paid a visit to Rav Dovid Barkin and informed him that there was a student in the yeshivah who was putting in way too many hours in the *beis medrash*.

Perhaps someone told him that I was endangering myself with sleep deprivation and had to be stopped before I caused myself serious damage. Whatever the reason, one day as I was sitting and learning with my *chavrusa,* another boy informed me that Rav Dovid Barkin wanted to see me in his office right away. I had no idea what he might possibly want and felt honored that Rav Dovid wanted to see me — and in his "holy of holies," no less!

I left my seat in the great hall, promised my *chavrusa* that I'd be back as soon as possible, and headed straight for Rav Dovid's inner sanctum and my personal audience with the universally acclaimed *masmid* of Telshe.

◆ ◆ ◆

I entered the room, not sure what to expect.

Maybe I thought there would be a *shalom aleichem*. After all, we had never really had a chance to meet until then. But no... there was no warm welcome from Rav Dovid. He began talking to me with little in the way of preamble.

"So I hear this new thing, that you're staying up very late hours learning. You should know that it's *mamesh* a *sakanah*, that you're endangering yourself. There are stories of boys who did such things and suffered nervous breakdowns in consequence."

He looked me straight in the eye.

"Binyomin," he said, his voice stern and authoritative, "I am not willing to take responsibility for such behavior. I'm giving you three choices. Either you promise me that you will be in bed asleep by 12:15 every night, or you ask your father to call me and tell me that he takes responsibility for your actions during the night, or" — a pause — "you leave the yeshivah."

Thus began my first conversation with Rav Dovid Barkin.

I was so disappointed. I tried to argue with him: I was young and naïve and tried to quote the Rambam...as proof...and how the Steipler used to learn 36 hours without respite...and how my strenuous learning was the only thing keeping me going...

He paused, then reiterated his earlier ultimatum. "You have an hour to make up your mind. When you're ready, come back to me and tell me your decision."

As I walked out of Rav Dovid's office, I was filled with righteous indignation at his ruling, and my gut feeling was to leave Telshe immediately. I had come to this learning methodology based on what I absolutely needed at the time, and the fact that those in positions of authority didn't understand this meant that maybe it was time for me to find another place where they *would* understand and not try to stunt me and my growth. I was leaving! And besides, I still hadn't really found my place in the yeshivah. Maybe leaving Telshe really was the best idea?

Before I made my final decision (I had an hour to decide, after all), I called the *yungerman* back at my previous yeshivah who had advised me to go to Telshe in the first place. When I heard his voice, I exploded in a burst of immature noise, taking him to task for sending me to Telshe: a place that didn't recognize true *hasmadah* and put spokes in the wheels of boys who were trying to grow and become great in Torah!

"There's no way that I'm going to get my father involved in this," I went on, all heated up. "That's it. I'm going back into that office, and I'm going to tell Rav Dovid that I'm out of here. Today!"

To his credit, the *yungerman* who sent me to Telshe heard me out, listened to all my grievances, and only then began begging me to stick it out.

"Binyomin," he said, "listen to me. Please. Remember how hard it was for you to get accepted to Telshe. You just got in, now you want to leave? Give it a chance! And besides, where exactly are you going to go from there? Don't be silly, don't make this mistake. Go back to Rav Dovid and promise him that you're going to go to sleep on time. I'm begging you. Don't make the mistake of your life!"

Basically he kept me on the phone until he managed to talk sense into me. In the end I promised him that I wouldn't ruin what we'd managed to accomplish, and that I'd give Rav Dovid my word that from that day on, I'd be in bed shortly after midnight every night.

"*Hatzlachah*," he said to me.

"You, too," I replied, then I hung up the phone, mustered my courage, and retraced my steps to the Telshe holy of holies, where Rav Dovid waited to hear my decision.

◆ ◆ ◆

Before I could even open my mouth, before I could even get one word out, I saw a different Rav Dovid Barkin. Gone was the tough-talking educator demanding complete and total obedience from a student. That Rav Dovid had been replaced by a soft-spoken man who began apologizing to me profusely.

"I feel so bad about how I just spoke to you," he said. "I was too harsh, too strong." He seemed beside himself with remorse. "You're going to be a *maggid shiur* one day... You're going to have your own students... You must not be so harsh..."

He was a different person. I had left the office with his words "This is the way it is — you have an hour to make up your mind" ringing in my ears and returned to a gentle rebbi who couldn't stop apologizing for the way he'd treated me. At some point in that memorable conversation, the tables turned and I began comforting him.

"It's okay. I understand why Rebbi did it. You meant it for my good..."

Seeing how a great man like Rav Dovid didn't hesitate to ask *mechilah* of a young student like me when he felt he'd been overly strict made an impression that has stayed with me since.

From that day on, Rav Dovid began treating me with more warmth. Because of this incident, I did return to the dorm at an earlier hour and (as Rav Dovid had undoubtedly realized would happen), my learning grew stronger and stronger — as did our relationship. He had grasped that here was a boy who really wanted to learn and who meant well, and he was worried that my natural tendency toward intensity might make me do things that weren't good for my health.

For example, I was very skinny in those years. I didn't particularly care for the yeshivah food and I wasn't eating well, and this was reflected in the fact that I appeared malnourished. Rav Dovid was concerned that I wasn't eating for spiritual reasons. He wanted me to eat enough and sleep enough and take care of myself. Rebbetzin Gifter shared his concerns (I know that she even spoke to him about me), and the two of them began taking a tremendous interest in my health. So much so that whenever I came to speak with him in learning, he'd say, prior to commencing our conversation, "The condition for us talking in learning is that you tell me that you had a piece of cake today!"

He used to force me to buy food from the canteen. "Binyomin," he said to me once, "when I'm looking for you, all I need to do is search for a sweater walking around and I find you right away."

Once, I arrived to speak to him in his room right when he was about to eat lunch. This ended up being a mistake on my part, because Rav Dovid simply took his lunch and forced me to eat it.

"I want you to eat this," he told me. "You need it more than me."

As the months moved on, I learned when I could go see him in his room and when it was off limits. Rav Dovid definitely began taking a much greater interest in my learning development and overall health and well-being due to that first "tough-love" conversation. It didn't happen overnight — he was still Rav Dovid Barkin, and there was still a distance between him and his students — but slowly we grew much closer, until we shared the relationship of rebbi and *talmid* that I had initially envisioned.

◆ ◆ ◆

One Shavuos night in Telshe I stayed up all night working on a certain *suyga* in *maseches Yevamos*. It was a very difficult piece of Gemara, and I worked on it the entire night, from after the meal until *Shacharis*. By morning, I had reached the point where I had gained a modicum of clarity in the *sugya* — and one very powerful question. After davening, I accompanied Rav Dovid back to his house. As you know, most people are more or less knocked out after staying up all night. I was about seventeen that year. Rav Dovid was in his mid-50's. Taking advantage of the fact that he was in my company and I was holding him captive, I shared my question on the *sugya* with Rav Dovid.

"Binyomin," Rav Dovid said to me after I'd explained my question to the best of my abilities, "in the *zechus* of your *kabbalas haTorah* this Shavuos night, you merited to ask the question of the Nachalas Moshe and the Keren Orah."

I cannot describe how impressed I was with Rav Dovid at that moment. Another person might have said, "Listen, I'm exhausted right now. We'll talk about this another time." Rav Dovid didn't say that. He had no problem discussing the challenging point that I brought up, and it didn't matter in the slightest that this followed a night of no sleep.

The second point that really struck home was the fact that he didn't just compliment me on having asked a strong question. Rather, he made a point of mentioning that I must have learned with special diligence that evening to have merited coming up with such a powerful question. It was phenomenal praise that would remain with me forever.

Third, in order for a person to be able to confirm on the spot that a particular question has been asked by both the Nachalas Moshe and the Keren Orah, he must know everything there was to know about this piece of Gemara, including the names of the only two commentaries who asked my question, though they had lived over a hundred years apart and had no real thread linking them to each other. And he was able to pull this off on the way home from shul on Shavuos morning, after not sleeping for an entire night! His knowledge was true. His clarity was awesome. He truly amazed me.

◆　◆　◆

Baruch Hashem, I have had the good fortune to share a wonderfully close connection to my *rebbeim* and many other great *tzaddikim*. I have been asked numerous times, "How does a young American boy who came to Eretz Yisrael become so close to one of the *gedolei hador*? Everyone wants to be close to Rav Chaim. What's so special about you?"

The answer to this question is very simple and applies equally to every one of my *rebbeim*. Every relationship has to be two sided. Most people who go to visit a *tzaddik* are there because they need something from him. They may have a question that needs an answer, or they want a *berachah* from him or an *eitzah*, but they are coming because they need something from the *gadol*. They are coming to receive. Generally the visit is a one-time deal, and they can't be expected to develop a relationship with the person they are coming to see.

I always had a different attitude toward these relationships. Of course, I was coming to these great men because I wanted to receive: to learn from them and study their habits and see what behavior had turned them into the giants they were. But I always searched for something that I would be able to give them in return, an action that would mean something to them and would develop our relationship to the point where it actually turned into a two-way relationship, something that was important to both of us!

Believe it or not, I was able to find something that little me was able to do for even the greatest person in *Klal Yisrael:* something that only I was uniquely capable of doing for him, something that meant the world to him. And the fact is, when it becomes a two-way relationship, it's a completely different game.

With Rav Dovid, there was another side to our *kesher.* Our relationship reached the point where we'd continue speaking on the phone after I'd already gone to learn in Eretz Yisrael, and when Rav Dovid came to visit, I'd escort him around the country and accompany him to the homes of many *gedolim* he was interested in seeing.

And all this came about because I never stopped thinking about what I could do for him. For example, Rav Dovid was a person who loved *sefarim*. Loved them with a passion. He'd purchase every new *sefer* that was published, and then he'd actually learn it. I'd always help him find new *sefarim* that he hadn't yet heard about, or help him collect works that were difficult to track down. Sometimes I'd travel to the home of the author of a *sefer* that was out of print to get a copy for Rav Dovid. At other times, I was able to obtain copies of manuscripts that hadn't yet been printed. I saw tremendous *siyatta d'Shmaya* in my quest to provide him with the *sefarim* that he loved so much.

Once, when I was already learning in Yerushalayim, Rav Dovid asked me to help him find a certain *sefer* written by Rav Moshe Blau, the famous Yerushalmi *askan*. Try as I might, it seemed the *sefer* wasn't available. After making extensive investigations, my search led me to the library at Hebrew University in Givat Ram, which did, indeed, have a copy. Upon my arrival at Hebrew U., I was planning to make a copy of the entire *sefer* for Rav Dovid, page by page, when all of a sudden I saw the slightly familiar face of none other than the grandchild of Rav Moshe Blau himself!

"*Shalom aleichem*," I greeted him.

He greeted me in return.

"You won't believe me when I tell you that I came here today to make a copy of the *sefer* written by your grandfather."

He held up his hand. "Wait, don't do anything," he instructed me, "they are about to reprint it." He gave me all the pertinent information, and I was able to pick up a copy for my rebbi a short time later.

I was always happy to do anything that I could for him. If he ever needed a messenger to ask a question from one of the local *gedolim*, I was his choice. Over the years I was willing and overjoyed to do anything I could for my *rebbeim* — and they felt it and appreciated my sentiments.

◆ ◆ ◆

I had been in the yeshivah for over two years when Rav Dovid called me into his private study one day for a serious conversation.

"Binyomin," he said to me, "you've been at Telshe for a while and have grown. I've kept a close eye on you throughout this time and have come to the conclusion that it's time for you to move on."

Now it so happened that the *roshei yeshivah* of Telshe were not in favor of boys going to learn in Eretz Yisrael at all. They didn't understand why *bachurim* — even boys who had reached the age of 22 or 23 — had to leave the yeshivah for an unsupervised environment. I, however, wasn't 22. I was 18 — and to leave Telshe to go study in Eretz Yisrael at 18 was unheard of! But here was Rav Dovid Barkin, the angelic *masmid* of Telshe, telling one of his closest *talmidim* that it was time for him to leave.

"What yeshivah does Rebbi want me to go to?"

"I feel that you will do very well at the Mir Yeshivah in Yerushalayim."

"Whose *shiur*?"

"There's a *maggid shiur* in the Mir named Rav Asher Arieli," Rav Dovid replied. "His *shiur* is famous around the world, and for good reason. I feel that it will be the perfect environment for you."

I was torn. On the one hand, Rav Dovid Barkin had already made up his mind that it was time for me to move on, despite the fact that I was only 18. On the other hand, others didn't agree with him. One *mashgiach* looked me straight in the eye and told me that he would "chain me down to the bench" before allowing me to leave Telshe. Rav Chaim Stein, one of the *roshei yeshivah*, also came out strongly against my leaving. You can imagine my dilemma. I respected the *roshei yeshivah* of Telshe immensely, and to disobey Rav Chaim Stein was unheard of!

I knew who Rav Chaim was. I had seen him in action. For a portion of the time that I was learning in Telshe, one of Rav Chaim's sons had been suffering from a difficult illness. Through those darkest of days, we could see the intensity of Rav Chaim's service of Hashem. We knew of his multiple fast days and how much he demanded of himself. We saw his exceptionally high level of accountability and intuitively understood that here was a man who was held in the highest regard by *Shamayim*. Nobody knew the exact details of the story, but in the end his son recovered, and there was no doubting his father's involvement or the vast amount of spiritual effort he had devoted toward saving his son's life.

On another occasion, Rav Chaim instructed a *bachur* who was returning to Monsey for Shabbos to wait until Sunday morning before making the return trip back to Cleveland. The student, who thought Rav Chaim was merely giving him a free piece of good advice, disregarded his words (no doubt due to having arranged transportation for an earlier return) and drove back to Cleveland that *motza'ei Shabbos*. Sunday morning, however, brought with it a phone call from home telling him that his grandfather had passed away and that he needed to make the trip back home once again for the funeral.

That was Rav Chaim Stein. A man who possessed wisdom so indisputable that I simply feared disobeying his direct command.

But Rav Dovid did not back down. Clearly he felt that as my rebbi he knew me and what suited me best.

◆ ◆ ◆

During my time at Telshe I had begun what would become a lifelong correspondence with one Rav Chaim Kanievsky of Rashbam Street in Bnei Brak. I was the type of *bachur* who was constantly looking into a wide assortment of questions on many different *sugyos* and enjoyed discussing my ideas and conclusions with the *roshei yeshivah* of whichever yeshivah I was in at the time. There happened to be a student from Australia studying in Telshe right then who informed me that I could write to Rav Chaim in Eretz Yisrael with my numerous *kasha*s and he would write to me with his answers.

And so it began. I wrote to Rav Chaim, including a self-addressed envelope in the letter, and received his response like clockwork two weeks later.

During the course of the "great Telshe argument" over my future, I had sent a letter to Rav Chaim, which had been returned to sender, apparently having not been addressed properly. This was my third letter to him; he'd replied to all of my questions in the first two in record time. I re-sent the third letter, and when his response arrived, I found to my great surprise that he had ignored the entire list of questions and written the following cryptic message:

"When you arrive in Eretz Yisrael, come in to see me."

I hadn't mentioned a word about leaving Telshe for Eretz Yisrael, and his response was extremely surprising, to say the least. I hadn't yet reached the point in our relationship where I was asking his advice — our correspondence had been devoted to clarifying my questions on Gemara and halachah — and yet here he was offering it to me, unasked!

I studied his one-line answer and repeated the words over and over to myself. *When you arrive in Eretz Yisrael, come in to see me.*

I carried Rav Chaim's missive to Rav Dovid Barkin, and said, "Rebbi, isn't this the clearest sign from Heaven that I should get on a plane and go to Eretz Yisrael?"

Rav Chaim Stein at a *siyum Mishnayos* that I made
for my great-uncle's *sheloshim*

"This is a *'ra'ayah she'ein aleha teshuvah*,' a proof that can't be dismantled," he responded after studying the letter closely. "A clear directive telling you to go."

That was that.

I didn't have the courage to ask Rav Chaim Stein for a letter of endorsement before I left, but I did go in to say good-bye and to thank him for two of the best years of my life. Rav Dovid did, of course, provide me with a beautiful letter of recommendation for Rav Nosson Tzvi Finkel, the *Rosh Yeshivah* of the Mir, as did Rav Isaac Ausband, another one of the Telshe *roshei yeshivah* with whom I had a close connection.

I was embarrassed to use Rav Ausband's letter of recommendation, being that he had written inside, "*Shelamad biyeshivah harbeh shanim*" — that I had learned in the yeshivah for many years. Since I had only been at Telshe for a little over two years, I was afraid to show this to any *rosh yeshivah*, who would take a look at my 18-year-old self and ask me what Rav Ausband had meant when he wrote "many years." To me it was clear that he had written those words due to the depth of our relationship. Even though I hadn't actually been there a very long time in physical terms, I had made the best of the two years and gleaned a tremendous amount from every one of the *roshei yeshivah* and staff, to the point where, in his eyes at least, it seemed like I had been at Telshe for "many years."

I still have Rav Isaac's letter. It occupies a beloved place in my heart, testifying to the fondness and love that came my way from the phenomenally great men of Telshe. No, it was never used as a recommendation. But I will always cherish it as a reminder of two amazing years of growth and uninterrupted learning alongside some of the brightest minds and loftiest spirits of the American yeshivah world.

It was now time for me to move on to Eretz Yisrael and the next part of my life. I boarded the flight to Tel Aviv, fingering Rav Chaim's letter as his words reverberated through my mind: *When you arrive in Eretz Yisrael, come in to see me.*

I could hardly wait.

Encounters with

Rav
Asher Arieli
שליט"א

Rav Asher Arieli at our *vort*

He walks the hallways of the Mir as if he's just another yungerman.

He teaches thousands without considering himself a cut above.

He is a man who doesn't waste a second, a rebbi par excellence, and a loyal, trusted adviser.

They call him Rav Asher. One of the most famous maggidei shiur in the world.

Rav Asher Arieli

Part A

Rav Asher Arieli, *shlita*, is arguably the best-known *maggid shiur* in the world, with the number of those attending his *shiur* topping 500. While times have changed since those early days when I arrived in Yerushalayim, and Rav Asher's *shiur* is now located in a spacious room with sufficient seats for anyone who wants to attend, back then he gave *shiur* in the yeshivah's bomb shelter and there was extremely limited space. Boys stood in the hallway and up the staircase leading to the first floor, while others listened to the *shiur* in their dorm rooms on an inhouse radio system that had been rigged for that express purpose.

While obtaining a seat was extremely difficult, developing a connection with Rav Asher himself seemed near impossible. The knowledge that I was attending a *shiur* given by a man of such capabilities gave me no rest. Here I was, hearing a daily

Rav Dovid Barkin in Rav Asher Arieli's *succah* —
I was privileged to introduce these two great *talmidei chachamim*

shiur from a man who possessed infinite reserves of Torah learning and from whom I could gain so much — if only I could find the key to open the door that was so firmly shut between us. Though discouraged, I did not consider giving up. If I had managed to develop a relationship with Rav Dovid Barkin while in Telshe, I'd do my best to make a *kesher* with Rav Asher Arieli here in the Mir.

No easy task, this: while Rav Dovid's *shiur* had been composed of 40 boys, Rav Asher was teaching 500 *talmidim* and seemed as busy an individual as I'd ever met.

Still, there were times when the *talmidim* were able to ask him questions, and I took my place in line, hoping for an opportunity to find my way into his heart. I knew that here was a great man, and that I wanted more than to attend his *shiurim*, important as they were. I wanted to know him and for him to know me. The only question was how to achieve the impossible.

After a while, I managed to obtain a seat close by Rav Asher, enabling me to ask questions. It was the beginning of a relationship, but I wanted something much more personal. I was at a loss as to how to achieve that which I so desired. And then one evening, everything changed. It was unexpected and unplanned. Nevertheless, it served as the catalyst for the relationship that I had been so hoping for.

After *shiur* had ended, I took my place in the line, determined to wait until I had a chance to speak with Rav Asher in learning. He spoke to each *talmid* with great patience, and the minutes slipped by. Finally, I was one student away from speaking with him. And then, just as the final barrier between us came down, Rav Asher glanced at his watch, gave me his shy smile, and said, "I'm sorry, but I have to leave now."

I confess my sins. I couldn't help it: a look of utter and abject disappointment crossed my face. And Rav Asher noticed it.

In my defense, the pace of Rav Asher's *shiurim* is extremely rapid, and this had been my chance to discuss that day's learning with him. The coming day would bring an entirely different *shiur* in its place. I felt that I was missing an opportunity that could never be reclaimed. I was still very young and didn't stop to think about the fact that Rav Asher had a life of his own and obligations to take care of. I was merely disappointed — and it showed.

When he returned to the yeshivah that night, a crowd of some 20 or 30 boys rushed over to speak with him. Once again I took my place in line, hoping to succeed where I had failed in the past. When our eyes met, however, I got the feeling that Rav Asher was not happy with me, that the look that had crossed my face that afternoon had not been well received by him.

Heart pounding with remorse, I waited around until everyone had finished talking to him. When it was time for Rav Asher to leave, I turned to him and said, "I sense that Rebbi is upset at me."

"I would like to talk with you," he replied. "I'm going home now. Would you like to accompany me? We'll have time to talk along the way."

I nodded my head vigorously, and we left the Mir together.

"You should know," he began, "that your look this afternoon gave me a very bad feeling. There's a *talmid* in the *shiur* whose mother is very sick. They made an emergency *minyan* to daven for her at the Kosel this afternoon, and he asked me to attend. I had to leave at that point, but you made a face as if I was doing something wrong!

"I never asked anyone to come learn by me, and I don't consider myself sufficiently worthy that people should want to come and learn from me. *Sach hakol*, I say that whoever's interested can come and learn together with me, and I learn out loud in front of a group of people. But that anyone should feel like I owe him something and should make me feel like I haven't acted properly, that's not okay."

I apologized profusely to him. "Rebbi," I said, "I've just come from Telshe where I had a very close relationship with my *rebbeim*. Not only that, my rebbi, Rav Dovid Barkin, sent me to learn by you! But try as I might, it seems almost impossible to develop a connection with you. That's why I was disappointed."

In the shadowy darkness of the silent Yerushalayim street, I could feel that my words, spoken from the heart, had made an impression. I could tell that Rav Asher was concerned by my revelations and especially by the fact that I had come to his *shiur* with certain expectations that had not been fulfilled.

"You should know something, Binyomin," he suddenly said. "I have never had complaints or a grudge against a person in my life. Not that I was never hurt by someone else, but I myself was never angry at anyone. You shouldn't feel, *chas v'shalom*, that I am at all angry at you in any way. I like you...I love you..."

With every word, Rav Asher was validating me as a *talmid*, talking to me in a loving voice, drawing me closer to his internal world. Our conversation continued until we arrived at his apartment building in Sanhedria. I could see that he was filled with remorse for having been "too harsh" with me.

"Binyomin," he said, "you should know that I love you very much!"

We then continued speaking for another few minutes and parted warmly from each other. I returned to the yeshivah knowing that a breakthrough had been achieved between Rav

Asher and myself. That conversation is something I'll treasure forever.

◆ ◆ ◆

The character trait that most characterized Rav Asher is his astounding humility. Despite having the Torah world running after him and close to 500 *talmidim* in his daily *shiur*, nothing went to his head. He eschews the typical and (even expected) frock of the *maggid shiur* and speaks with one and all as if they were his equals.

When I first arrived in Eretz Yisrael, my father told me to look up an old friend of his with whom he had learned in Chevron. His name was Rav Yehudah Dvir. A famous personality in the Torah world, Rav Yehudah is the author of a widely accepted *sefer* on *Shas*, *Beis Lechem Yehudah*. We got to know each other and before long had become close, our relationship culminating in a learning *seder* every Friday night in *Ramban*. Rav Yehudah would go on to publish a set of *sefarim* on *Ramban* that he entitled *Beis HaYayin*, part of which was based on our Friday-night sessions. The Dvir family lived in Sanhedria, and Rav Yehuda and Rav Asher davened in the same shul.

One Friday night, when I was staying at the home of the Dvir family, I accompanied Rav Yehudah to shul. After *Ma'ariv*, I went over to Rav Asher to wish him a *"gut Shabbos."* Rav Asher, however, was in a private discussion with someone I did not know. Not wanting to intrude and realizing that the conversation might take a while, I joined Rav Yehudah for the short walk back to his home, slightly disappointed that I hadn't been able to use the opportunity to exchange a few words with Rav Asher.

We sang *Shalom Aleichem* and *Eishes Chayil*, and Rav Yehudah made Kiddush, when there was a knock. One of the children ran to open the door, and there, standing in the doorway, was Rav Asher Arieli, who had walked a block and a half out of his way to come wish me a "good Shabbos."

His arrival took us all completely by surprise.

"I'm so sorry," he kept repeating. "I just couldn't stop in the middle of my conversation with that man…"

It was pure humility without a trace of personal motivation or pride.

It was a classic Rav Asher moment.

◆ ◆ ◆

A few years ago the Mir learning cycle came around to *maseches Bava Basra*. I was no longer learning in the Mir, but I felt a desire to hear Rav Asher's *shiurim* once again; a nostalgic longing for the sound of his voice and the magic of his *chiddushim*. My weekly schedule didn't allow me to attend his daily *shiur* at the yeshivah, but I listened to his *shiurim* on Kol Halashon. One Thursday night, however, I boarded a bus to Yerushalayim to join a private group of close *talmidim* in Rav Asher's home, where he'd share some original *chiddushim* with the 30 or so regulars who attended. It was a serious group of men, some of whom had been attending this particular *shiur* for years.

I had been out of the Mir for about 15 years by then and didn't recognize anyone in the room. "By the way," one of the assembled said to me, "there are set places here. Every seat is taken."

I nodded. It made sense. With 15 chairs and 30 participants, half of those attending were forced to stand. It didn't bother me at all. In fact, it helped me feel like I was a *bachur* again, standing on the staircase of the bomb shelter, craning my neck to hear Rav Asher's words, just like old times.

I stood alongside the regulars and enjoyed Rav Asher's Torah. It was over at 11 o'clock, and most of the men left, with a few remaining behind to clarify a few points with Rav Asher. Since I had a long bus ride ahead of me, I wished him good night and left for the bus stop.

Rav Asher called me the next day.

"I feel so terrible. I don't know what to do. A *chashuve* guest comes to the *chaburah*, and I didn't even give you a chair to sit on. It's not right. I simply didn't know what to do. The others have their usual places, and I couldn't take one of their chairs away from them. But how did I let you stand for the whole time? I'm going to go out and buy a special chair just for you!"

"Rebbi, please don't buy a chair just for me. Please! I can stand just like everyone else!"

"*Chas v'shalom*, I'm buying you a chair. Next time you come, you'll have where to sit."

I begged him not to buy me a chair, promising to take care of the matter myself — and I did, by purchasing my own stool, which I left in his home to use on Thursday nights, knowing that Rav Asher would have no peace of mind until I had a place to sit.

◆ ◆ ◆

One Thursday evening the weather turned stormy during the *shiur*. It had been dry when I left my home hours before, and I had neglected to bring an umbrella with me. Rav Asher was very concerned.

"Here, here," he said, handing me his own raincoat and umbrella.

There was no way in the world that I would ever consider accepting his offer.

"Reb Binyomin," he entreated me, " '*anashim achim anachnu*' — we're brothers!"

He was seriously expecting me to accept his own raincoat and umbrella! (It wasn't a game with him; he really, really meant for me to take his personal belongings.)

"Rebbi, thank you, but I'll manage. Don't worry."

"At least allow me to give you money for a taxi from Sanhedria back to Beit Shemesh!"

It took time, but eventually I was able to convince him that I'd be O.K. Then I left his home, bracing myself against the cold wind and filled with the warmth of his love.

◆ ◆ ◆

For Rav Asher Arieli, life is divided into two distinct categories: during the *zeman* and *bein hazemanim*. During the *zeman*, his mind is 100 percent focused on his learning and teaching, to the exclusion of everything else. When a member of the *shiur* produced a musical album, of course he presented Rav Asher with a copy. A few weeks later I asked Rav Asher's son whether they'd already opened the CD.

"No," he answered, shaking his head in the negative, "my father told us to wait until *bein hazemanim*."

Question: Who in the world waits for *bein hazemanim* to open a CD?

Answer: Rav Asher Arieli and his family.

◆ ◆ ◆

On one occasion, before leaving to the States for a visit, I asked Rav Asher what I could bring him back from America.

"*Chas v'shalom*, Binyomin, we have everything we need."

Despite his protestations that the Arieli family was blessed with anything and everything they could possibly ever want or need, I did manage to think of a useful gift to bring them. I had noticed that during Rav Asher's Thursday night *shiurim* the phone, which was attached to the wall, would ring many times, but Rav Asher's wife wasn't able to answer because the room was crowded with *yungeleit*. A set of cordless phones would be the perfect gift for the Arieli family.

I knew that if I suggested an upgrade from their phone on the wall to a modern cordless, Rav Asher, who personified simplicity itself, wouldn't see the need, so I purchased it on my own initiative.

Rav Asher was taken aback. "It probably cost a fortune!"

"No, Rebbi, today they're not expensive."

"Let me pay you for it."

"Out of the question."

And so on.

A couple of months later I asked Rav Asher if they ever started using their new phone. He answered in the negative.

"Why not?"

"We have to bring a handyman to break the wall."

I was shocked. "Why do you need to bring someone to break the wall?"

"Because the plug doesn't go in. It's built for an American outlet."

"Rebbe," I said, "you can buy the plastic piece you need to adapt the plug for the Israeli electrical system in any hardware store for two shekels."

In the end I bought one for him myself so they could begin using the phone, and I never forgot his beauty and purity: how his essence was so completely immersed in Torah learning that he really didn't know that the adapter he needed was available at the corner store for a few pennies.

◆ ◆ ◆

When my wife was first starting out in her chosen field of reflexology and massage therapy, she was offered a job in the school where she had studied. The pay wasn't much, but we looked at it as a way for her to build the clientele she needed before striking out on her own.

Many of her fellow workers weren't religious, and when she told me some of the topics they spoke about during the day, I became uncomfortable with the situation. She'd studied there

Rav Asher visiting us in our home

without mishap, but now she was suddenly becoming exposed to many things that she had never been exposed to before. The more I heard about the atmosphere at her job, the more I felt that it was not the kind of place that was healthy — from a spiritual standpoint.

When I broached the idea of her leaving the job, some of our acquaintances objected that it would be crazy to give up such a wonderful job: the money, the experience... "You don't just throw something like that away!" they said.

Parnassah is parnassah, I said to myself, *but it can't be allowed to come before a person's spiritual growth.*

Wasting no more time, I put my wife on the phone with Rav Asher. He asked her to describe the atmosphere at the job and what type of discussions and conversations were normal among the other workers.

"If I were you," he told her after she'd finished describing the scene to him, "I would leave there yesterday!"

That was that. Of course, it was hard for us to make such a decision, but the *psak* was clear and we followed through. Having no choice, my wife threw herself into the deep water of private practice. It was very hard in the beginning. She was a newcomer in the field, and people hesitated to spend their hard-earned money on someone they had never heard of.

Baruch Hashem, she slowly built up her reputation, and she now has a thriving practice. The fact that she had forced herself to leave the "safe" confines of her job served as the catalyst to much greater growth for her in her private practice. Even more, she had been forced to become a much more confident and proactive person. All this stemmed from following Rav Asher's *da'as Torah* and doing the right thing, even when it seemed so difficult to do.

I still ask Rav Asher's opinion and advice on a regular basis. Though young — he is only in his mid-50's — he is a truly great man, and I have been fortunate to share a deep rebbi-*talmid* relationship with him, which I hope will continue for many, many years to come.

Encounters with

Rav
Chaim Kanievsky
שליט"א

Sharing a special moment with Rav Chaim

At the end of a simple street, there stands a small building. People wait for hours outside that building. This is the home of HaRav Chaim Kanievsky. Son of the Steipler Gaon and son-in-law of Rav Elyashiv, Rav Chaim is himself recognized as a master of every area of Torah. Who hasn't heard of Rav Chaim?

As with all of the greatest people, Rav Chaim has never looked for or sought attention in any way. But it comes to him...as endless lines of people and thousands of letters can attest.

Enter the Kanievsky home.

This is where miracles happen.

Rav Chaim Kanievsky

Part A

One of the most famous addresses in the Jewish world today is 23 Rashbam Street. Located within the confines of Bnei Brak, on a street pulsing with the authenticity of genuine Torah life, the house and its adjoining neighborhood are a throwback to a time of simplicity and purity: to the years of the Steipler Gaon, the Chazon Ish, Rav Shmuel Greineman, and Rav Shach. This is the world in which Rav Chaim Kanievsky grew up, the city where he lived with his Rebbetzin and raised his children, the city from which his light has spread forth to every corner of the world.

Though the Bnei Brak of today is most certainly not the Bnei Brak of 30 years ago, there are parts of it that have managed to retain the original magic. And Rechov Rashbam, home to the Kanievsky family, the Lederman Shul, and countless families of sincere *bnei Torah*, is one of those.

◆ ◆ ◆

Of course, I went to see Rav Chaim Kanievsky as soon as possible after my arrival. After all, in a very real sense, it had been his timely letter that had made my coming to Eretz Yisrael a reality. Clutching his precious missive in my hand, I alighted from the Number 400 bus on Nechemyah Street, crossed over to the other side, and found the entrance to Rechov Rashbam. As I walked past the Lederman Shul, I caught a glimpse of Rav Chaim leaving his home and getting into a waiting car.

Hurrying over to the car before it drove away, I stuck my hand through the window and handed him "his" letter (with its request that I come to see him), my "passport," as it were, into the home and life of Rav Chaim Kanievsky.

Upon reading the letter, Rav Chaim treated me to a big beautiful smile, told me that he was just leaving for a *bris*, and would be back in about half an hour. He asked me to wait at his home until he returned.

I did. That was the first encounter of many.

While visiting Rav Chaim Brim, *zt"l*, one of Yerushalayim's most respected *talmidei chachamim*, a few days after my arrival in Eretz Yisrael, I related the story of Rav Chaim's letter and how it had alleviated any doubts I might have had about following Rav Dovid's advice to leave America for the Mir in Yerushalayim. Rav Chaim Brim was obviously impressed by what he perceived as another example of the *ruach hakodesh* (those were his words!) that Rav Chaim Kanievsky possessed.

"What a *moiridige* (awesome) story about Rav Chaim," he enthused. "Tell me more stories, please, about Rav Chaim. Tell me more!"

I didn't have more stories at that time, but it wasn't long before I could tell stories about Rav Chaim. Many, many stories.

◆ ◆ ◆

The average visitor who crosses Rav Chaim's threshold and enters his home doesn't get a chance to know him at all. When I first began visiting Rav Chaim, I'd get a few minutes to spend with him, just like everyone else. It was impossible to catch a real glimpse of Rav Chaim's personality in so brief an encounter. But those who are fortunate enough to spend more time with Rav Chaim when it's not overly busy in the house, or when he's not under tremendous pressure, find themselves in the company of a very relaxed and caring person, since Rav Chaim is one of the nicest, sweetest people one could ever hope to meet.

Sometimes a visitor will present himself to Rav Chaim, never dreaming that on the previous night Rav Chaim had slept all of one hour. Though his schedule is such that he almost never sleeps more than three hours a night, there are nights when he barely manages one. There's a reason for this. Rav Chaim has imposed upon himself a non-negotiable schedule of learning that he must accomplish every single day. The greatest pressure for Rav Chaim is when he has fallen behind in his learning schedule. It might be 50 *blatt* of *Yerushalmi* or half a *Bavli masechta*, but Rav Chaim considers his learning obligations a *chov*, a debt, and cannot rest or sleep until his "debt" is paid.

Rav Chaim's learning is often interrupted by visitors, some from abroad, some bearing life-and-death questions, so being sleep deprived is a normal state for him. But when the doors are closed, and there aren't many people around and his "debt" has been paid, he has all the time in the world to give to those who are close to him.

There was one time, however, when Rav Chaim wasn't himself, and that was when the Rebbetzin passed away. Rav Chaim lost weight drastically, to the point where those around him were worried about his health. He couldn't stop crying during the *shivah*. Though some may have had the impression that they barely spent time together, that wasn't true. Rav Chaim and the Rebbetzin had their special times together, and those moments were sacrosanct. Theirs was a relationship that radiated mutual love and respect. When she passed away, Rav Chaim was broken, almost inconsolable. When I came to see him during the *shivah*, I was shocked at how he looked; he was utterly bereaved and bereft.

The family set up a rotation system so that the thousands of people who were pouring in — ordinary people (is there such a

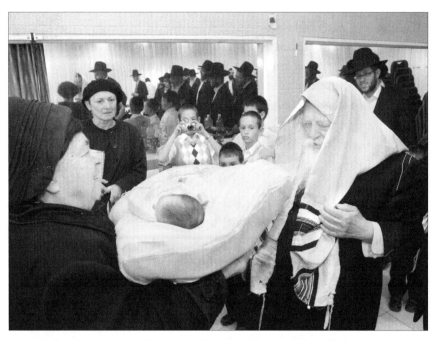

Honored as *kvateren*, the Rebbetzin hands our baby to Rav Chaim, *kvater* and *sandak*, at our son's *bris*

thing as an ordinary Jew?) alongside the leaders of the generation — could all pay condolences to their beloved Rav Chaim. Each visitor was able to stay for a minute or two before regretfully taking leave while trying to convey just how sorry he/she was.

I passed before him. I could see how broken he was. The tears were streaming down his face. Just seeing Rav Chaim in such a state brought tears to my own eyes, and I didn't know what to say. My mind went completely blank. I, who always had plenty of words, was speechless. But Rav Chaim knew just what to say. Meeting my gaze, the venerable *gadol hador* uttered but a few words.

"I received your letter," he said to me.

For the last 15 years I had sent Rav Chaim letters filled with Torah questions on a regular basis. I had written thousands of questions to him, and he had replied with thousands of answers. (Many of those *teshuvos* would eventually be turned into a *sefer*.) Obviously he'd received that week's letter and wanted to let me know. Even while sitting *shivah* for his beloved Rebbetzin, he'd possessed the presence of mind to tell me that he'd received my letter! A true *gadol*.

◆ ◆ ◆

I heard the following story while sitting with Rav Chaim and the Rebbetzin at their Shabbos table.

A child born at the Mayanei HaYeshuah Hospital in Bnei Brak was very ill, and the doctors had almost given up hope of his survival. Ultimately, though, the child recovered. All who witnessed the story agreed that it was nothing short of a miracle.

When the family was checking out of the hospital with their newborn, they made sure to thank the devoted staff who had been instrumental in saving their child's life. When they went in to say good-bye to the head of the department, a nonreligious woman, she told them, "Your child is alive. It's clearly a miracle, without a medical explanation. But there is an explanation of a different kind. When Dr. Rothschild, the founder of the hospital, was in the process of establishing Mayanei HaYeshuah in Bnei Brak, the Steipler gave him a blessing that no baby should ever die in the *machleket yoldot,* the maternity ward. We have assisted thousands of women to give birth in our wards," she told the parents, "and until this day no baby ever died in the maternity ward at Mayanei HaYeshuah!"

From Rav Chaim's reaction, I couldn't tell whether he had already known about his father's *berachah*, but he smiled broadly upon learning that in all the years since Bnei Brak's famous hospital had been established, no baby had died in that particular ward.

◆ ◆ ◆

Another time a man came in to see Rav Chaim when I was there. The man was suffering intensely from cellulitis. After explaining his medical condition in detail, he related a story he had heard that might have a direct bearing on his condition.

The man told Rav Chaim the story of a certain Sephardic Jew from Bnei Brak who had been in the cemetery when the *chevrah kaddisha* had brought in Rav Chaim's father, the Steipler, for burial. The cemetery had suddenly become filled with people, and someone told this man that the crowd was there for the *levayah* of the Steipler, known as one of *Klal Yisrael's* greatest leaders.

After a few minutes, it became clear that there was a serious problem. It seemed that Arabs had broken into the cemetery on the previous evening and stolen all the equipment, making it extremely difficult to bury the Steipler. Without proper shovels, preparing the Steipler's grave became a backbreaking and time-consuming task that the *chevrah kaddisha* was ill equipped to handle.

Watching the proceedings, this Sephardic Jew soon came to the conclusion that the Steipler Gaon's burial might have to be pushed off to a later time — a terrible dishonor for such a *tzaddik* — if the proper tools weren't located and soon. It so happened that this man's father was a successful contractor who owned a lot of equipment. Without wasting any time, and despite the fact that it was difficult for him to move quickly due to the fact that he was suffering from cellulitis, the man left the cemetery, contacted his father, and arranged that his workers quickly bring as many shovels as they might possibly need to bury the Steipler with the proper respect.

That night, the Steipler came to this Sephardic Jew in a dream.

"I have tremendous *hakaras hatov* to you for what you did for me today," he told the man. "You are suffering from cellulitis on your foot. I am now going to place my hand on your foot, and when you wake up, your foot will be completely healed. Not only that, from now on, if a person suffering from cellulitis comes to see you and you place your hand on the affected spot, he will be cured. His cellulitis will disappear!"

"Rebbi," said the man to Rav Chaim, "this is the story that I have heard. I, too, suffer from cellulitis. Should I go see this man and have him place his hand on my foot, or not?"

I was very curious to hear Rav Chaim's reaction.

"Why not?" Rav Chaim responded. "Try it!"

The man left to follow Rav Chaim's advice. I met the man a while later once again at Rav Chaim's home.

"Did you ever have that Sephardi Jew place his hand on your foot?" I asked.

"I did," the man replied.

"Did it help?"

"It could be, but since I was taking antibiotics at the same time, it's difficult to know if that was the only reason it was healed. Still, it did disappear in a way that could definitely be attributed to the man's *berachah* from the Steipler — even if the *berachah* had been granted in a dream."

◆ ◆ ◆

Though Rav Chaim's focus is almost completely Torah related, to the exclusion of everything else, there are certain times — mainly Shabbos meals, when he's surrounded by family and those close to him — when he will recount a personal story or two. Those are moments to cherish, for they are rare and pro-

A Torah moment with Rav Chaim

vide a candid look into Rav Chaim's world. On one occasion, Rav Chaim related the following incident from his youth.

"When I was child growing up in Novaradok," he said, "there was another youth in the town who, instead of growing taller as he grew older, was gaining inches around his waist. He was growing wider and wider instead of taller. He became heavier and heavier, his girth so large that it became difficult for him to walk. The family summoned doctors from all over Europe to come and see him; the truth is, it wasn't difficult to convince them to come because they wanted to study this unique medical and scientific phenomenon.

"At some point, the situation became so bad, with his bodily dimensions so out of proportion, that the boy was no longer able to sit or stand, but could only lie on a bed, barely able to move.

"On Purim the community collected money for this boy's medical expenses, and the people, knowing how desperate a situation it was, donated as generously as they were able. At some point," Rav Chaim continued, "my father, *zt"l*, and our family moved to Eretz Yisrael, and after our arrival we no longer heard news about this boy.

"The war broke out not long afterward, and then, of course, we lost all semblance of a connection to that part of the world. Though I wondered what happened to that boy from time to time, I never dreamed I'd ever hear the end of the story.

"But in the years following the war, we heard the story's surprising conclusion. When the Nazis came to Novaradok, they gathered all the town's boys, who were either shot or deported to places unknown, *Rachmana litzlan*. But when the SS troops arrived at this boy's house and saw a human mountain lying immovable in his bed, they saw no reason to waste their time and ammunition on him, seeing that he would no doubt die if left to fend for himself.

In an awesomely unexpected turn of events, the boy, whom everyone (even the Nazis) had given up on, somehow survived the war, moved to Eretz Yisrael, and, amazingly, reverted back to normal health. He stopped growing sideways, put inches on his height, and became the picture of good health. He married, had children, and lived a life of utter normalcy in every way.

"When my father heard the whole amazing story," Rav Chaim concluded, "he couldn't believe it. If we hadn't known the details, it would have been one thing, but we were there, we had seen him, we knew what he'd been like. My father called it a *nes galui*, an open miracle."

Rav Chaim became very emotional when he related this story.

"I remember how everyone talked about this boy, how everyone went to gawk at him and stare at him as if he were an exotic animal in the zoo...and *davka* this boy ended up surviving. It was as if Hashem chose to gift him with a physical deformity so that he'd survive the war and help rebuild the Jewish people."

◆ ◆ ◆

Rav Chaim is wont to stress that nothing a person does is ever forgotten and that Heaven is extremely *makpid* that every person pay back his debts, even if the amount is minuscule, and even if the loan had taken place a long time before. Nothing is forgotten and nothing is erased.

"To the point," Rav Chaim says, "where a certain Jew who lived next door to a family who owned a number of chickens found himself facing a very strange and ongoing occurrence. Every morning one of the family's hens would leave its master's fenced-off area, make its way into the man's courtyard, and lay an egg before returning to his yard. The man informed the family and asked them to please take the necessary precautions to make sure their hens weren't able to run free and wild, yet somehow, no matter what the family did, the hen still managed to enter the neighbor's courtyard and lay its daily egg.

"Seeing that the matter wasn't being resolved by normal means, the man began devoting more and more thought to the bizarre daily encounter with the hen, trying to figure out why this could be happening. And then, suddenly, it came to him. He remembered that he'd lent his neighbor a sum of money, and that the man had passed away before returning it to him. Feeling bad about raising the matter with the man's children, he had let the whole thing drop.

Maybe, he said to himself, *the reason the hen keeps on coming to lay eggs in my yard, day after day, is to pay back the money its master owes me.*

"The man decided to try an experiment. The next day when the hen arrived, he was waiting for it.

"'Listen to me,' he said to the hen, 'if you are coming to my house because of the money your master owed me, know that I am *mochel* the debt *b'lev shalem,* with a whole heart. You do not have to come here any longer.'

"The hen apparently understood and stopped coming.

"The fact is," Rav Chaim continues, "my father, the Steipler, came to me in a dream a short while after he passed away to tell me that he owed someone money and that I had to take care of the matter as soon as possible."

Which Rav Chaim did.

He'll relate this story or that story, savoring the lesson and enjoying the message. Even his stories are all Torah.

◆　◆　◆

"Your mother was my *shadchan,*" someone told Rav Chaim, "and I never paid her a *shadchan's* fee. Since you're the heir, I would like to give you a gift. What would you like for *shadchanus?*"

Rav Chaim knew that this particular individual had known the Chazon Ish. "I would like you to write down for me everything you ever spoke about with the Chazon Ish. Every question you asked and every answer he gave. This will fulfill your *shadchanus* obligation to me."

When Rav Chaim related this story, he explained that his mother used to manage a school for orphan girls in her younger years. She cared for the girls until she saw them standing under the *chuppah* with a husband. The man who paid his *shadchanus* fee by sharing memories of the Chazon Ish had been engaged to one of her girls.

"A short while after their engagement," Rav Chaim continued, "the *kallah* swallowed a needle by mistake. This placed her in terrible danger; the needle's sharp point was capable of puncturing a vital organ."

The *chasan* and his *kallah* immediately went to confer with the Chazon Ish, who told them there was nothing to worry about, that the needle would emerge safely prior to the wedding. As per the Chazon Ish's promise, the needle emerged on the day of the wedding, exactly as he'd said it would.

"Unfortunately, the *shidduch* was not successful and ended years later in divorce. The reason for this," said Rav Chaim, "can be attributed to the fact that everyone in the city had been talking about the miracle that had taken place in their midst and the Chazon Ish's uncanny ability to predict the future. All this attention to the young couple was the source of an *ayin hara* that adversely affected their marriage."

As this story shows, Rav Chaim strongly feels that sometimes when someone is the recipient of a clear miracle, he should downplay his experience and not draw attention to himself so as to avoid any *ayin hara.*

◆ ◆ ◆

Another story: A man came from America especially to see the Steipler's Rebbetzin, Rav Chaim's mother, to ask her to find him a *shidduch.* She threw her prodigious skills into the challenge, suggesting one girl after another for the young man, but nothing came of any suggestion, and despite her best efforts, every idea fell flat as quickly as it had been raised.

At one point, as they sat together trying to figure out what was wrong, the man told the Steipler's Rebbetzin that he thought he knew what was holding him back.

"I was engaged once before," he admitted.

"When?"

"It happened back in Vilna."

"Why did you break off the *shidduch*?" the Rebbetzin wanted to know.

"Because I noticed a certain — how should I say this delicately — lack of normalcy from time to time. There were periods of complete lucidity, and other times when I sensed there was a problem. When I understood what was going on and what I had gotten myself into, I decided to visit Rav Chaim Ozer and ask his advice."

"What did he say?"

"Rav Chaim Ozer told me to marry her. Clearly he was hoping that her mental situation wasn't as bad as I imagined and that I would eventually become accustomed to it. Better that I marry her than break the engagement. I listened to Rav Chaim Ozer — a technical type of listening. I married the girl. And although he clearly meant that I should give the marriage a chance, I divorced her right away. Married her and divorced her. Technically I had fulfilled the mandate handed me by the *gadol hador* of Lithuanian Jewry. On the other hand, even I knew deep inside that this was not what Rav Chaim Ozer had meant.

"From the day I divorced my wife, nothing has worked out for me in the *shidduch* department. It's as if a brick wall has been erected between me and any possible success in matrimony. That's why I've come to see you, hoping that you'll have some success in helping me break through this spiritual blockage."

"My mother tried to help this man," Rav Chaim told his listeners, "but even she wasn't *matzliach* with him. When it comes to certain extremely delicate matters, one must be so, so careful with every move we make. In the end, he remained single for the rest of his life. People have to remember that the honor of a *bas Yisrael* is regarded very seriously by the *Ribbono shel Olam*."

◆ ◆ ◆

Though Rav Chaim is for the most part a person who looks at life with extreme seriousness, he is eminently capable of displaying a wonderfully developed sense of humor. On one of my frequent visits to the Kanievsky home, I asked Rav Chaim a halachic *she'eilah*. He responded by telling me that it boiled down to a question of *gezel akum,* stealing from a non-Jew. When I pressed him for a *psak*, he said, "I'm not a *posek*. Go ask my *shver*." (His *shver* — his father-in-law — was, of course, Rav Elyashiv, *zt"l*.)

I told him I'd go.

"You know that my *shver* lives in Yerushalayim?"

I nodded.

"You live in Beit Shemesh, correct?" (This was already after I had married and was living with my family in Beit Shemesh.)

Once again, I nodded my head in the affirmative. Then Rav Chaim asked me a very strange question.

"Where is Beit Shemesh? In America?"

I was completely at a loss for words. What kind of a question was that? What did he mean?

"Rebbi, Beit Shemesh is located between Bnei Brak and Yerushalayim."

"Oh, so it's close to Yerushalayim... So you can go and ask my *shver*."

I wasn't sure what to make of his words. I told them over to a few people, and every one of them was perplexed by Rav Chaim's reaction. Especially considering the fact that Beit Shemesh is clearly mentioned in *Tanach*, and Rav Chaim is just as much an expert on *Tanach* as he is on every other part of the Torah!

I wasn't able to rest until I had some kind of clarity. The very next time I wrote to him, I made sure to mention his comment and ask for an explanation.

(As an aside, Rav Chaim once told me that he receives between 50 to 100 letters a day. It's very difficult for him to answer all of them. "I try to answer as many as I can, but I don't have time to answer them all. I always answer your questions," he continued, "because you write in a very concise style, and I can answer your questions without looking things up." It took me time to understand exactly what kind of questions to send him in writing, but once I grasped what he preferred, I made sure to follow those guidelines.)

Rav Chaim's response to my question about his Beit Shemesh comment arrived a few days later. It was succinct and to the point.

"Yesh od Beit Shemesh b'chutz la'aretz — There is another Beit Shemesh located outside Eretz Yisrael. Look at *Yirmiyah mem gimmel, yud gimmel (Yirmiyahu* 43:13)."

I looked up Rav Chaim's source and discovered it referred to a Beit Shemesh located in Egypt, of all places! Then it dawned on me that Rav Chaim had been making a joke, and that this was his way of showing me his sense of humor.

"Which Beit Shemesh? The one in *chutz la'aretz*?" It was Rav Chaim's type of humor. He was enjoying the bit of knowledge that almost nobody else remembered: yes, there was another Beit Shemesh, and that while it was not situated across the ocean in the United States, it was most certainly nowhere near the flatlands of modern Beit Shemesh.

Rav Chaim had made a joke...and the joke was on me.

◆ ◆ ◆

Not far from Ramat Beit Shemesh is a picturesque little village called Beit Chilkiya. A quiet corner with beautiful fields and orchards nearby, Beit Chilkiya is the perfect place for working with animals, and indeed some years ago one of the families living there opened a farm where boys who haven't been able to find themselves in the regular school system can go and forge a connection with nature. One of my neighbors had a son living and working on the farm, so we took the children on a family outing there during vacation time.

We were warmly greeted by our neighbor, who asked the kids if they wanted to take a ride in one of their donkey carts.

"Of course," they chorused enthusiastically.

The boy hitched the donkey to a wagon and then drove us out into the fields surrounding Beit Chilkiya. This is moshav territory, with Yesodot and Chafetz Chaim not far away. With its verdant foliage and sloping hilltops abounding with flowers, the views are simply magnificent, and we were enjoying ourselves immensely.

I had always imagined the donkey to be a slow, plodding animal, but with our driver's prodding and direction, boy, was that donkey galloping along. The wagon jounced and bounced over the bumpy road; it really was quite a thrilling ride, except for the fact that we felt bad for the donkey, who was not enjoying itself as much as we were.

When we arrived home, I said to my wife, "The kids had such a great time, part of me even wishes that we could go out and buy our very own donkey!"

We laughed together, picturing a donkey residing in our backyard...and that was the end of the matter.

The next day I traveled to Bnei Brak to visit Rav Chaim. I had a number of issues to discuss with him. One of them was a question that I'd been considering for quite some time. I had owned a car in the past and was strongly leaning toward purchasing one again. As an American, owning a car was in the realm of the norm, but before I went out and committed myself, I wanted to ask Rav Chaim for his opinion. My mother-in-law was very much against us having a car — there had been a few horrific car accidents in the area just a short while before — and I was undecided.

"Rebbi," I said to Rav Chaim, "I want to purchase a car, but my mother-in-law is concerned."

"What do you need a car for?" Rav Chaim replied. "Just buy a donkey."

"*What?*" I said, taken aback by his response and recalling my donkey ride of the day before.

"Get a donkey," he repeated himself.

He had nothing more to say on the topic, and I wasn't sure where to go from there. Rav Chaim sat there smiling, a twinkle in his eye. Just get a donkey, the simplest thing in the world!

I didn't know what to make of this. We sat there for 30 seconds, after which he again reiterated his earlier piece of advice: "Just get a donkey."

"But, Rebbi, I need to get my family around!"

He considered that for a few seconds, then amended his earlier reply. "So get a horse."

"A horse?" I was at a loss for words at this bizarre conversation.

"Yes," he clarified. "The Mishnah says that the *olei regalim* used to ascend to Yerushalayim via horse. Get a horse."

Again I had no idea what to say or do. Was I supposed to answer? Where was this going? And all the while Rav Chaim was smiling to himself. Finally he stopped laughing and became serious.

"You're an American, right?"

I nodded.

"For an American, it's not a *chisaron* to buy a car."

"What should I do about my mother-in-law's concerns?"

"Only drive where you have to go. If you are careful to only use the car when you have to, you don't have to worry."

Once again, Rav Chaim showed me a rare flash of humor. That, plus the fact that his donkey comment came the day after our donkey encounter and my subsequent comments about donkeys and their benefits, ensured that I never forgot that particular interchange.

Rav Chaim Kanievsky

Part B

Does Rav Chaim have *ruach hakodesh*? He himself writes in his *sefer Orchos Yosher* that the sages of past generations sometimes exhibited *ruach hakodesh*, but that today we are living in times of concealment, of *hester panim*. And yet...

Ruach hakodesh doesn't necessarily mean that a person looks at your face and says, "Let me tell you what's going to happen to you tomorrow." Rav Chaim tailors his answers to every person in a uniquely individual manner. And in those answers one can't help but feel that *HaKadosh Baruch Hu* gave him the words that He wants the person to hear.

◆ ◆ ◆

Rav Chaim's usual *berachos* consist of two words: *berachah v'hatzlachah*, blessings and success. There are times, however, especially when it comes to matters of *shidduchim*, where he uses

Rav Chaim donning his tallis at our son's *bris*, where he served as *kvater* and *sandak*

the word *b'karov*, shortly. When he utters the word *b'karov*, you know it's time to start planning the *vort*. Of course, by now people know the code words and enter his study filled with hope that he will use them. When he says those words, they possess the power of dynamite. But there is no way to manipulate Rav Chaim and convince him to say what you want to hear. It just doesn't work that way, because Rav Chaim is no one's puppet.

Once he gives a *berachah*, he will not change his choice of phrase. You can try and try to convince him to add or subtract a word, but it's an impossible mission. I've seen people try three or four times, but he will almost never budge from his original position.

On one particular visit, I brought in a man who was seeking Rav Chaim's *berachah* for both his daughter and his daughter-in-law. The two of them were expecting, and the man wanted Rav

Chaim to give them a *berachah* for a *"leidah kalah,"* an easy birth. While translating the visitor's words into Yiddish for Rav Chaim's benefit, I mistakenly used the wrong words, and — as I realized only later — Rav Chaim thought I had said that they were seeking a blessing for children.

"They should check their mezuzahs" was Rav Chaim's response.

Rav Chaim often advises people who don't have children to check their mezuzahs, and I finally understood that Rav Chaim was under the impression that these two women were childless and that my translation had been faulty.

Meanwhile, the visitor was taken aback by the interchange. On the return trip to Yerushalayim, he kept asking me if I thought that Rav Chaim had seen or sensed that something was wrong. This was one nervous father. After all, he'd entered Rav Chaim's study merely seeking a blessing for an easy birth and had instead been told to check his mezuzahs, which could be an indication of impending problems. A sense of foreboding filled his heart.

I tried to reassure him. "Don't worry about it," I said. "It was all a misunderstanding."

But nothing I said made any difference.

"We have to go back to Rav Chaim," he said at last. "We need to go see him and ask him if he sees that there's something wrong!"

Instead of traveling all the way back to Rav Chaim's house, I called one of his grandsons, who had been there during our meeting and who had heard the entire conversation.

"Please go back and tell Rav Chaim what happened. Once you have clarified the situation, ask him whether this man has something to worry about or not."

The grandson did as I asked him.

"So many people ask me questions every day," Rav Chaim replied, after his grandson explained the situation. "I can't remember exactly how the question was asked. Whatever I understood at the time is how I answered it..."

The grandson returned to the phone.

"Reb Binyomin, you know my grandfather. If he said something, then it's worthwhile to pay close attention. He told the man to check his mezuzahs. What does he have to lose? Let him check his mezuzahs!"

The man returned to the States the next day. He called me up a few days later.

"Reb Binyomin, you're not going to believe what happened!"

"What happened?"

"You have to understand something. I purchased these mezuzahs myself. They were the most expensive mezuzahs I could find, the best the *sofer* had for sale. Somehow," he went on, "when the mezuzahs were rolled up and placed into their cases, the corner of one mezuzah was bent upward by mistake, cracking right through a letter. I purchased these mezuzahs only a year ago, and one of them was completely *pasul*! That was in one of my children's homes.

"In the second home, this one a rental, one of the mezuzahs had been placed inside its case upside down, and when my kids opened up another one of the cases, they found that it was completely empty, with no mezuzah within, either kosher or *pasul*! Since it was a rental, and the owner of the home was a Jew, they hadn't even thought to check them in the first place, and here they were, living their lives with real problems in the mezuzah department...and it was only due to Rav Chaim's 'mistake' that this was all discovered!"

All in a day's work in Rav Chaim's world.

On a different occasion many years ago I brought a friend who didn't have children to see Rav Chaim. He told him to check the mezuzahs, which they did. They found a problem, fixed it, and found out not long afterward that his wife was expecting. Excited by how quickly the situation had turned around, I returned to the Kanievsky home to share the good news with them, marveling at the miracle.

To my surprise, the family members found my excitement and wonder amusing.

"These are *ma'asim b'chol yom*," I was told. "Stories that happen every day."

◆ ◆ ◆

In general it's always a good idea to go see Rav Chaim with someone who knows how to speak to him. Many times I've seen people come in and begin describing the nature of their issue to him. Rav Chaim is hard of hearing in one ear. If the person doesn't talk loud enough, Rav Chaim will have trouble hearing his visitor, and at some point he will say, "What?" This confounds the person, who doesn't know where to start from. Many times the person gets all confused and loses his thread, and that's the end of the conversation. It is therefore imperative to visit Rav Chaim with someone who knows how to present your question.

I always tell people, if you're going yourself, write your request as a letter and place it before him. He will read it and give you an answer. Presenting a question to him without prior experience often does not work out. Just something for the prospective visitor to keep in mind.

◆ ◆ ◆

A relative of mine who teaches at a certain out-of-town school called one day. The community where she lives is off the beaten track, and it's not a simple thing to find a job in the area. Though people like living in the community, it's difficult to live there without being employed locally. She had been teaching in the community school for a couple of years with no trouble at all when suddenly problems began.

The principal, a veteran educator whom she respected and admired, began disagreeing with her decisions and then constantly finding fault with her. It was becoming impossible to work under such conditions, but she knew that giving up her job meant that the family would have to move from their community and home. It was a tough decision. She called me, terribly disturbed over what was taking place, especially since she and the principal had always gotten along before, and this seemed to be coming from out of nowhere and for no reason.

"Please go to Rav Chaim and ask him for a *berachah* for me."

I promised to do my best.

I went to Rav Chaim shortly afterward and told him the story, explaining how her boss had suddenly turned against her with no explanation.

As was his wont, Rav Chaim kept the wording short and to the point. "Hashem should help her," he said.

I called her back and related what Rav Chaim had said. She thanked me and we hung up.

My relative called me back within the month.

"Thank Hashem, I never had a lack of *emunas chachamim*," she began, "but I also never saw such a thing in my life, and I still can't believe what is happening!

"Shortly after you spoke with Rav Chaim, I heard that the principal had gotten into a major disagreement with the board, and that one of them is going to have to give in. Rumor has it that the board is bent on firing the principal if he insists on getting his way. What makes the story even stranger is the fact that the principal has been at his post for 15 years and is the absolute and undisputed backbone of the school. He built the school from nothing and developed it into something special, and his job has never been in jeopardy. Suddenly, however, things seem to be changing.

"If he doesn't back down, the board will fire him. That's what everyone's saying. If that happens, all my problems are solved."

She called me back two weeks later.

"He didn't back down and the board fired him."

"I guess that takes care of things for you."

"Yes — not only is he unable to cause me any more difficulties, he's actually leaving the community and moving away!"

I had struggled with the situation in the first place, unsure whether I should present her side to Rav Chaim without the principal being there to defend himself. In the end, her suffering left me no choice; I would tell Rav Chaim everything she told me and let him decide what to do. Obviously Rav Chaim had the ability to see the reality for what it was and phrased his *berachah* accordingly. Looking back, it was clear that Rav Chaim's choice of words had been extremely accurate and unerringly on target. It was yet another example of the tremendous *siyatta d'Shmaya* that guides his every word.

◆ ◆ ◆

There was a couple who had been married for 10 years without children, and the doctors had basically given up all hope for a turnaround. One of their family members wrote a letter to Rav Chaim, a letter that contained an original piece of Torah.

"Why do we find that Yitzchak davened for Rivkah to be blessed with offspring, and Yaakov davened for Rachel, but we never see Avraham Avinu davening for Sarah Imeinu?"

The man went on to explain that in his opinion the reason stemmed from the fact that while Rivkah and Rachel were suffering from fertility issues, Sarah was incapable of having children because she did not have a womb. While there was a reason for Yitzchak and Yaakov to daven for their wives, in Avraham Avinu's case, it would have been a wasted prayer, since Sarah was not physically capable of bearing children.

He then went on to ask Rav Chaim, "Now that the doctors have *paskened*, as it were, that my relatives are not capable of having children, am I still allowed to daven for them, to ask for a miracle, though my *tefillah* might perhaps belong to the category of a *tefillas shav*, a wasted prayer?"

Rav Chaim wrote back a few terse words.

"*Ein harofim yodim klum* — The doctors do not know anything!"

A short while later this man's relative found out that she was expecting. At their son's *bris*, which was held about nine and a half months after this question was posed to Rav Chaim, the man who had sent Rav Chaim his letter rose to speak, sharing his letter with the assembled and especially Rav Chaim's one-line response: *The doctors do not know anything.*

This was a couple who were desperately trying to have children for 10 years with no success. Then Rav Chaim wrote one line and...everything changed.

I related this story to a family member of mine, who listened with interest and then said, "Great story. Let me tell you my own personal encounter with Rav Chaim."

I hadn't known that he had gone to Rav Chaim and listened carefully.

"As you know," he said, "my wife and I have been blessed with a fairly large family. For some reason, however, a few years ago the wellsprings suddenly dried up, and we stopped having children. Instead of healthy births, there were miscarriages. Eventually we went to the doctor for an overall checkup, where we discovered to our horror that there were complications in her blood work, and that it was very dangerous for my wife to ever have another child.

"Not yet ready to accept this, I went to Rav Chaim for a *berachah*. Hearing how many children we had — nine, *bli ayin hara* — Rav Chaim laughed. 'What, you need a *minyan*?' he said. Then he became serious and uttered his usual two-word blessing: '*Berachah v'hatzlachah*.'

"I said *amen* to Rav Chaim's *berachah*," he went on, "but then I said, 'Rebbe, what should I tell my wife? She so much wants another child, but the doctors say it's dangerous. What should I tell her when I get back home?'

"'*Yiheyeh b'seder*,' Rav Chaim said. 'It will be all right.'

"My wife found out she was expecting within a week of that meeting. In the past, when she was expecting, she suffered with terrible morning sickness, but this time around it went absolutely smoothly. No throwing up, no nothing. During her fifth month, it became time for them to deal with the blood complications that the doctor had warned us about. When we presented ourselves at our regular doctor for a consultation, we were advised to go to a medical center that specialized in that field.

"We made an appointment and arrived at the center armed with all prior medical documentation. The doctor welcomed us into his office and began examining the files and previous blood work. After frowning down at the papers for a few minutes, he turned to us.

" 'I don't really understand this,' he said. 'According to what your doctor writes, you are suffering from a rare blood complication. But I've just looked over the documentation from the last blood test that you did, and it came back from the lab negative!'

" 'Maybe the complication disappeared?' I said.

" 'Not possible,' the specialist said. 'In the case of this kind of blood complication, once you have it, it's there for life. And yet it's not showing up! Please return to the hospital and bring back every single bit of documentation that exists in your file. Something doesn't add up here.'

"We returned with the documentation. The doctor studied everything. In one file, the blood tests had come back from the lab positive, while in the next they were negative! The two sets of tests were contradictory! The doctor had never seen anything like it, and he was stymied.

"I, on the other hand, had no questions," my relative concluded with a smile. "It was a simple thing. Rav Chaim told me, '*Yiheyeh b'seder*,' that everything would be okay. What more could I possibly want or need than a promise from Rav Chaim?"

❖ ❖ ❖

One morning a brand-new father was called up to the Torah in the Lederman Shul, where he proceeded to make a *Mi Shebeirach* for his newborn daughter. After davening, the glowing father approached Rav Chaim. "Rebbi, do you remember me?"

Rav Chaim took a good look at the man, then shook his head in the negative.

"I came to Rebbi a year ago with a *she'eilah*," the man explained. "My wife and I had been married already for five years without children, and we had been seriously considering a number of options and assorted courses of treatment. One of the main possibilities involved a trip to the States for an expensive and drawn-out procedure, and we wanted a *berachah* for success in achieving our dream.

"You heard me out," the man continued, "and then you gently informed me that there was no way you could possibly give me a *berachah* for success in this particular treatment, since your father, the Steipler, *zt"l*, had been 100 percent against this type of medical procedure.

"At the time," the man went on, "I said to Rebbi that I hadn't come for advice, but rather for a *berachah*. If I would have come to ask whether I was allowed to do this, then I would have been obligating myself to follow your advice whatever it was. But here we had already decided to do the procedure and were merely requesting a *berachah* for its success,

" 'I'm sorry,' you told us, 'but I can't give you a *berachah* for something my father held was completely forbidden to do.'

" 'What should I tell my wife?' I asked you. 'She's *mamesh* a broken person right now.'

"Rebbi, you then said the following words: 'If you don't fly to the States to do the procedure, then *Hashem ya'azor* — Hashem will help.'

"It's now a year later," the man concluded. "We did not go to the States, and we are finally holding our very own newborn baby in our arms. I came to make the *Mi Shebeirach* here at Lederman Shul and to thank you for the *berachah* that changed our lives!"

◆ ◆ ◆

Allow me to describe a normal, everyday scene in Rav Chaim's home. There are 30 people waiting in the anteroom outside. I am standing beside Rav Chaim, watching his every move. In general, when it comes to speaking with Rav Chaim, there isn't much privacy, and people have to know that most likely there will be other people standing in close proximity who will hear whatever it is that they want to discuss. Especially today, when unfortunately it's not safe to leave a *gadol* unprotected, there are always other people around. If it's something especially private, a person can write the problem on a piece of paper and hand it to him.

The first person on the line enters the room.

"Rebbi," he begins, "I'm married for seven years, and we still haven't had children yet."

"You should do *shiluach hakein*," Rav Chaim instantly replies, as if his answer is the most obvious thing in the world.

The man leaves and the next five people enter, ask their questions, receive their answers, and leave.

Number seven enters the room. It's the same heartbreaking issue that supplicant number one spoke of: he and his wife have been married for years and have not yet been blessed with children. I'm waiting to see if Rav Chaim will tell the man to do the mitzvah of *shiluach hakein*.

He does not.

"Do you fulfill the mitzvah of Havdalah with wine?"

"Not always. Sometimes we use grape juice."

"Only wine from now on."

The man nods his head. It will be only wine in their home from that day on.

Ten additional people enter, receive *berachos* and *eitzos*, and leave.

The 11th person has come about children. Will Rav Chaim instruct him to do *shiluach hakein*? Will he tell him to use only wine for Havdalah?

"Are your beds situated between north and south or between east and west?" Rav Chaim wants to know, and proceeds to give specific instructions.

Among the many people who came to see him that night, five turned to him for help with having children. To each, Rav Chaim gave another answer and different advice. How did Rav Chaim know that this one needed to fulfill *shiluach hakein*, and that one needs to make Havdalah on wine? No one knows.

When the fifth man told Rav Chaim how they were still childless and needed a *berachah*, Rav Chaim looked him in the eye and said, "You can daven."

"I can daven?" The terribly disappointed man repeated Rav Chaim's words. "Of course I daven."

"You're allowed to daven," Rav Chaim reiterated.

The man understood that Rav Chaim was refusing to give him a *berachah* or an *eitzah*, and he started to cry.

"Why doesn't the Rav want to give me a *berachah*?" he asked, his voice shattering every heart in the room.

Rav Chaim's warm gaze met the tear-filled eyes of his supplicant.

"The Chafetz Chaim used to say that sometimes it's better not to have children. You don't know who their friends will be, you don't know if they'll be good children, sometimes a person's children aren't well… You're allowed to daven."

Five different people. Five different examples of the same scenario. One received a *berachah*, one a word of advice. And to one, Rav Chaim was unwilling to give anything.

Is this *ruach hakodesh*? Does he use special X-ray vision to look at people's faces and discern what it is that they need? Obviously Hashem is putting the correct message that each needs to hear into Rav Chaim's mouth at the exact time that the person needs to hear it.

◆ ◆ ◆

Rav Chaim himself says that a *tzaddik's berachos* are fulfilled based on how much *emunas chachamim* the person receiving the *berachah* has. It is therefore important to strengthen your *emunah* before going to see a *tzaddik*, to resolve to truly accept whatever he tells you, and to actually follow his advice even if it seems strange to you. Coming to a *gadol* means putting his understanding of your situation before yours; if you can't do that, why are you coming to see him?

A *bachur* in his 30's asked Rav Chaim for a *berachah* for a *shidduch*. Rav Chaim took a good look at him. "If you start to grow a beard," he told the man, "you will find your *kallah* very soon."

"It's impossible for me to grow a beard," the man protested. "Please give me something else to do."

"No," Rav Chaim replied firmly. "You have to grow a beard; your *kallah* is waiting for you to grow a beard! If you grow a beard, you will find her!"

"It's impossible for me to do that! Nobody in my family has

a beard. Anything but that. Give me anything else to do and I'll take it on, but this is one thing I just cannot do!"

Rav Chaim looked him in the eye and said with uncharacteristic firmness, "If you don't grow a beard, you will remain single until 120!"

Everyone standing around him was shocked to hear Rav Chaim make such a statement and with such assurance. Rav Chaim saw that the young man wasn't convinced. He repeated it a second time. The *bachur* started to cry. He literally broke down in tears.

Rav Chaim's grandson approached to try and intervene.

"Saba," he told his grandfather, "the *bachur* is crying!"

"*Az mah*," Rav Chaim responded. "This is what he needs to hear. This is the truth! *Lo karah klum*. He can cry." Then he said it yet again: "If he doesn't grow a beard, he is not going to get married until 120."

In the end, the young man left Rav Chaim's house, upset at the person who had brought him and unwilling to hear what Rav Chaim was telling him.

"What did you get me into?" he yelled at the man who'd accompanied him. "Take me to a different *gadol*!"

"No *gadol* will tell you that you don't have to grow a beard once Rav Chaim said that you should. You're talking about someone who is known worldwide as a *ba'al ruach hakodesh*. Do you really think anyone will challenge his words? Rav Chaim doesn't tell this to every person who walks through his doors. Obviously he sees that this is holding you back on some level. Do you want to get married or not?"

Bottom line, if you're choosing to ask a *gadol*, you have to be ready to follow his advice. Rav Chaim himself says that you don't have to ask every question. But once you ask, be prepared to listen.

(As a postscript, one of the editors working on this book mentioned this story about growing a beard to a friend of hers. Her friend started to laugh. It turns out that her son, who was in his early 20's, had gone to Rav Chaim before leaving Eretz Yisrael and setting out on *shidduchim*, and Rav Chaim gave him the same *eitzah*: grow a beard. Her son was reluctant to do so, as he claimed that the type of girl he was looking for wouldn't want to go out with a bearded boy. One year passed, two years, four years… The boy was almost 26, and though he was a top *bachur* from a great family and received many suggestions, nothing worked out. Finally, he went to Rav Mattisyahu Salomon, *shlita*, for a *berachah*. He mentioned that Rav Chaim had advised him to grow a beard. "Rav Chaim," said Rav Matisyahu, "is a very holy man." This time the boy got it right: he grew a beard and is now happily married to the second girl he went out with after following Rav Chaim's advice.)

Recently a woman called me. We were on the phone for an hour and a half. It was a sad situation, and she needed to unburden herself.

"My husband and I like each other very much," she told me, "but he has very serious problems, and I'm not sure I can live with these problems for the rest of my life."

Bottom line, there was a real case in this situation for divorce.

"Logically," she said, "the answer seems pretty clear, but I can't base my decision on pure logic here. I need the *da'as* of a *gadol*, someone who can tell me with assurance what it is that Hashem wants me to do. Is my lot to live with the issue, or does Hashem want me to cut my losses and move on?"

It was a valid question.

Before we went any further, I felt I had to clarify my position regarding a visit to a *gadol* from someone seeking advice.

"You have to understand something," I told her. "If we ask Rav Chaim and he answers that you should get divorced, that's what you're going to have to do. Before you take this step, make sure that you have made the necessary mental preparation to follow through, whatever the ramifications."

Suddenly she became very nervous. "I don't know if this is the right move."

"I agree with you," I replied. "You really have to be sure."

End result, she didn't ask the question, because she wasn't sure that she could handle hearing the answer. And you know something? That's fine. Better not to go if you don't feel capable of upholding the answer that you get.

◆ ◆ ◆

On another occasion I took a prominent artist to visit Rav Chaim for a *berachah* for *parnassah*. (Being a prominent artist doesn't necessarily translate into financial success.) The man was a very capable artist with many pictures to sell and a huge portfolio — but, bottom line, he wasn't doing well. He asked me if I could take him to see Rav Chaim, and I agreed.

At the meeting Rav Chaim listened attentively, and he seemed excited when I mentioned that the visitor was an artist.

"He should draw a picture of the Beis HaMikdash," Rav Chaim exclaimed.

Although this wasn't the type of subject that the artist normally painted, you would think that he'd rush to follow Rav Chaim's advice and sit down at his easel first chance he got to draw his own rendition of the Beis HaMikdash. This was Rav Chaim's advice, and it made sense to follow it, whether you understood it or not.

The artist did not draw the picture. I bumped into him half a year later, and he still hadn't done it. I met him a year later, and, no, he had not managed to find the time. Our paths crossed three years later, when we ran into one another once again; he still wasn't making money and, no, he still hadn't bothered to follow Rav Chaim's advice.

The man occasionally calls me and wants to go back for another *berachah*! It's beyond my understanding: you didn't follow his advice the first time around, so why do you want to go back again for Round 2?

◆ ◆ ◆

I receive calls from people I know and people whom I have never met in my life. Almost all the calls have to do with Rav Chaim. Everyone wants to go to Rav Chaim or needs me to go see him on their behalf. It's one of my missions in life, and I accept it with love.

The phone rang a few months ago.

"Our son has just recovered from a serious illness, and we are bringing him to Eretz Yisrael to thank Hashem for all the miracles we have seen. Would it be possible for you to take us to see Rav Chaim?"

We made up a date and time. On the way to Bnei Brak, they related the entire story from beginning to end. It was a miraculous story. Twists and turns. Impossible to ignore the Hand of Hashem throughout.

"We plan on making a *seudas hodayah* (a festive meal of thanksgiving) when we return to the States."

"I know that making a *seudas hodayah* is not always such a simple thing," I told them. "Even if a person was the recipient of a miracle, it's not always such a good idea to make everyone aware of what went on. *Ayin hara* and so on. Here's what I think. You're going in to see Rav Chaim. Ask him what he thinks about making a *seudas hodayah* for your son."

They agreed that this was the perfect idea.

We entered Rav Chaim's study, and I introduced the child to him, explaining the incredible turn of events that had led from his doctors predicting his demise, to the point where he was able to stand, unaided and healthy, before the *gadol hador*.

Rav Chaim wanted to know how old he was.

"Nine years old."

Rav Chaim gave him a *berachah*.

"Rebbi, the parents want to know whether they should make a *seudas hodayah* when they return to the States."

"At his bar mitzvah."

The boy was nine. He would be celebrating his bar mitzvah in four years' time.

"They should push it off for that long?"

"At his bar mitzvah," he repeated. "And they should celebrate the bar mitzvah in Eretz Yisrael."

We left the room and descended the narrow flight of stairs to the street. I could see that the parents were very happy.

"What are you so excited about?"

"First of all," they replied, "the fact is, our son has still not received a final clean bill of health. By telling us to celebrate his bar mitzvah in Eretz Yisrael, Rav Chaim has basically promised us that he will still be alive in four years' time to celebrate! This is huge news!

"Second, our son just underwent a treatment of radiology. The doctors told us that we won't know for sure whether his treatment was successful for at least another three years. In our hearts, we flip-flopped back and forth on the whole subject of a *seudas hodayah*, because we really weren't sure of the proper thing to do. Now we know. We wait until his bar mitzvah, at which point we will see whether or not the treatment was successful, all the while holding on to Rav Chaim's 'promise.'

"Lastly, we had been debating all along whether we should celebrate his bar mitzvah in Eretz Yisrael, and now Rav Chaim erased any doubt or hesitation that we may have had on the subject!"

Nobody had spoken about a bar mitzvah or about flying to Eretz Yisrael to celebrate it. But Rav Chaim apparently knew.

◆ ◆ ◆

I heard the following story from one of Rav Chaim's grandsons:

"Someone told me that the family of a soldier who had been very badly wounded came to my grandfather for a *berachah*. Rav Chaim gave the soldier a *berachah*, and he recovered against all odds. After the soldier had been released from the hospital, he arrived, along with his family, at Rav Chaim's home as an act of *hakaras hatov*. Upon seeing the recovered soldier, Rav Chaim recited the *berachah* of *baruch hatov v'hameitiv*."

"I wanted to verify the story," the grandson told me. "I went to my grandfather, and I asked him if it was accurate."

Rav Chaim told him that the story was genuine and even added a few salient points.

"When they came to see me the first time," Rav Chaim said, "they were desperate. The doctors had all given up hope for their son's life and were recommending that they take him off life support.

" 'We're sorry, but your son is already in the next world,' they said, 'and there's no reason to keep him attached to the machines any longer.'

"I told the parents not to listen to the doctors; that their son would yet have a complete recovery and that he would be *bari v'shalem*, healthy and whole. Seeing such an obvious miracle certainly necessitated the recital of *hatov v'hameitiv*."

◆　◆　◆

X-ray vision. That's the perfect term to use to describe Rav Chaim's unique ability to take one quick glance at a person and see things that are hidden from everyone else.

Recently a visitor brought his son to Rav Chaim for a *berachah* just prior to his bar mitzvah.

"And what about you?" Rav Chaim asked the father.

"What about me?"

"Did you have a bar mitzvah?"

It turned out there was a question regarding the conversion of this man's grandmother. The Bnei Brak *beis din*, with whom he'd conferred, ruled that he should go through a form of *geirus* as well, just in case, making his original "bar mitzvah," in a sense, misplaced. He hadn't mentioned a word about this to Rav Chaim, who once again had seen things without having to be told.

Another time a nonreligious Israeli came to ask Rav Chaim for a *berachah*. Like many traditional, if not fully practicing Jews, the man knew enough to don a yarmulke when coming to see the *gadol hador*.

"Are you *shomer Shabbos*?" Rav Chaim wanted to know.

Overcome with embarrassment, the man lied. "Yes, I am."

Before he left, the man asked Rav Chaim for a *berachah* a second time.

"When you begin keeping Shabbos," Rav Chaim replied, "the *berachah* will be *chal* (actualized)."

◆　◆　◆

A certain Bnei Brak bank found itself facing a severe problem. Many of its employees were suffering from a spate of foot-related illnesses: broken legs, among other things. This had been going on for a while, and as a last resort they appointed a spokesman for all of them and sent him off to visit Rav Chaim.

"Is your bank open on *Chol Hamo'ed*?" Rav Chaim asked the man.

The man nodded in the affirmative.

"That's the reason."

"How does Rebbi know this?"

"It's a *Yerushalmi*," Rav Chaim replied simply. "The Gemara makes a *hekesh*, a correlation, with the words *regel, regel*, comparing the word *regel* that means 'yom tov,' to *regel*, 'feet.' If so many people are suffering from medical issues having to do with their feet, it can surely be traced back to their lax approach regarding the sanctity of *Yom Tov*."

This is a somewhat typical response for Rav Chaim. In many instances, his answers to people can be sourced in a *Gemara*, halachah, or *derush*. His encyclopedic grasp of the entire Torah leaves one astounded and amazed.

Another individual came to Rav Chaim complaining of a cough that had confounded the doctors and that refused to go away no matter what he tried. His suffering was immense, especially since no matter whom he consulted, no one was able to help him.

"Drink milk directly from a goat," Rav Chaim advised him. "Spritz it out of the goat's udder straight into your mouth."

Everyone looked at Rav Chaim, trying to understand why he'd suggested such a thing. "It's a *mefurishe Gemara*," he explained. "There was a story of a certain righteous individual who was suffering from the exact symptoms that you are describing. He asked the doctors what to do, and they told him to drink fresh goat's milk…"

Indeed, Rav Chaim relates to everything that he sees through a prism comprised of *Gemaras*, *Tanach*, and *midrashim*. One Purim, Rav Chaim saw a child walking the streets of Bnei Brak in a fish costume.

"What are you dressed up as?" he asked the child.

"A *dag* — a fish."

"No," Rav Chaim corrected the boy with laughter in his eyes, "you're Yonah in the stomach of the fish!"

◆　◆　◆

On one occasion, Rav Chaim wasn't feeling well and was taken to the hospital for tests. After he was examined by the medical team, and they had decided on their diagnosis, the lead physician invited Rav Chaim into his office, where he explained their diagnosis and what they felt had caused the medical issues in the first place. When he concluded his analysis, he asked Rav Chaim if he had any questions.

"Yes," replied Rav Chaim, "I have questions...in Torah."

Rav Chaim Kanievsky

Part C

As I've stressed time and again, it's a good idea when visiting a *gadol* to ask yourself what you can do for the *tzaddik* you are coming to see. Walk into his home and introduce yourself as a doctor; perhaps something is bothering him and you can help. If you're an accountant, mention it and offer to help him with your services. Maybe this *gadol* needs someone with just your level and area of expertise to help him with something right now!

Rav Chaim has his own private doctors and medical staff, who treat him with the highest level of devotion. But even with all that care, there was a period of time when I was able to tell he was feeling weak. Concerned for his health, I conferred with a top nutritionist, whom I know, to try and get to the root of the problem, and I arranged for him to accompany me to visit Rav Chaim.

The nutritionist sat down with the person in the household who is in charge of everything related to Rav Chaim's physical condition. Together they went through every relevant document. It didn't take him long to conclude that Rav Chaim was low on certain vital nutrients. He explained to the *gabbai* what had to be added to Rav Chaim's diet, and the *gabbai* faithfully followed his instructions.

Baruch Hashem, Rav Chaim looks much better these days, and I am filled with inner joy every time I see how healthy he appears. My point is, this was something I was able to help him with!

Every person comes with unique strengths and should offer whatever services he can. You never know. You might have the *zechus* of helping a *tzaddik* so he can continue to help *Klal Yisrael*.

◆ ◆ ◆

There's another very important thing one should do before entering a *tzaddik's* presence: take a minute and ask the person bringing you inside, "Is there anything I should know about this *tzaddik*?" For example, is there anything he doesn't like that people do, such as taking a picture? Even today, there are still certain *gedolim* who do not like being photographed. The last thing you want to do is visit a *gadol* and upset him in his own home!

It's crucial that people remind themselves before entering a *gadol's* home that they are about to enter the private world of someone very special, and they should do their best to act accordingly and in a way that won't offend their host.

◆ ◆ ◆

Another piece of advice: If you asked a *gadol* for a *berachah*, and your request is ultimately answered, tell him. Let him rejoice with you.

I met a newcomer to my neighborhood who had moved to Eretz Yisrael from Italy. Everything was wonderful, except that he still hadn't managed to find a job. Feeling bad for him, I offered to take him along with me the next time I went to visit Rav Chaim. He jumped at the opportunity. When we arrived, I explained the situation to Rav Chaim: how all the jobs the man

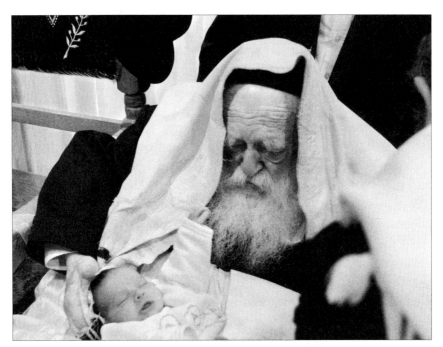

Sharing our joy: Rav Chaim as *sandak* at our son's *bris*

was being offered were far away from his home, which would mean many hours of commuting. Rav Chaim's response was typically terse.

"You should find a job near your house."

Unfortunately, most people don't get back to you when there's good news and their prayers are answered, and I am uncomfortable calling people up to hear the end of the story, but I do avail myself of the opportunity to find out what happened when and if I run into them. Two or three months later, I ran into the Italian Jew at a local shul.

"Whatever happened with the whole job situation?"

His face took on a surprised look. "I didn't tell you?" He seemed surprised by the fact that he hadn't gotten back to me.

"Tell me now," I said.

"Well, about a week after we went to Rav Chaim, someone called me up and offered me a job about 100 meters from my house!"

I couldn't help but marvel at Rav Chaim's power. But shouldn't this man have let me know earlier so that I — and Rav Chaim — could have shared his happiness?

◆ ◆ ◆

Rav Chaim is extremely insistent on not breaking a *kevius,* a set time of learning. He backs up his position with a quote from the Gemara that discusses what the heavenly court will ask each and every one of us when we arrive in *Shamayim* after 120.

"*Kavata itim laTorah*? Did you set aside specific times to learn?" is one of the questions that we will be asked under interrogation. Rav Chaim explains that the Torah's usage of the terminology *kavata* — "did you set aside specific times" — is alluding to the fact that there is something particularly powerful and important about a person's insistence on treating his learning hours as immutable, something he will not miss no matter what.

This lesson was brought home in a very personal way when Rav Chaim set up a daily learning session with a new *chavrusa* with whom he'd never learned before.

"There's one thing you have to know before we begin," he told the prospective *chavrusa.* "I am very *makpid* on never missing a day. A time is a time, and there's no such thing as missing it!"

"This concerns me," replied the *chavrusa.* "You see, every winter I am usually hit with a bad case of the flu that knocks me out for at least a few days. There's no way for me to guarantee that I won't have to cancel."

"You don't have to worry," Rav Chaim reassured him. "If you commit and keep your word to never miss a day no matter what, you'll be fine."

They began learning together and, indeed, winter arrived. The harsh rains of the Israeli winter of yore drenched Bnei Brak with unyielding force, yet the study partner never got sick, enjoying instead an unaccustomed stretch of perfect health.

One day something came up, and Rav Chaim's *chavrusa* wasn't able to come and learn with him. For the first time, he was forced to cancel their *kevius* together.

The next day he woke up with a terrible case of the flu. Rav Chaim's protection had been based his commitment to never breaking the *kevius*. Apparently, the promise had been compromised, and the special protection had worn off. When Rav Chaim was informed that his *chavrusa* was laid up in bed, he said that it was clear that his illness had come about because he had been derelict with his commitment to their learning session.

"He would never have gotten sick," Rav Chaim said decisively, "if he had kept his *kevius* with dedication."

As a young *bachur*, I had the *zechus* of learning *b'chavrusa* with my *Rosh Yeshivah*, Rav Shmuel Miller. We learned together every afternoon for a few hours at a stretch, and Rav Shmuel was extremely particular about never canceling our time in the *beis medrash*. One day, however, Rav Shmuel didn't show up to second *seder*. It was most uncharacteristic behavior on his part, and I was surprised because he had never, ever missed learning with me before.

At 11 o'clock that evening I was in the dorm, already in my pajamas and about to go to sleep, when I heard a soft knock on my door.

With my rebbi, Rav Shmuel Miller

Opening the door, I saw an exhausted-looking Rav Shmuel standing there.

"What's the matter, Rebbi?" I asked him in alarm.

"Nothing's the matter," he replied, "except that we were supposed to learn together this afternoon and I never showed up."

I waited to hear what he wanted from me.

"I would like to learn with you now instead."

"Now?"

"Yes, we have a *seder* together, and there's no way I can disregard a *seder limud*."

I promised to meet him in the *beis medrash* and went to get dressed. We ended up learning for about half an hour. He was red eyed and clearly exhausted, but he soldiered on after a day of nonstop action. When we finished and he had closed the Gemara, he turned to me.

"Binyomin, I want to apologize to you for missing our time together today. I have to pay the *kollel* tomorrow, and I was under incredible pressure to raise the necessary funds. That's why I couldn't make it."

Rav Shmuel's arrival on my doorstep at 11 o'clock at night left a lasting impression on me, showing me what dedication to Torah was, as well as what it meant to take a *kevius* seriously. I never forgot his 11-o'clock knock or the fact that he pushed himself to learn when he was so, so fatigued. This is the kind of lesson that remains with a *talmid* for life.

◆ ◆ ◆

As everyone knows, Rav Chaim is one of the great *masmidim* of the generation. His diligence is simply legendary. The sole activity with which he occupies his days (other than seeing people who seek advice or *berachos*) is learning. He sees Torah in everything.

People think that Rav Chaim has a phenomenal memory, but I'm not sure that it's so much a superlative memory as it is an incredible capacity to forget! His ability to forget information is not to be believed. Anyone who knows Rav Chaim can attest that what I'm saying is true. Talk to him about anything that's not *mamesh* Torah and he will forget what you discussed a few minutes later. Come back an hour later and ask him if he recalls what you spoke about, and he will have zero recollection, as if the conversation never happened!

People have asked Rav Chaim about this phenomenon, and he explained that he makes a point of not remembering anything that's not Torah, because the Midrash writes that when you have a barrel filled with oil, every drop of water that falls in means there will be room for one less drop of oil. Rav Chaim doesn't want to use his memory space for anything other than Torah. His power of forgetfulness in this area is simply unbelievable!

One time someone close to Rav Chaim told a friend about this unique trait.

"I don't believe it," the man replied.

"I'm telling you," insisted the first one. "You can come to Rav Chaim and put down tens of thousands of dollars on the table, and an hour later, he'll forget that the incident ever happened."

"It can't be, it's impossible," the man protested. "Tens of thousands of dollars, and he'll forget about it an hour later?!"

"Do it and see for yourself."

The man was wealthy enough to agree. Taking a considerable amount of money with him, the two men entered Rav Chaim's study, and the wealthy man was introduced to Rav Chaim. He put the money down on the table, making it clear that he was donating a very large amount of money to Rav Chaim to distribute for *tzedakah*.

Rav Chaim accepted the money with a gracious "*berachah v'hatzlachah*," and everyone parted with much goodwill. They returned an hour later. The wealthy man introduced himself and reminded Rav Chaim that he had been there an hour earlier and had given him a very generous donation.

"I don't recall," Rav Chaim said. "I believe you; the person whom you are here with is a trustworthy individual, and if he backs you up I believe him, but I personally don't remember this at all."

The Rebbetzin used to tell people that Rav Chaim goes so far as to daven to Hashem to help him forget all unnecessary information so that it will not affect his learning.

◆ ◆ ◆

Rav Chaim's *hasmadah* was already very much a part of him from a very young age. When his IDF draft papers arrived in the mail, Rav Chaim presented himself at the local Lishkat HaGiyus (IDF Recruitment Center), where he found a corner to learn until his name was called. Eventually he found himself sitting before a private, who had a number of questions for him.

"Where do you live?" the soldier wanted to know.

"My yeshivah," he replied.

"Where is your yeshivah located?"

"I don't know. I know how to get there from my house and back, but I don't know the name of the street."

The soldier took a good look at the *bachur* sitting there and said to himself, *Here's a boy who's been learning at the same yeshivah for a good few years yet doesn't know the name of the street it's on...* And he quickly issued a deferment."

And that's the reason Rav Chaim was released from army service. But he wasn't kidding. There was no reason for him to know the name of the street. It was extraneous information, and Rav Chaim saw no need to process it.

◆ ◆ ◆

Since Rav Chaim is such an incredible *masmid*, people may think that he can't relate to the normal person with all his *nisyonos* and challenges. They are wrong. Completely. Despite being who he is, Rav Chaim has no trouble comprehending that the vast majority of *Klal Yisrael* is not holding on his level, and he gives everyone advice according to the person's needs.

One of his children once asked him where he had celebrated his bar mitzvah.

"My bar mitzvah? We celebrated my bar mitzvah at Yeshivas Beis Yosef, where my father, the Steipler, was a *maggid shiur*."

"What was served?" the son wanted to know.

"There was wine and cake," said Rav Chaim, smiling in fond memory of his special day.

"Who came to your bar mitzvah?"

"The Chazon Ish, the Ponevezher Rav, and a few of my friends from cheder."

That was Rav Chaim's bar mitzvah, and it had been perfect in his mind. On the other hand, when one of Rav Chaim's children chose not to make a reception when his son turned 13, Rav Chaim was disappointed that he hadn't treated his son to the type of bar mitzvah that all the boy's friends had.

"Why didn't you make him a real bar mitzvah?" he chided his son.

"It was O.K. with him," the father defended himself.

Rav Chaim was not convinced. "No, you can't do that. You have to make him a bar mitzvah just like everyone else."

Because this grandson hadn't been given the same type of affair as his peers, Rav Chaim decided to make it up to him. How? By presenting this grandson with a bar mitzvah present (a *sefer*, of course) with a much more detailed inscription than he usually writes for the grandchildren. The grandson was also invited specially to Rav Chaim's house for a personal slot of time, so his grandfather could hear him say over his *derashah* in private.

And even after it was all over, Rav Chaim still insisted that forgoing a bar mitzvah celebration had been the wrong thing to do.

"Never treat one child with less honor than you treat another," he reiterated time and again. "Every child must be treated with equal love and respect."

For a long time afterward, Rav Chaim kept on inquiring about that particular grandson's welfare, making sure that he was O.K. and not negatively impacted by what he had missed out on.

His interest and concern regarding a bar mitzvah reception were all the more impressive for a person wholly uninterested in matters of the mundane. This was the same person who didn't even have a bar mitzvah in the modern sense of the word! No dinner, no *kiddush*. Just a few pieces of cake and a bottle of wine.

But he didn't look at it that way. When he was a child, things had been done in a certain way. Today things are done differently, and every child should receive no less than anyone else.

Yes, Rav Chaim may be standing with a foot in a different world, but he still understands the world the rest of us inhabit.

◆ ◆ ◆

Rav Chaim's entire essence is interwoven with the Torah that he studies. Anyone who lives in the Kanievsky residence can tell you (and I've heard this numerous times from key members of the household) that Rav Chaim dreams quite often. In his dreams there is a recurring theme of Torah learning. He will delve into a *sugya* from start to finish. At times, Rav Chaim will awaken and tell those around him that he studied a particular *masechta* in a dream or even that he just celebrated a *siyum*! Sometimes his dreams deal with complicated questions in halachah, and when he wakes up he runs to find the *sefarim* dealing with the issue so as to clarify matters immediately.

Once, after waking up, Rav Chaim told some members of his family that he'd dreamed that a certain grandson had just written him a letter containing 100 questions on topics in the Rambam's *Hilchos Melachim*. Rav Chaim was perplexed by the choice of *Hilchos Melachim* and shared his puzzlement candidly. Later that day, this same grandson came to Rav Chaim's house to daven *Minchah*.

"Tell me," his grandfather asked him, "did you write me a letter recently dealing with *Hilchos Melachim*?"

"I didn't write Saba any letter," his grandson replied, "but just last week I was busy learning *Hilchos Melachim*."

"Why?"

"Because someone I know is working on a *sefer* about *Hilchos Melachim*, and he asked me to help them with the details."

◆ ◆ ◆

Another dream tale: Rav Chaim is meticulous about reciting 100 *berachos* every single day. Weekdays are easy enough, and he gets by without too much effort, but on Shabbos he usually finds himself actively on the lookout for his final 20 *berachos*. He keeps track of every single *berachah*, and, of course, there are always fruits to eat if he finds himself short.

Once, on the first day of Succos, Rav Chaim returned home from shul after davening and went to lie down in the *succah* for a short nap. When he woke up, he told his family that he had dreamt about his *berachos* obligation for the day. In his dream, he'd been told that he'd already taken care of 10 *berachos* out of the 20 that he normally lacked on a Shabbos or *Yom Tov*. Wanting to see if his dream had been correct, Rav Chaim sat down with one of his grandchildren to make the *cheshbon*.

Five from *maftir*.

Two from Hallel.

Two on the *lulav* and *esrog*.

A *leishev ba'succah*.

Ten *berachos* accounted for.

Even in his dream, he'd been right on the mark.

◆ ◆ ◆

On one occasion, after the Kanievsky family had married off a child, Rav Chaim turned to his new *mechutan* and apologized to him in advance for the fact that he wouldn't be able to attend every one of the *sheva berachos* celebrations since he was a *ba'al chov,* someone in debt.

The *mechutan* looked at Rav Chaim with sympathy, no doubt feeling bad that Rav Chaim was struggling with his financial obligations and all the stress that accompanies paying off the wedding debts. Seeing his reaction, one of Rav Chaim's family members explained that he had misunderstood.

"Rav Chaim isn't referring to money matters at all," he told the man. "When he uses the word *chov*, he's referring to his Torah obligations: to the pages of Gemara and halachah that he needs to learn and catch up on. These are Rav Chaim's debts, and he simply can't sleep knowing that he still 'owes' any learning to his heavenly bank account."

◆ ◆ ◆

Years ago, when Rav Chaim was a young man, he was learning in Kollel Chazon Ish late one night with a group of some of the finest young *talmidei chachamim* of the city. It was wartime and the night was filled with the sounds of exploding ammunition. The group tried to learn while ignoring the booming artillery, but it was very difficult. When they looked over at Rav Chaim, however, it was clear that he was his tranquil self.

"Rav Chaim," they asked him, "why aren't you scared?"

"*Rabbosai*," he replied, "the only thing pertaining to us right this second is whether a tank is *mekabel tumah* or not."

◆ ◆ ◆

At times Rav Chaim feels pressured due to the amount of learning he still needs to accomplish, and yet a *yeshivah bachur* will enter his office and Rav Chaim drops everything and gives him his full attention. He's patient and calm, and you can be forgiven for thinking that here sits a man with nothing on his mind other than helping this *bachur* through whatever it is that's bothering him.

I have witnessed *bachurim* sitting with him and asking him question after question, and I know Rav Chaim is waiting for everyone to leave so he can go back to finishing his daily quota. Yet, even after all the questions, Rav Chaim will turn to them and say, "Is there anything else you want to ask?"

So, on the one hand, he's juggling unlimited responsibilities, and on the other hand, he's capable of granting a *yeshivah bachur* unlimited time to speak with him in learning. As soon as the people leave, Rav Chaim turns back to his Gemara and finishes learning his 50 *blatt* for the day. If he didn't manage to cover everything, he won't go to sleep.

It's something to see. Here's an elderly man and he doesn't stop — and he knows so much — and he's constantly learning it all again and again.

◆ ◆ ◆

Rav Chaim is not impressed by anything other than Torah. He will never give a person respect merely because the individual is wealthy and occupies a position of power.

One day a very rich man came to see him for a *berachah*. This particular person had a reputation for philanthropy and for supporting many yeshivos with his financial largesse, and he was treated with kid gloves and copious respect from all who crossed his path.

When he entered Rav Chaim's study, the people who brought him were hoping that Rav Chaim would accord him honor for all the *tzedakah* he gave. Rav Chaim however, does things his own way. After being introduced to the wealthy man, Rav Chaim looked him in the eye and said, "Tell me, do you have the opportunity to learn Torah yourself? After all, that's really the main purpose of our lives."

The man hemmed and hawed, and Rav Chaim understood that he himself was not involved in learning on a regular basis.

"You have to find time to learn," Rav Chaim told him decisively.

This was the last thing the people who'd brought him were expecting to hear. Rav Chaim had given this wealthy man *mussar* instead of honor and had taken him to task for ignoring his own obligations. The rich man's "handlers" were extremely embarrassed. At the end of his visit to Eretz Yisrael, however, the wealthy man told those who had accompanied him that of all his visits, he had most enjoyed his encounter with Rav Chaim, who had seen fit to "hit him with the truth with no regard to the politics of the situation."

A postscript: In the end, those few minutes with Rav Chaim paid off, and the wealthy man did find the time to learn.

◆ ◆ ◆

As a young man in yeshivah, Rav Chaim shared a room in the dorm with Rav Moshe Soloveitchik of Switzerland, scion of one of the leading rabbinical families in the Orthodox world. At the time, the yeshivah was suffering from an invasion of mice, and the administration handed mousetraps to the student body, with clear instructions to drown any mouse that was caught.

To one particular mouse's good fortune, it got itself caught in Rav Chaim's room, where neither Rav Chaim nor Rav Moshe were capable of drowning any creature, mouse or not. In the end, they left the mouse in the cage where it had been trapped until they could figure out what to do: a decision that caused Rav Chaim to arrive at a practical halachic *she'eilah.*

Maybe I have to feed the mouse, he mused to himself. *Otherwise I could be transgressing the aveirah of tza'ar ba'alei chaim.*

This question called for expertise and insight, and the soft-hearted Rav Chaim went to ask the Chazon Ish if he was required to provide the mouse's sustenance. The Chazon Ish ruled that Rav Chaim was not obligated to take care of the mouse's *mezonos.* Having received a clear *psak* from the Chazon Ish, the two room-mates went about their business, while their guest proceeded to go on a diet. Within a day or two, the mouse had lost so much weight that it became thin enough to slip through the bars of the cage — which it lost no time in doing.

Rav Chaim reacted to the bizarre incident by quoting a midrash on *Koheles*: "A fox found a vineyard that was all fenced in, with all entrance denied him. Unwilling to concede defeat, the fox circled the vineyard repeatedly, until he managed to discover a hole, which could serve as a possible entranceway. The challenge: he wasn't skinny enough to fit through the hole. The fox gave the matter some thought and eventually decided to abstain from all food for a day or two. It wasn't long before he was able to fit through the hole."

"That is exactly what happened here," concluded Rav Chaim. Classic Rav Chaim: finding a Torah source for everything that happened in his life.

Many years ago Rav Chaim went to the zoo with his family for an outing on *Chol Hamo'ed*. As the family made their way from cage to cage, Rav Chaim told his children every place the particular animal they were looking at was mentioned in *Tanach* and in *Shas*, and everything about it from a Torah per-spective as quoted by *Chazal*. It wasn't long before a sizable crowd was following along with the Kanievsky family, intent on hearing the explanations of their extremely *chashuve* "zoo-logical expert."

◆ ◆ ◆

Rav Chaim once mentioned to someone who had come to him for an *eitzah* that a person can't learn Torah while pressured to do so. "A person's learning has to come from a desire to immerse himself in Torah study."

He then made the following powerful statement: "If you would tell me now that I had to learn for the next four hours, I wouldn't be able to learn for one more minute! If you tell me nothing, I'll be able to learn for 10 hours straight, because it's my choice and I know that I can get up at any point and do anything I want."

This is the *masmid* of the generation talking. *Kal va'chomer* is this true of the average individual.

An added detail: The Rebbetzin never, ever told Rav Chaim to go and learn. She made sure to remove any trace of household obligations from his shoulders, leaving him free to devote his days and nights to Torah. But not once did she ever give him *mussar*, or tell him how to spend his time. Any pressure that Rav Chaim has when it comes to learning is self-imposed and internal.

Rav Chaim studied the entire six orders of Mishnah with some of his sons before their bar mitzvahs. With others, he learned through the entire Mishnah twice. With one particular son, he studied all of *Talmud Bavli* before the boy's bar mitzvah. Further-more, Rav Chaim related that the Steipler studied with him whole sections of *Tanach* prior to his bar mitzvah, every single Mishnah, and numerous *masechtas* in *Shas* as well. Yet when people come to see him and make statements like "My son is 11 years old and just wants to play; I can't get him to want to learn," Rav Chaim will answer, "Give him till his bar mitzvah. . ." "Don't pressure him..." "He's a child, let him be a child."

◆ ◆ ◆

Chazal wrote, "*L'olam al yeshaneh adam bno bein habanim* — A person should never treat one child differently from one another"

(*Shabbos* 10b) — a warning that a person must not show favoritism toward any child above another. Rav Chaim gives the same present, a siddur, to every granddaughter on the occasion of her bas mitzvah. So cognizant of this exhortation of *Chazal* is he that when one of his granddaughters was coming over to his home to receive her bas mitzvah gift, Rav Chaim requested that she bring the siddur he had given her older sister as a present a few years earlier.

There was a simple reason for his request. Rav Chaim wanted to check the inscription that he'd penned in the flyleaf of the first sister's present to ensure that he didn't write anything for the next sister in line that could be construed in any way as liking one of them more than the other.

◆ ◆ ◆

As a young child, the Steipler put Rav Chaim to bed with a lullaby comprised of all the names of the *masechta*s of *Shas* and the *parashiyos* in *Chumash*. As a child of 5, Rav Chaim once approached a guest in his home and requested that the man test him on all of *Shas*. The guest was taken aback. He knew Rav Chaim was a bright kid, but all of *Shas* at 5 years old? In the end, Rav Chaim explained that he was referring to the names of all the *masechta*s and *perakim* in *Shas*.

The Steipler did not use electricity on Shabbos. On Friday night, when it was dark and they couldn't see the words of a *sefer*, the Steipler would tell his son the names of *tzaddikim*, of *Tanna'im* and *Amora'im*, instilling in him the basis for all the knowledge that would come in the future.

Rav Chaim continued his father's tradition in his own home, and the Kanievsky family would sing those lullabies around their Shabbos table until every child knew the name of every tractate in *Shas*. After someone rebound Rav Chaim's *Shas* and replaced the *sefarim* on the shelf in his library, one of his daughters commented that the man had replaced them in the wrong order.

"How do you know that?" Rav Chaim asked her.

"We grew up on the songs of the *masechtas*," she replied. It might have been more than 50 years earlier, but she remembered every name of every *masechta* as if it were yesterday. This was the way Rav Chaim was raised and the way he raised his children, but that didn't mean that he felt the same approach applied to every child.

As an aside, someone mentioned to Rav Chaim that he'd heard that he devotes time to reflecting on the names of the *Tanna'im* and *Amora'im*.

"Yes," Rav Chaim answered with a nod, "I think about those names after I've said *HaMapil* — before I fall asleep — and in the morning before *Birkas HaTorah*."

◆ ◆ ◆

As I mentioned earlier, many times people have asked me, "How have you managed to build a close relationship with so many *gedolim*?" and I tell them how I did it, but the truth is, as worthwhile as it is to be so close to so many Jews of caliber, it also puts a tremendous obligation on a person.

The Gemara tells us that when Rav passed away, his students gathered together and decided to apportion the 10 "*mili dikedu-shah*" — the 10 special holy practices that Rav had taken on himself — among themselves. Every one of the group accepted one of Rav's practices. Rav Sheishes, the Gemara tells us, accepted the practice of *shemiras einayim,* of guarding one's eyes from sights of impurity. But when he found he wasn't able to follow this practice as his rebbi had, he blinded himself so as not to be derelict in the mission he had undertaken.

You have to realize, it's not just about developing a connection with these holy people; it's also a real obligation.

After Rav Yitzchok Nosson Kupershtok (more about him later) passed away, I poured out my heart to Rav Asher Arieli about how hard his passing had hit me. We'd been so close, with an almost father-son relationship. Rav Asher uttered a line that really hit home and resonated with an ultimate truth.

"Now it's our job to make new Rav Yitzchok Nossons," he said.

So, yes, having these kinds of relationships can be a truly unbelievable part of a person's life, but at the end of the day, one has to realize that they obligate him as well in a very real way.

Rav Chaim Kanievsky

Part D

The average visitor to Rav Chaim is treated to a quick conversation before the next person is given a turn. It's simply a matter of math. There are so many people coming to see Rav Chaim on a regular basis that it would be impossible to give more time per person. As it is, Rav Chaim already devotes many, many hours every day toward speaking to those who need his counsel, and the pressure on him is enormous.

Those who have managed to develop a closer relationship with Rav Chaim, however, come in contact with a side of him others rarely see. They see his softness, his giving nature, and his patience with people, which is difficult to discern when the *gabbaim* are hurrying everyone in and out. Being with him on more private occasions grants you the chance to see other sides to Rav Chaim's personality.

One character trait that stands out is Rav Chaim's keen humility, which I have been privileged to witness time and again.

◆ ◆ ◆

Being part of a Shabbos *seudah* with Rav Chaim is a unique experience. Since he is surrounded by his family and close confidants, Rav Chaim will sometimes relate a few personal stories between *divrei Torah*. On one occasion, Rav Chaim recounted the following incident from his younger years.

He began by telling us how someone once bemoaned the fact that Rav Chaim had never been a *rosh yeshivah*.

"Imagine how many *talmidim* you might have had, had you been a *rosh yeshivah*," the man said in a mournful tone.

"You are absolutely wrong," Rav Chaim replied. Then he clarified his statement. "In my youth I was offered many positions as a *rosh yeshivah*, but my father never allowed me to even consider them.

" 'It's not for you,' he said. 'You should just sit and learn.'

"The truth is," continued Rav Chaim, "my father was 100 percent correct. How do I know this? When I was still a *bachur* learning in yeshivah, one of the *maggidei shiur* at a local *yeshivah ketanah* (yeshivah high school) wasn't able to come to teach due to a family emergency. One of the administration asked if I would be a substitute for the day. Feeling bad for the yeshivah, I agreed to teach the class for one day.

"The class was learning *Perek HaMekabel* in *Bava Metzia* at the time. A short while after I started to teach, a boy raised his hand and asked me if he could leave the room.

"I gave him permission.

"The class immediately realized that I was the sort of rebbi who didn't have much in the way of control. In the minutes that followed, the majority of the class raised their hands and asked to be excused as well.

"I let every boy go.

"It wasn't long before there was only one *bachur* left in the classroom. Most probably he remained in the room," said Rav

Chaim with a twinkle in his eye, "because he felt bad leaving me completely alone. I looked at the boy. He looked at me.

"'You don't have to go to be excused?'

"'Actually, I do,' he answered.

"'Go,' I told him. He left the classroom and I opened my own Gemara and carried on learning by myself. I managed to teach them all of one *mishnah* from *Perek HaMekabel* before my entire teaching effort unraveled and everyone disappeared. That teaching experience was enough for me to trust my father when the offers to be a *rosh yeshivah* came in through the years and he told me to stay at home and learn. Because instead of me teaching them, those boys taught me. They taught me that I wasn't meant to sit in front of a classroom and teach."

It takes authentic humility to be able to discuss what some might perceive as a weakness, and Rav Chaim has no problem relating stories that show his human side and admitting that there are some things that are difficult for him to do.

◆ ◆ ◆

Somebody informed Rav Chaim that Rav Yechezkel Abramsky had learned his *sefer Taama D'kra* and praised it greatly afterward. Rav Chaim responded, "It must be because I brought down some *chiddushim* from the Chazon Ish."

Chas v'shalom for him to attribute any honor to himself.

◆ ◆ ◆

Rav Chaim is very careful to respond to the letters that come to his home on a daily basis from around the world. Since he doesn't know the people writing to him on a personal level, he generally doesn't use titles when addressing the person he's corresponding with. If there's a question, he devotes his attention to answering it and moves on to the next letter.

On one particular occasion, Rav Chaim was very impressed by a point someone had made to him in a letter, and he addressed that person with the impressive title of "*hagaon hagadol*," the great sage.

Rav Chaim's grandson, who happened to see this, knew how unusual it was for his grandfather to use such language, and he asked, "Why did this person merit such a title?"

"What's the big deal?" Rav Chaim replied with a twinkle in his eye. "People write that about me, too!"

Another time a *bachur* wrote Rav Chaim a letter and addressed it to the "*Rashkebahag*," which stands for "*Rabban shel Kol Bnei HaGolah*," leader of all Jews, wherever they may be. It's the type of salutation that one would have given to the Chafetz Chaim or Rav Chaim Ozer and is among the highest forms of respect. Rav Chaim was taken aback when he saw the greeting and thought about it for a few seconds before replying to the *bachur* using the same exact title.

When asked why he'd addressed a young man with such a prestigious choice of words, Rav Chaim replied, "He used the title for me, so I used the same one for him!"

❖ ❖ ❖

Rav Chaim ran a lending *gemach* in his home for many years. Not long ago, when he started feeling his age, Rav Chaim asked his son to take over. As Rav Chaim was handing over the documents and information, Rav Chaim shared an important piece of information with his son.

"The Arizal tells us," he said, "that if someone lends another person money and the money is not paid back, then both of them — the borrower and the lender — are forced to return to this world so that the borrower can repay his loan. The reason the lender has to return," explained Rav Chaim, "is because he is also culpable for not being *mochel* the debt."

His son waited to see where Rav Chaim was going with this.

"Look here," Rav Chaim said, showing his son a list of names. "These names are the people who borrowed money from my *gemach* and never repaid the loan. They haven't paid until now, and chances are that it may never happen. I would like to be *mochel* their debts, but this money belongs to charity and I'm not able to do so.

"Please take this money," and here Rav Chaim handed his son a stack of his own personal cash, "and pay their debts to the *gemach*, so that neither I, nor they, have to return to this world to deal with the matter in the future."

◆　◆　◆

It was Shabbos HaGadol at the Lederman Shul. The large room was packed with its usual wide range of honorable Bnei Brak personages, and Rav Chaim was honored with *maftir*. When he returned to his seat, he turned to the man sitting next to him and said, "I don't understand why they gave me *maftir*. I'm not a *rav*, I don't say a *derashah*. Why did they give me *maftir*?"

Why indeed?

Nobody tried to answer him. Sometimes, you see, a question is better than any possible answer can ever be.

◆　◆　◆

Rav Chaim is constantly being invited to different events. At one particular event, Rav Chaim surprised those in the know by remaining much longer than he normally does.

"Saba," his grandson asked him, "why did you stay so long?"

"There were a lot of speakers," Rav Chaim replied. "I was afraid that if I left in the middle, no matter where or when, someone would be offended, perhaps thinking that I'd stayed until that point out of respect for the speaker before him and that he wasn't worthy enough for me to remain. In the end, I just couldn't leave for fear that I'd hurt someone's feelings."

"But you are so pressured for time," his grandson protested.

"It doesn't matter, not if someone's feelings are hurt because of me."

◆　◆　◆

"I'm the one who tells my grandfather when it's time for him to go downstairs to Lederman's for davening," Rav Chaim's grandson told me.

"One day, I miscalculated. I told him to go down for *Minchah*, and when we reached the shul I realized that I had erred and been off by about 10 minutes. You have to understand something. My grandfather is capable of learning an astounding amount of Torah in 10 minutes. This is not a negligible thing. Every moment of his is so precious, it represents so much Gemara, I felt terrible.

"When I realized my mistake, I immediately began to apologize, but my grandfather cut me off with a wave of his hand.

"'It's not so bad,' he comforted me. 'A few more Yidden will be able to receive a *berachah*.'"

This is Rav Chaim. *Klal Yisrael*'s Rav Chaim. The *tzaddik* they turn to and call and write to and pour out their hearts to and seek advice from.

They feel he is theirs. And he agrees.

Encounters with

Rebbetzin
Batsheva Kanievsky
ע"ה

Rebbetzin Kanievsky examining the *sefer* Rav Chaim asked me
to revise and expand

*In a world where the focus is constantly and consistently
on the "I," Rebbetzin Kanievsky lived her life continuously
thinking of others, while at the same time doing her all to
ensure that her husband, Rav Chaim, shlita, had the peace
of mind to learn and serve Klal Yisrael.*

*This "eim b'Yisrael" — this mother of Israel — cherished
everyone who crossed her threshold, seeing in each of
the thousands who turned to her an individual, a holy
neshamah, a Jew who needed help.*

That was the Rebbetzin. All that and much, much more.

Rebbetzin Batsheva Kanievsky

Part A

When I arrived in Eretz Yisrael over 17 years ago, Rav Chaim Kanievsky was already very well known. He wasn't yet receiving the huge volume of mail that is delivered to his door today, but he was already famous as one of the leaders of the generation.

Rebbetzin Kanievsky, on the other hand, had not yet taken her unique place in *Klal Yisrael*'s heart. People respected her and knew that Rav Chaim's Rebbetzin was something special, but she had not yet become an official stop for people visiting from overseas. This developed gradually, with the Rebbetzin ultimately becoming renowned in her own right.

The first time I met the Rebbetzin was on the night of Hoshana Rabbah, shortly after my arrival in Eretz Yisrael. I had come to Bnei Brak to see Rav Chaim, but was informed, along with all the other people waiting to see him, that Rav Chaim was resting in preparation for staying up the entire night of Hoshana Rabbah.

"After he wakes up," the *gabbai* explained, "someone will open the door, and you'll know that Rav Chaim is seeing people again."

Meanwhile, however, the door was closed and the lights were off.

All of a sudden a little girl about 7 or 8 appeared, seemingly out of nowhere, and positioned herself directly in front of the Kanievskys' front door. She proceeded to pound on the door while yelling without letup, "*HaRabbanit! HaRabbanit!*"

The three or four people waiting at the top of the staircase next to the door tried to convince her to desist by telling her that Rav Chaim and the Rebbetzin were resting and shouldn't be bothered. The little girl was undeterred. She completely ignored all the bystanders and continued pounding away, determined to see the "*Rabbanit.*"

Standing there watching this determined little creature, I couldn't help but wonder if there was an emergency in the neighborhood that could only be dealt with by the Rebbetzin's capable hands. The Rebbetzin's young visitor eventually succeeded in getting her way. The door opened up, and we found ourselves face-to-face with Rebbetzin Kanievsky.

It was obvious that she had been woken up. There was an expression of surprise on the Rebbetzin's face when she realized who it was who had been pounding at the door, but when she opened her mouth to speak, she was in full control of her emotions. She may have been sleeping just a few moments before, but now she was up and quick to welcome her unexpected guest into the house without a hint of displeasure or anger.

It was my first time seeing the Rebbetzin, and in those few seconds I immediately realized that here was a unique and spiritually exceptional individual. As we read in the many articles and books that were written about her after her passing, she succeeded in loving everyone who passed through her door, like a mother and then like a grandmother.

Over the next years I spent a lot of time with the Rebbetzin. Sometimes I would sit and shmooze with her at length in her

A palpable *kedushah*: Rav Chaim Kanievsky

kitchen and domain. Those conversations were emblazoned into my mind, to be recalled in later years with fondness.

In those early days before I was married, I tried my best to come see Rav Chaim and the Rebbetzin at least once or twice a month. I'd take a *sherut* (taxi) from Rechov Strauss in the middle of the night, leaving myself sufficient time to reach the Lederman Shul so I could daven *vasikin* with Rav Chaim. There's a special beauty to be found in the Bnei Brak early-morning glow, and I'd stand beside a *gadol hador* and daven *Shacharis*, enjoying my physical proximity to a man who was much more than a man.

After davening, I'd accompany Rav Chaim to his home and discuss with him whatever questions I had prepared on Gemara or halachah. It would have been nice to eat breakfast with him, but Rav Chaim doesn't allow anyone to watch him when he eats.

The Gemara implies that it is inappropriate for a *talmid chacham* to partake of food in public, and Rav Chaim makes sure to eat in private. I've eaten Shabbos meals in the Kanievsky home, and then, of course, Rav Chaim does eat with everyone else, but never during the week.

Talking with Rav Chaim was always an experience, and when we were done, I would linger for a nice, long conversation with the Rebbetzin. You'd enter that famous kitchen, and there it was: the feeling of coming home to unconditional love and acceptance and warmth. To the magic of the Rebbetzin.

Once in a while I'd get the chance to help: she might ask me to take down the mixer from a shelf or return it to its place. But no matter why I had come, or whether I had come alone or brought others with me, I'd never leave their home without receiving a *berachah* from Rav Chaim *and* the Rebbetzin. It was obvious to me from the first second that I met her that here was a woman eminently worthy of emulation, specifically in the area of patience and her love for all creations. It seemed clear that she had received those outstanding character traits from her grandfather Rav Aryeh Levin, *zt"l*, with whom had she had been very close and who had a significant influence on her way of life.

Anyone who is familiar with stories about Rav Aryeh Levin knows that there was something unique in his very genes when it came to the mitzvah of loving his fellow man, and this character trait was passed down intact to the Rebbetzin. But it wasn't merely heredity; the Rebbetzin worked to become who she was. In particular, she was enamored with the *Iggeres HaRamban*, devoting time to study it every day. The *Iggeres HaRamban* discusses ideas such as seeing the good in every person, not getting upset with people, and recognizing that every person has something he excels in.

In his *Iggeres* the Ramban writes that one should read it every day, and on the days that a person studies it, he promises that his prayers will be fulfilled. I once suggested to Rav Chaim that the secret of the Rebbetzin's power might very possibly lie in the fact that she devoted such unbridled attention to the *Iggeres*, thereby becoming the recipient of the Ramban's promise.

Rav Chaim didn't disagree.

◆ ◆ ◆

I remember when the Rebbetzin collapsed one day and was taken to the hospital for tests. The doctors told her in no uncertain terms that she was working too hard and that she wasn't sleeping nearly enough. It so happened that they were correct. The Rebbetzin was on her feet almost the entire day and barely slept at night, and that, combined with her many hours of seeing people, had taken a toll on her health.

"You're going to have to cut down on your hours for seeing people," the doctors informed her.

I was there in the house when she arrived home from the hospital. The moment she walked through the door everyone wanted to know what the doctors had said.

"They told me that I have to cut down the hours that I spend with people," she replied.

"What are you going to do? Are you going to listen to the doctors?"

"What's the question?" she shot back. "I'm going to add to my hours of seeing people!"

And that was exactly what she did, because she felt that if such a thing had happened, it was an obvious sign from Heaven that she needed to increase the hours she donated on a daily basis to *Klal Yisrael*.

◆ ◆ ◆

Since I merited a special relationship with Rav Chaim and the Rebbetzin, there were many times when I was in the house during off hours, at the times of day when people were asked to give the family their privacy. Of course, almost every neighbor felt that she was an exception. This one was her best friend, and that one needed to borrow something, and the stream of people that flowed in and out of the house during the "off" hours was amazing to see.

There were times when it took the Rebbetzin an hour to get home from shul — and she lived a two-minute walk away. She'd exit Lederman Shul half an hour after Rav Chaim, and there would be people waiting outside the shul to see her. (Rebbetzin Kanievsky went to shul, which was right across the way, for all three *tefillos* each day. Of course, when I knew her, this was already when her children were grown, and she could attend shul freely.) It could be mid-morning before she'd sit down with the first cup of coffee of the day, even though she'd left the house before the sun rose. And though she might be hungry and tired, she greeted every person along her short/long route home with such love and joy that they never knew or imagined that she might be ready for a much-needed rest even before she began what was sure to be another arduous day.

Not everyone who visited her knew to come dressed in a way that was appropriate for their surroundings. At times secular women braved the "wilds" of Bnei Brak for an audience with the Rebbetzin, and they emerged all the richer for their experience. She'd hug and kiss them, treating them like her long-lost daughters.

◆ ◆ ◆

The Rebbetzin was a person of great spiritual stature, whose *berachos* and insights seemed to issue from a higher place. In much the same way that Rav Chaim would at times make statements that were diametrically opposed to what doctors had told a patient, so would the Rebbetzin, and so she, like Rav Chaim, would inevitably be proven right.

How did the Rebbetzin reach such lofty heights?

Rav Yonasan Eibeshitz, in his classic *sefer Ya'aros Devash*, discusses the words of the Gemara: "What merit propels women to the World to Come? In the merit of waiting for their husbands and sons to come home from the study hall and by sending them to learn Torah every single day..." (*Berachos* 17a).

Rav Yonasan offers an incredible insight on this Gemara. "As the husband grows in Torah and *avodas Hashem*, so does his wife. As the man becomes greater in Torah, so does his wife."

As Rav Chaim developed into one of the *gedolei hador*, Rebbetzin Kanievsky experienced exponential growth at the same time, to the point that some of the things taking place in their home were almost unbelievable.

I was once visiting their home when a woman limped inside to see the Rebbetzin. She was clearly expecting and was crying hysterically. I was standing beside the Rebbetzin at the time and understood that the woman had come straight from the hospital, where the doctors had just informed her that they weren't hearing a heartbeat and that they feared the child was no longer alive.

Rebbetzin Kanievsky laid her hand on the visitor's heavy stomach and then exclaimed in a loud, confident voice, "It's not true! *Yeled bari v'shalem, bari v'shalem.* Go back to the hospital and tell them that your child is healthy and whole!"

Never mind the fact that the doctors were emphatic. So was she. They had done tests while she had simply laid her hand on the mother. Yet she knew what she was saying and confidently transported countless individuals — including this frightened mother-to-be — out of trouble and into realms of good health and *mazel*.

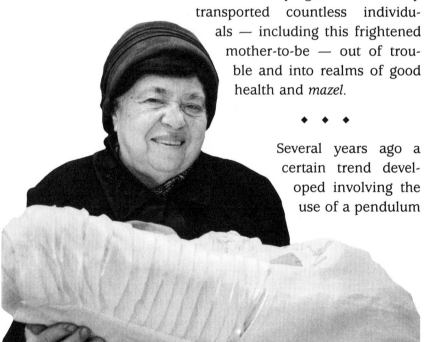

♦ ♦ ♦

Several years ago a certain trend developed involving the use of a pendulum

The Rebbetzin honored with serving as *kvateren* at our son's *bris* (essentially a necklace with a charm suspended from it). Known as "pendulum testing," the facilitators would give answers to people's questions based on the direction that the pendulum swung in response to the question. Many religious women were consulting with the facilitators, and it had become very popular within the *chareidi* population. Often they used this approach to address their health concerns.

There was a certain woman who was employed by a company where she and her *frum* female coworkers relied on the pendulum method to determine answers to key questions that they had. This woman explained to me how popular pendulum testing was becoming. It wasn't difficult to use, the whole procedure took just a couple of minutes, and the information was usually accurate. What did I think about it?

I found the concept of pendulum testing very strange, and it set off a host of warning bells in my head. I described the pendulum-testing method to Rav Chaim in a letter and asked him whether this was an acceptable method for determining answers to questions. I waited eagerly for his response.

It arrived a few days later.

"*Chalilah* to use this."

Armed with Rav Chaim's response, I informed my source that she had better let her colleagues know that Rav Chaim was 100 percent against the trend and had said it was forbidden to practice it.

"But the women who do it told me that Rebbetzin Kanievsky does it herself!"

"I find that hard to believe. I visit Rav Chaim and the Rebbetzin often, and I have never seen the Rebbetzin do something even remotely similar to what you are describing. In my opinion, there's not a chance in the world that Rebbetzin Kanievsky would be doing such a thing."

"I believe you," she replied, "but if I tell the women at work what you said, they won't be impressed because they don't know who you are. The only way I'll be able to make inroads with my friends at work is if I go visit the Rebbetzin and ask her myself."

"Not a problem." I gave her clear directions, arranged an appointment for her, and off she went.

The woman arrived at the Kanievsky home in Bnei Brak. She was expecting a child at the time and no doubt figured that it was a good opportunity to get a *berachah* for herself as well. She showed the Rebbetzin exactly what the ladies were doing and asked her if it was true that she herself was a pendulum practitioner.

The Rebbetzin laughed. "Of course not," she replied. "Never. Anyway, why would anyone want to use such a device?"

"The ladies at work use the pendulum to determine whether they are going to have a boy or a girl."

The Rebbetzin smiled at her. "You want to know what you're having?"

The lady nodded.

"Turn around."

She did so.

The Rebbetzin took a good look at her. "You're having a boy."

Of course, she had a boy. Without having to use the pendulum. For the Rebbetzin, looking at a person was more than enough.

◆ ◆ ◆

The Rebbetzin spoke about her famous grandfather Rav Aryeh on more than one occasion. She loved telling stories about him and his saintly ways and relished speaking of his *tzidkus* and lofty character. One morning she shared the following story: one that she'd heard directly from her father, Rav Elyashiv.

"My grandfather used to collect money for the poor of Yerushalayim. One *erev Pesach*, try as he might, he was unable to raise the amount he needed to provide for all the families who were counting on his help so desperately. The very thought of failing all these people who depended on him made him miserable. On the day before Pesach," she went on, "my grandfather was standing at a Jerusalem bus stop when an Arab he had never met before approached him, handed him an envelope without saying a word, and disappeared.

"My grandfather opened the envelope to discover the exact amount of money he had been missing, and he was able to meet all his financial obligations in time for *Yom Tov*. As everyone knows," the Rebbetzin concluded, "the Gemara writes that Eliyahu HaNavi appears to people at times dressed up as an Arab."

Was it Eliyahu HaNavi? Draw your own conclusions.

◆ ◆ ◆

"One Shabbos the gas went off for whatever reason," the Rebbetzin once told me. "In the morning, when I checked on the cholent, I saw that it was cold. That week," continued the Rebbetzin, "Rav Chaim ate a lot more than he normally did. When I questioned him, he told me that he liked the cholent better than usual because 'he likes his cholent cold.'

"It was *pashut* to me," concluded the Rebbetzin, "that he didn't want me to feel bad for serving him cold cholent and that's why he ate more."

◆ ◆ ◆

The Rebbetzin once confided to me that she and Rav Chaim had been married for a while before having children. "Someone told Rav Chaim that he knew of a *segulah* that might help us.

" 'What *segulah*?' Rav Chaim asked the man.

" 'Try to make your wife happy,' he answered.

" 'How do you make a wife happy?'

" 'Buy her a present.'

"Rav Chaim thought for a while about what to buy me. In the end he decided to buy me a siddur. Except that this was Rav Chaim, the *masmid* of the generation. What did he know about buying presents? As soon as he made his decision, he went to one of the used *sefarim* stores in Bnei Brak and bought a siddur for me. When he brought it home and presented the used siddur to me, I laughed so hard, it really did make me happy!"

◆ ◆ ◆

There's a very famous story about Rav Chaim and a grasshopper. I know that it was written in a number of *sefarim*, and has been told through the years with many versions and variations, but the Rebbetzin related it to me herself one Shabbos when I was staying at the Kanievsky home, and I feel that it's worthwhile to record it here again.

"Many years ago," the Rebbetzin began, "Rav Chaim undertook to write a certain Torah *kuntres* entitled *Karnei Chagavim*, literally translated as 'horns of grasshoppers.'

"The *kuntres* dealt with the signs needed to identify which grasshoppers are kosher and which are not. Obviously Rav Chaim was not planning to permit the consumption of grasshoppers, since that isn't Ashkenazic tradition. But this was Torah and thus needed to be clarified. There was no decisive work on the subject, and Rav Chaim labored extensively to reach the root of the matter.

"While engaged in his research, Rav Chaim came to a standstill. According to the commentaries on the subject, Rav Chaim believed that the grasshopper should have certain *simanim*, certain conclusive signs. He asked his daughters to please bring home books from the school library with pictures of grasshoppers so he could check to make sure his conclusions were correct.

"Rav Chaim's daughters did, in fact, bring home books with pictures of grasshoppers. After diligently studying the pictures, Rav Chaim found himself stymied, since the pictures did not match the way a kosher grasshopper was supposed to look according to his calculations. Not knowing what else to do, and unwilling to publish something on which there were any doubts, Rav Chaim decided to shelve the project.

"And then, one day, while he sat and learned in his study, a grasshopper suddenly flew into the room and landed on his table. Though grasshoppers are not commonly seen in Bnei Brak, here was a real live grasshopper sitting on his table, content to allow him all the time he needed to verify any questions that he had on the subject. After studying it for a while, Rav Chaim concluded that his earlier calculations had been correct. He also decided that the grasshopper's sudden appearance was a sign from Heaven that he should, in fact, publish the *kuntres*.

"A few days later, Rav Chaim ran into another difficulty and was unsure how to proceed — and again, a grasshopper flew into his room and came in for a landing on his table. This unprecedented occurence was of exceptional assistance to him, and Rav Chaim was able to publish the *kuntres* a short while later.

"When people questioned him about the story," said the Rebbetzin, "his usual response was 'Do you think I remember things that happened a hundred years ago?'"

Anyone who knows Rav Chaim well understands that this type of response is typical Rav Chaim: admitting without admitting.

"A man, a *talmid chacham*, once told over this story in Bnei Brak in front of a whole gathering of people," the Rebbetzin added. "The majority of those who were there loved the story and accepted it as yet another example of Rav Chaim's greatness and high standing in *Shamayim* (who, after all, sent the grasshopper right to his study?). But one of the people who heard the story was unwilling to accept that it was true, considering the story a *bubbe ma'aseh*, and something that couldn't have happened, 'because these types of stories do not happen today, even to people like Rav Chaim.' "

"Unfortunately for him, he voiced his comments out loud. And in public.

"When he came home," said the Rebbetzin with a twinkle in her eye, "he found to his horror that his entire house was infested with grasshoppers!

"Unwilling to make something of what could very possibly be an everyday occurrence, the man got out the phone book and called an exterminator. Three different exterminators were summoned to deal with the situation over the next three days, with no success. The grasshoppers were oblivious to anything the exterminators threw at them and were seemingly content to remain exactly where they were, with no intention of moving. Eventually the man arrived at a different conclusion. He returned to the man who had related the story. He admitted how he had scoffed at its validity and told him of the instant repercussions.

" 'By stating in public that you don't believe Rav Chaim worthy of such a miracle,' said the *talmid chacham* who had originally retold the story, 'you have belittled his *kavod*. *Shamayim* has taken umbrage at your actions. It seems to me that you have no choice but to go and ask Rav Chaim for forgiveness.'

"The man presented himself to Rav Chaim and asked him for *mechilah*, and the grasshoppers disappeared the same way they had appeared. Instantly and with no remaining trace.

"There is a postscript to the story. Every single week, at the same exact time, a solitary grasshopper would show up on the windowsill of the scoffer's home. It came in winter and summer, on beautiful spring days and in the harshest of stormy weather. People began to come to see the grasshopper that serves as a reminder of the miracle that took place in that home.

"Not only that," the Rebbetzin said with a smile, "the woman of the house takes a picture of the grasshopper every week and brings the pictures to show me. At some point, the family needed to move to a larger home, but the mother wasn't sure that this was a good idea, since she didn't want the grasshopper visits to cease. Who could move away from such a revelation of *hashgachah*? In the end, after much deliberation and sheer necessity, the family decided to move. And lo and behold, the same grasshopper — well, who can really tell if it was the same one? — landed in the same windowsill spot at the same exact time every week to remind one and all of what had happened in their home."

◆ ◆ ◆

It's brought down that there's an ancient *minhag* to burn one's *lulav* along with the *chametz* on *erev Pesach*. It's not an obligation, but is a highly recommended practice. As a Jew who follows every nuance of halachah and *minhag*, Rav Chaim always burns his *lulav* faithfully on *erev Pesach*. Rebbetzin Kanievsky related the following incident, illustrating Rav Chaim's devotion toward even the smallest *minhag*.

"It was the ninth of Nissan," she said, "and I returned home at 12 o'clock after a long day.

"'Where's Rav Chaim?' I asked my grandson.

"'Saba wasn't feeling well and went to sleep early.'

"I entered the bedroom, and I saw right away that Rav Chaim was still up, that he was bothered and not his peaceful self.

"'What's wrong?' I asked him.

"'I can't find the *lulavim* I was saving to burn with the *chametz*. They aren't where I left them!'

"'Most probably the cleaning woman moved them somewhere else. Wait until tomorrow morning and we'll find them then.'

"Rav Chaim listened to me, heard me out, but he wasn't calm. 'Don't worry,' I told him, 'we'll find the *lulavim* in the morning. You're so tired right now, just go to sleep.'

"I woke up at 1:30 in the morning," the Rebbetzin continued, "and I saw that Rav Chaim's bed was empty. Knowing that Rav Chaim had gotten up made me too nervous to sleep, so I got up myself and went to find him. I looked around the apartment, but I couldn't find him anywhere. Then I saw that the light was on upstairs, and I figured that maybe he went up to his study to learn a little. All of a sudden, the door opened, and Rav Chaim entered the house from outside.

"'Where did you go?' I asked.

"'I went downstairs.'

"'Why now, at this time of night?'

"'I went down to the garbage Dumpster to see if maybe someone threw out the *lulavim* there.'

"He hadn't managed to find the *lulavim*, and he was simply beside himself. I tried to convince him to go back to sleep; burning a *lulav* is a beautiful thing, but it's just a *minhag* after all. Rav Chaim, however, couldn't hear a word I was saying. Burning his *lulavim* at *sereifas chametz* was something he'd always done, and he couldn't imagine missing doing so this year. There was nothing to talk about, no way for him to return to bed until those *lulavim* had been found.

"Rav Chaim didn't rest. He searched in every nook and cranny, every closet, on top of every bookcase. It was like *bedikas chametz*, except more intense. In the end, Rav Chaim found the *lulavim* in some overlooked corner at 3 o'clock in the morning. His face was the picture of happiness and satisfaction. Tranquillity and peacefulness returned to his *neshamah*. He was calm once again."

Why the anxiety? Why the angst? Because Rav Chaim took his *minhagim* as seriously as he takes his halachah. What could sleep possibly mean to Rav Chaim Kanievsky when faced with the "Case of the Missing *Lulavim*"?

◆ ◆ ◆

After Rebbetzin Kanievsky passed away, a number of DVDs were circulated with footage of the Rebbetzin in her kitchen, and I received numerous messages from people who told me that I had been filmed talking with the Rebbetzin, though I don't recall seeing anyone with a video camera. Yet though I had been in her home countless times and shared many a conversation with her, the Rebbetzin never once asked me my name! If someone would have mentioned my name to her, she would not have known who they meant.

I gave much thought to this unusual phenomenon and came to a conclusion: the reason the Rebbetzin didn't know my name, though we had spoken so many times, was because it made no difference to her. She recognized my face, but my name was not important. Why? Every Jew who entered her home held the same importance in her eyes and received the same respect. Every single Jew deserved her undivided attention, and it didn't matter whether your name was well known and important or if you were someone who was completely unknown. To the Rebbetzin, every single Jew deserved the same warm and wonderful treatment.

◆ ◆ ◆

As I mentioned earlier, I always sought ways to do something for the *gedolim* whom I knew. I was never content when my relationship with someone was all "take" on my side.

With the Rebbetzin, I knew it would take me some time to think of the perfect gift. What can you give to someone who has everything? Here was a person who was so happy with her lot in life, she needed absolutely nothing! One day, though, it dawned on me. I happened to notice that in the Kanievsky home there was always a shortage of pens. There was a reason for this. Since countless people passed through their home, and many times people needed pens with which to write down their requests for *berachos* from Rav Chaim, the Kanievsky pens disappeared with alarming frequency. It was nobody's fault really, but many times, after using one of the Kanievsky pens, the visitor would slip it absentmindedly into a pocket and leave.

With this in mind, I purchased a huge bag of Bic pens and presented them to the Rebbetzin, feeling a little self-conscious as I did (after all, what kind of a present was a bag of pens?), but her reaction made me realize that I had made the right move. She was so happy with her present! She never asked anyone for anything, ever. But her *hakaras hatov* when something was presented to her was palpable.

"*Eizeh matanah yafah!* What a beautiful gift!" she enthused. You would never imagine that someone would make such a big deal over such a simple gift, but the Rebbetzin never took anyone or anything for granted.

◆ ◆ ◆

Pens aside, it was very difficult to find things that I could do for Rav Chaim. Every wealthy Jew in the world would have been glad to run and buy him whatever he wanted if he just gave the slightest hint. This was a man who had anything and everything he could possibly want. Yet I truly wanted to do something for him and to turn our relationship into one that was a two-way street.

For a while, I was stymied. Eventually I came to the realization that the only thing I could do for Rav Chaim was to give him a stream of well-presented and thought-out *he'aros* (comments) on his *sefarim*.

For example, Rav Chaim raised a question in one of his *sefarim* and suggested an answer. I found the same concept in a *sefer* written by a *Rishon*. I brought the *sefer* to Rav Chaim, and when I showed it to him, he gave me such a warm "*yasher ko'ach*" that the Rebbetzin, who had been entertaining a group of visiting women in the other room, came rushing in to find out what had just occurred.

"The Rav wrote a certain *chiddush* many years ago," I told her, "and I just showed him that the same *chiddush* was written in a *Rishon*'s *sefer*."

She was overjoyed. Returning to the group of women she said, "Ladies, do you hear what just happened? This *yungerman* just brought proof from a *Rishon* to something that my husband wrote many years ago! He deserves a round of applause!"

The entire group began clapping, while the Rebbetzin stood alongside, beaming with pride and happiness.

When I saw how much enjoyment this brought Rav Chaim and the Rebbetzin, I invested much time and thought in this direction, and ultimately that is what built the biggest connection between Rav Chaim and myself. My involvement with his *sefarim* led to my being privileged to actually revise and expand one of Rav Chaim's *sefarim*. It was entitled *L'Mechaseh Atik*, which means "to uncover that which is hidden."

My involvement in the project came about in an interesting way. The *sefer* deals with cryptic *pesukim* in *Tanach* that need explanation. Rav Chaim provides these explanations through quotes of *Chazal* uncovered from the encyclopedic library in his brain. I loved this *sefer* and wrote him extensive comments on it.

Once, when I came in to see him, he said to me, "I received your letter with the comments, and many of them are very good. In fact, I added them into the *sefer*."

Then he added another shocking line.

"Truthfully, the entire *kuntres* should be done over. I don't have the strength to redo it. Why don't you take on this project?"

I accepted the offer joyfully. I had written many comments through the years in my copy of the *sefer*, and Rav Chaim lent me his copy with all of his comments and additions, and I got to work. This meant seeing Rav Chaim a lot more than before, since there were constant questions that needed to be addressed

regarding what exactly to put into the revised version and what to leave out. It became an exciting *"chavrusashaft"* that I treasured and that brought a new dimension to my life.

One day, when we were sitting together, Rav Chaim turned to me and asked, "Do you think people are really going to purchase this *sefer*?"

Mazel tov! Rav Chaim examining our newly published *sefer*

"I think yes," I replied.

Rav Chaim remained unconvinced. "I'm not sure," he said, reiterating his earlier doubt.

Since then I have thought about Rav Chaim's statement many times, and I think that the reason he said those words was because he didn't want me to be disappointed if, after all the work I put in, the *sefer* wouldn't sell well. The fact is, when the *sefer* was finally published, the entire printing was sold out within two months. I added more material and published that as well and, *baruch Hashem*, the second edition is also almost gone, and we are about to release a third edition with a large quantity of new information.

After the *sefer*'s success had become an obvious fact, I returned to Rav Chaim and said to him, "In the 15 years since I've known the Rav, every single thing he told me was always 100 percent correct. There was only one time that his words weren't completely accurate."

"What do you mean?" he asked me.

"When we were working on the *sefer*, the Rav asked me if I thought it was going to sell and I told him yes, and then Rebbi said that he wasn't sure if that was indeed going to be the case."

The fact is, I went on, the *sefer* sold out immediately.

Rav Chaim then did an extraordinary thing. Putting his arm around my shoulder, he uttered a few words that I would never forget.

"*Dos is in ayer zechus*. That is in your merit."

The humility inherent in those few words is not to be believed. Yes, I took a 30-page pamphlet and turned it into a 200-page *sefer*. And, yes, Rav Chaim had provided me with a beautiful letter of *haskamah* for the *sefer*, as if it were my *sefer* and Rav Chaim had nothing to do with it. Regardless of that, it's clear as daylight that the *sefer*'s success can only be attributed to its connection with Rav Chaim. For Rav Chaim to say such a thing, to look me in the eye and to say, "*Dos is in ayer zechus*" — and really mean it — was a level of humility that astounded me and still does to this very day.

Encounters with

Rav
Refael Levin
זצ"ל

Rav Refael Levin at my *chuppah*

Jaffa Road, in the center of Jerusalem, is a busy street filled with pedestrians rushing here and there, all intent on making their purchases. The noise level is always high, and the scene is one of frenetic energy.

There is a shul on this bustling road. Upon entering its doors, you find yourself walking straight into another world. Here is genuine quiet, a serenity that is a throwback to a time when things were more simple, and more real.

Step inside, and you have entered another universe: the world of Rav Refael Levin.

Rav Refael Levin

Part A

I was fortunate to develop relationships during my years in yeshivah and afterward with many of Yerushalayim's "hidden *tzaddikim*." These were men who overwhelmingly chose to shun the limelight, eschewing fame and honor for the privilege of remaining unknown, relatively anonymous, and left undisturbed within their sheltered Yerushalmi neighborhoods.

People have asked me many times, "How did you find these people? How did an American *bachur* become friends and even a close confidant of quite a few *tzaddikim* from Batei Broide and Batei Nathan, the strongholds of Yerushalayim's Old Yishuv?"

Others have asked me how I even knew where to look for Yerushalayim's hidden *tzaddikim* in the first place. These are all reasonable questions, with a fairly reasonable answer.

You know what they say about *shidduchim:* All you need is one.

It's pretty much the same thing when it comes to *tzaddikim*. All you need is one to serve as the starting point. Once you have a relationship with one *tzaddik*, you're bound to hear about his friends and even meet them. And as I've found, the friend of a *tzaddik* is usually a *tzaddik* himself. It's just the way things are. People are usually friendly with others who share similar interests and passions.

Once I began visiting Rav Yitzchok Nosson Kupershtok on a regular basis in the central Jerusalem enclave of Batei Broide, it wasn't long before I met his friend and lifelong confidant Rav Zundel Kroizer, who was also a resident of Batei Broide.

During *bein hazemanim* I had gotten into the practice of davening every day at a different *vasikin* (sunrise) *minyan*. One of the rules when it comes to *tzaddikim*: most of them daven *vasikin* every day. Once there, it was a simple matter of scouting out the assembled. After that it wasn't difficult to bridge the age and culture gap.

◆ ◆ ◆

Jaffa Road, in the center of Jerusalem, straddles the Machaneh Yehudah *shuk* and is home to numerous businesses. With the opening of the Jerusalem Light Rail, the standstill traffic and suffocating exhaust fumes that were once part and parcel of this particular artery are a memory of the past, and Jaffa Road has become a pleasant place to stroll.

Despite its outer facade, Jaffa Road — either along the road itself or on the many small streets adjacent to it — is home to quite a few shuls and yeshivos. The most famous of these is no doubt Yerushalayim's Etz Chaim *cheder*, which had been located right off the main road for decades, but there are many other points of interest, too. From a historical perspective, Jaffa Road with its narrow alleyways is a gold mine of facts, stories, and anecdotes that tell a tale of days long gone and figures shrouded in mystery.

There was one shul in particular that called to me. It was known in Hebrew as "Zoharei Chamah" and in English as the "Sundial Shul."

Zoharei Chamah's building is well known due to the giant sundial on its upper story. The shul itself hosts both Sephardi and Ashkenazi *minyanim*. I had met a *bachur* in yeshivah whose interest in *tzaddikim* came purely from the angle of a photographer (he loved taking pictures of great men). It was he who told me about the Zoharei Chamah's "Rav," a holy Jew by the name of Rav Refael Levin, the son of Rav Aryeh Levin, who was famous in his own right as a man whose blessings came true.

Rav Rafael was very similar to his father in both his general outlook toward life and in the way he treated those whom he encountered. If there was any one individual who was accepted as this shul's rabbi, it was he.

◆ ◆ ◆

Rav Asher Arieli delivered a heated *shmuess* prior to the onset of the winter *zeman* in which he exhorted his students to take care of everything that needed doing before the onset of the semester, to ensure that they'd be free to be totally focused on their learning during the *zeman*. After hearing his words, I gave some thought as to whether there was anything that I needed to do before the *zeman* started. I could only think of one thing, and that was a wisdom tooth that needed to be dealt with. With Rav Asher's words ringing in my ears, and the tooth making its presence known with increasing frequency, I decided it was time to take care of it.

There was one impediment in my path toward dental bliss: the issue of money. How to pay to separate me from my ailing wisdom tooth. And as He'd done many times before, Hashem stepped in to take care of it for me.

Yitzchok Honig, a good friend of mine, had cousins who lived in Nachlaot. A friend of theirs in Sha'arei Chesed was making a wedding one night that week and needed someone to "babysit" their home during the actual evening of the *simchah* to thwart anyone who planned on robbing them during their big night. They were willing to pay whatever the going rate was for a house sitter.

Everything fell neatly into place. I'd babysit the house and receive sufficient remuneration to pay for the removal of my wisdom tooth. Yitzchok's cousins even gave me the name of a trustworthy dentist.

I spent the night in the Sha'arei Chesed home, learning at the dining-room table as they danced the night away. When they finally made it home well after midnight, they invited me to sleep there. It was a gracious offer and I accepted. I ended up leaving their home in the early hours of morning to find a *vasikin minyan*. Zoharei Chamah on Jaffa Road was not really close by, but I was already up and ready to daven and I couldn't think of anywhere else to go. The sky was just beginning to change color as I stepped out of their home and into the chilly streets of Sha'arei Chesed, the morning birds keeping me company as I walked through the silent streets toward my destination.

◆ ◆ ◆

Zoharei Chamah was already in full operational mode as the regular morning worshipers hurried in, took their seats, and commenced davening. I had been carrying the *sefer K'Motzei Shalal Rav* on *Chumash* with me that morning, and I set it down on the table beside me as I wrapped my tefillin around my arm.

As I wound, a Yerushalmi gentleman approached me and happened to glance down at the *sefer*, which had just been published. In classic Yerushalmi fashion he lifted it up and began leafing through the pages. I would later find out that this was Rav Yaacov Marcus and that he was the Rav of Bikur Cholim Hospital.

After a minute or two he turned to the first page of the *sefer*, where he found my name. He stared at it and then his expression proceeded to light up like a bulb.

"Wait here," he commanded.

I hadn't been planning on going anywhere, and I waited patiently to see where this interchange was leading. He returned about 15 minutes later holding two *sefarim* in his hands. He showed me the name written in both covers and then said, "Do you know this man?"

"It's my father," I replied, astonished.

"Twenty-eight years ago," he said, "your father learned at the Chevron Yeshivah here in Yerushalayim."

I nodded.

"At the time," he went on, "I had been searching for these two *sefarim* when someone told me that your father owned a copy of each. I borrowed them from him, and when I returned to Chevron a while later, they told me that your father had since left the yeshivah. I had no way of contacting him to return his *sefarim*. I have been waiting for 28 years to return them — and now here you are!"

The Zoharei Chamah *vasikin minyan* was small enough that everyone present grasped that something of interest had just taken place. Genuine Yerushalmi products to a man, the assembled didn't rest until they had heard all the details of Rav Marcus's successful *sefarim* return. As Rav Refael Levin, who of course was also present, was in some ways the quintessential Yerushalmi, he wasn't satisfied with the bare details. He questioned me for a while afterward until we both felt like we had gotten to know each other.

When I left Zoharei Chamah later that morning and stepped out into the fragrant early-morning Yerushalayim air, I knew that here was one man and one shul to whom I would be returning again and again.

It was just that kind of place.

◆ ◆ ◆

And so I began frequenting Zoharei Chamah on an ongoing basis. Since I didn't allow my fascination with the great men of Yerushalayim to interfere with my yeshivah obligations, I would head over to Rav Refael's shul after *Minchah* on Shabbos afternoon. We'd learn together until *Ma'ariv*, after which I'd make Havdalah for the people in the shul (including Rav Refael's wife, who attended all three prayers with her husband), since Rav Refael didn't want to drink the wine. After Havdalah I'd accompany him back to his home near David Yellin Street, where we parted ways: me to return to yeshivah and Rav Refael first to the

Kosel and then on to visit his brother-in-law, Rav Elyashiv.

Rav Refael was someone who possessed copious inner amounts of passionate, sizzling *ahavas Yisrael* for every Jew he met. In this, he was very much following in the ways of his beloved father, Rav Aryeh Levin, who was known throughout Yerushalayim as the rabbi of widows, orphans, and prisoners. Rav Aryeh's smile and soothing presence brought a calming spirit to the war- and poverty-stricken Jerusalem of yore. There were many men of stature and wisdom in Jerusalem, but none were as beloved as Rav Aryeh Levin. And his son followed in his ways.

Though Rav Refael was the unofficial Rav of the *minyan*, there was a unanimous unspoken policy to always wait for a certain man in the *minyan* to finish reciting the *Shema* or *Shemoneh Esrei*. To me this was an unfathomable decision since the man whom everyone waited for was a businessman and not a rav or *rosh yeshivah*. I wondered about this for months before finally confronting Rav Refael about it.

Rav Refael explained his reasoning to me.

"The man whom the *minyan* waits for suffers from a heart condition," he said. "I knew that if we could somehow make him happy, he'd be able to recover and strengthen his heart. I gave the matter some thought and eventually reached the following conclusion.

"How do you make a person happy? What is the true-and-tried solution? The answer is by making him the recipient of true honor. Once the answer came to me, I informed the members of the *kehillah* that we would be waiting for this man to finish saying *Shemoneh Esrei* from here on.

"I cannot even tell you how this honor changed his life. People heard about it. The news of his 'promotion' reached his children. Wherever he went, he was receiving honor from people who knew about his standing at Zoharei Chamah. He had become someone special, and it literally changed his life. The end result," concluded Rav Refael, "was that the physical condition of the man's heart really did improve."

Not that Rav Rafael needed backup for the things he said, but I did find later a statement by the Rambam in *Hilchos Yom HaKippurim* that says how giving honor to a person can save his life. This story exemplified Rav Refael's philosophy in life. It was always about the other person. Always. I loved the story and found myself revering him all the more.

◆ ◆ ◆

On *motza'ei Shabbos*, Rav Refael waited until every single person in the *minyan* finished davening *Shemoneh Esrei*. Even for the people who took a very long time. Even though he was in a rush to get to the Kosel and from there to Rav Elyashiv's home.

The fact that he had many obligations didn't matter in the slightest. Since it was his tradition to wish every member of Zoharei Chamah "*a gute voch*," there was no way in the world that he'd ever agree to exit the shul before giving his personal *berachah* to every single person. Rav Refael feared that if he missed wishing "*a gute voch*" to one of his regulars, this might be interpreted as something personal and might cause mental anguish to another Jew.

So he waited.

And he waited.

Until everyone present had taken three steps back and was available for comment. Then he wished them all blessings for the upcoming week. And nobody ever felt slighted or overlooked. Not at Zoharei Chamah. Not in the house of Rav Refael Levin.

Once an American man came to daven at Zoharei Chamah for *Ma'ariv* on *motza'ei Shabbos*. Rav Refael waited for everyone to finish davening, as was his *minhag*, but this particular individual was davening a very, very long *Shemoneh Esrei*. Rav Refael knew that someone was arriving shortly to take him to the Kosel. Wishing everyone "*a gute voch*" is a beautiful thing, but not at the expense of someone who has expressly come to drive you somewhere and will have to wait.

I could tell that Rav Refael was agitated. On the one hand, he couldn't imagine leaving without wishing the guest from America "*a gute voch.*" On the other hand, his consideration was causing an inconvenience for the designated driver.

"Rav Refael," I said to him, "I know this man and I will make sure to tell him that you waited a long time in order to wish him '*a gute voch*,' but you simply had to go."

Rav Refael only calmed down once he had my assurances that I would take care of the matter, and he made sure to follow up with me, asking me whether I had remembered to speak to the man. It had been on his mind, and he wouldn't rest until he verified that the man knew and understood why the Rav had left Zoharei Chamah without saying good-bye.

◆ ◆ ◆

When Rav Refael arrived at the Kosel, people would be waiting for him and asking him for *berachos* as he walked from the car. It took him a long time just to reach the Wall, where he'd recite a few *kvitlach* of *Tehillim* and retrace his steps for the short journey to his next stop.

I recall one week when Rav Refael told me he really wasn't feeling well and had no strength to go to the Kosel.

"I'm going even though I don't feel up to it," he told me.

"But you're so weak," I protested.

"I don't feel well enough to go," he said, "but there are many people coming especially to see me, and they will feel let down if I don't show up."

In the end he went, elderly and bent over though he was, and you could tell that every step was torture, but he went anyway. Because the people were waiting.

◆ ◆ ◆

There was an elderly Yerushalmi Yid who used to frequent Zoharei Chamah during the same hours that Rav Refael and I would be learning together. Rav Refael was always meticulous about making sure that any *chiddush* or piece of Torah that I shared with him was said in a loud enough voice so that it would seem as if I were sharing it with both Rav Refael and the elderly Yid.

On one occasion I brought a letter from Rav Chaim Kanievsky to show to Rav Refael.

"Bring it over to him, too," Rav Refael commanded me.

Zoharei Chamah had two entrances, one on either side of the building. One Shabbos afternoon, Rav Refael unlocked the door and we entered the shul. As we stood there beside his chair, Rav Refael noticed the door at the opposite end of the room opening and our "*chavrusa*" entering the room.

"Binyomin," he whispered urgently to me, "let's sit down quickly so that we can rise in his honor when he reaches his seat!"

One can only appreciate how impressive this behavior was for him, when you knew how truly difficult it was for Rav Refael to sit down and stand up. But I knew, and I had never seen anyone display such caring for one's fellow man before. There was an emphasis on giving sincere *kavod* to every individual in a way that would make them feel extra special.

◆ ◆ ◆

An older, unmarried *bachur* was another frequent visitor to the shul for *Ma'ariv* on *motza'ei Shabbos*. Every time he'd see the *bachur*, Rav Refael would shake his hand warmly and say the following words to him: "*Lamed vav tzaddik! Lamed vav tzaddik.*"

Evidently Rav Refael knew that the road to this man's heart lay through the utterance of those three words, and indeed the man's face would light up and start to shine whenever they shared the familiar refrain.

Every week Rav Refael would repeat his line as if it was being said for the first time. And every week the *bachur* would smile and glow with pleasure as if he were hearing Rav Refael's compliment for the first time.

◆ ◆ ◆

On another occasion, as we were walking home from the shul together, we were approached by one of the familiar beggars from the Zichron Moshe neighborhood of Jerusalem. Every article of clothing was mismatched, his shoes had many holes, and the aroma that preceded him was that of unwashed humanity laced with a strong dose of alcohol. Needless to say, this was the type of person that most people stayed as far away from as possible.

When we were close enough to hear him, the man whose entire being screamed of neglect opened his mouth and shared a little Pesach-themed *vort* with Rav Refael.

"*Shacharis*," the beggar said. "The word *shacharis* is the *roshei teivos* of the four sons from the Haggadah: *she'eino yodei'a lishol*, *chacham*, *rasha*, and *tam*."

Cute though it may have been, it was appropriate for Pesach and had nothing to do with our time of year or anything that we'd been discussing. Still, Rav Refael beamed his approval at the man and thanked him profusely.

I walked Rav Refael home from shul almost every *motza'ei Shabbos* over the next two and a half years. Throughout that time, whenever he saw the man coming from a distance, Rav Refael would already be calling out as if in greeting, "*Shacharis, Shacharis, roshei teivos!*" reminding the forlorn Yid that here was one man who never forgot the Torah thought he'd shared with him and who appreciated his acumen and intelligence. Inevitably, the man, who for all practical purposes was invisible to the world, would break out in a giant smile.

The message of the smile was there for all to see.

"I'm a person, too," it said. "I have self-worth just like everyone else. Look, even the great Rav Refael Levin sees me as a friend and as someone worthy of his respect!"

◆ ◆ ◆

There was a certain member of the *minyan* who was a stickler for coming on time, a real Yekke when it came to *zemanim*. Every time the man would enter the room, Rav Refael would glance at his watch and then back at him and say, "*Punktlach, punktlach*, right on time!"

It was the most meaningful compliment he could have paid the man, who'd smile back at him from ear to ear. With Rav

Refael it was all about finding the one point that was important to a person and with which he could brighten up his day.

◆ ◆ ◆

When my mother came to Eretz Yisrael for a visit, I made sure to introduce her to Rav Refael and his Rebbetzin. At that time Rav Refael had many financial responsibilities on his shoulders. He'd undertaken complete responsibility for a *kollel* of *talmidei chachamim* that he'd established in Beis Aryeh, the yeshivah founded by his father and run by his brother-in-law, Rav Leizer Pluchinsky. The yeshivah was located on Rav Aryeh Levin Street, just off the Machaneh Yehudah marketplace (Rav Nosson Tzvi Finkel actually learned there for a time in his youth). My mother wanted to show Rav Refael her *hakaras hatov* and to help him out with a $100 donation, to be given to whatever cause or person he felt needed it.

Rav Refael accepted the money with a smile, and nothing more was made of the matter.

Together with Rav Refael on Purim, in the courtyard of his house

Two years later, after I became a *chasan*, I was walking Rav Refael home from shul one *motza'ei Shabbos*. Generally we'd part at his doorstep and go our separate ways, but that week he stepped out of character.

"Wait here," he instructed me.

I waited in the entranceway of his home while he entered the apartment and began searching through a drawer for something. Eventually he found what he was looking for, and he returned to me holding a $100 bill in his hand.

"Here," he said, handing me the money that my mother had given him two years previously. "You're a *chasan* now and you need this."

He'd held on to the money for years, with the intention of presenting it to me when the right time came. His thoughtfulness was simply outstanding.

◆ ◆ ◆

Rav Refael had certain hours every day when he'd see people at Beis Aryeh. He had an interesting practice that I saw him do on many occasions. Every time a person left him, he'd hand him a shekel to put in the *pushka* so that the *berachah* he'd given the person would have something to "rest" on, and he would also give his petitioners a candy. It was a little bit of a funny thing, seeing a *rav* handing out candies to adults, but that was his *minhag*. Once, I decided to ask him why he did this.

"Binyomin," he said, "I don't know what my *berachos* are really worth, but the main thing in my eyes is that a person who enters my room with a sad face should leave with a smile, and receiving a candy puts a smile on a person's face.

"Remember this," he concluded. "Anything you can do to put a smile on another person's face is worthwhile.

"Do you remember the story of Nachum Ish Gam Zu," he continued, "when a poor man asked him for food while he was unloading his donkey? Nachum told him to wait until he finished unloading the donkey, but by the time he was ready to help the man, he'd already passed away from starvation. My father, *zt"l*, studied this Gemara and came to the conclusion that a person must always have something on hand to give to poor people who ask you for help.

"Recently I was on a bus," he went on, "and there was a child who was upset about something. He was screaming and annoying the entire bus with his unceasing tantrum. Everyone was becoming testy, and the mother, sensing the tension throughout the bus, yelled at the kid to be quiet and, when that didn't work, gave him a *patch,* which made the situation even worse. So I went over to the family," Rav Refael said, "and I handed the child a candy. His face lit up with a smile, the mother's face lit up with a smile, and the entire bus calmed down. Simply because of the power of one piece of candy!"

◆ ◆ ◆

Once, as we walked through the twisting Yerushalayim alleyways, a man approached Rav Refael, and they began shmoozing as if they were good friends. When they finally parted with warmest wishes on both sides, I asked Rav Refael how the man was related to him, because by the way they were conversing I was sure that they were *mishpachah* (as is half of Yerushalayim).

"Truthfully," he confessed to me, "I don't know who he is."

"But you spoke with him as if you were his brother!"

"I have a *kabbalah* from my father," he explained, "that when a person comes over to you and acts as if he feels he knows you, you reciprocate and give him the feeling that you are the best of friends."

◆ ◆ ◆

The only time I ever heard Rav Refael complain about other people's behavior — and I have heard this from other *gedolim* as well — was when he told me, "So many people come to see me. They ask me for *berachos* of all sorts, and they tell me all their problems. I hear about *tzaros* that *pashut* tear me apart. They don't realize that I literally take their hardships and difficulties to heart. They don't grasp that I accept their pain upon myself, that I feel for them and remember them. And they never return to tell me that things have improved in their lives.

"It's like the Gerrer Rebbe used to say, '*Chachamim heim l'hara u'leheitiv lo yada'u* — people come to see their leaders when things are bad, but fail to return when things get better.'

"Many times when I finish seeing people," he told me, "I feel like I'm going to faint from all the troubles they just shared with me. My heart pounds from their pain, and my head becomes dizzy. All I ask in return is that they come tell me when things have turned around, but that rarely happens."

Rav Refael Levin

Part B

Rav Refael held different positions in the Torah world through the years. He was a *dayan* on a *beis din* and a *maggid shiur* in Yeshivas Etz Chaim for many years. He was a respected *talmid chacham* and a *tzaddik* on such an exalted level that other *gedolim* used to confer with him, especially when it came to the removal of *ayin hara* from people.

Rav Refael possessed an additional area of expertise that was uniquely his: his connection with the *goral haGra*.*

The *goral haGra* was implemented throughout the generations by *gedolim* of a certain caliber. Only people who conducted their lives with the highest level of sanctity were willing to undertake the *goral haGra* for their supplicants. In a playing field consisting

---

* The *goral haGra* is a rare and esoteric method for determining answers to difficult questions through pages and verses in *Tanach*.

of a precious few, Rav Refael was the undisputed leader. A person has to really know what he is doing. More than that, a person must possess a *mesorah*, a tradition, in the *goral haGra,* and Rav Refael's *mesorah* when it came to the *goral haGra* was impeccable.

One of the more famous stories about Rav Aryeh Levin took place after one of the Haganah's early battles prior to 1948. And entire group of 35 soldiers fell in that particular skirmish. The bodies of 23 of the soldiers had been identified, but the bodies of the remaining 12 bodies could not be identified. The families of these 12 men turned to Rav Tzvi Pesach Frank, Rav of Yerushalayim, for help. He directed them to Rav Aryeh Levin, with instructions that Rav Aryeh use the *goral haGra* to identify the bodies.

With two witnesses present — including his son Rav Refael — as well as the bereaved fathers of two of the dead soldiers, Rav Aryeh proceeded through every phase of the *goral,* one for each of the soldiers. Every one of those times the *goral* directed them to a specific *pasuk* that clarified the matter in a precise manner, leaving no room for ambiguity.

Rav Aryeh would choose a particular set of remains and be directed instantaneously to a *pasuk* in *Tanach* whose significance was impossible to ignore. Thus, when identifying one soldier, the *goral* came out with the *pasuk* "And Yosef said…" — and the martyred soldier Yosef Baruch was identified. "And Eliyahu took the son…" identified Eliyahu Hershkowitz. On and on, repeating the *goral* 11 times (because, obviously, the 12th body was that of the remaining soldier).

Rav Aryeh took careful notes of the entire *goral.* When the results were shown to Rav Tzvi Pesach Frank, he ruled that they should be accepted without question.

Like his father, Rav Refael also practiced the *goral haGra.* He used a *Tanach* that had been handed down from his father, who had in turn received it from Rav Chaim Berlin, who had brought it from Volozhin. He was particular to use this *Tanach*, and he was very careful to do the *goral haGra* only when he felt its use was merited. He used clear guidelines to determine when to use this special weapon and resource.

Since we were so close, I merited to watch him and eventually to actually help him carry out the *goral*. Those moments are ingrained on my memory as times when our world and that of Heaven intertwined in a rare exhibit of coexistence.

◆ ◆ ◆

One day someone approached me in the Mir with a tragic story. A man had been out shopping in one of the European capitals with his wife. He left the department store for what was supposed to be a minute or two, but when she went outside to look for him, he had disappeared.

Four days went by with nail-biting tension. The family had no clue where their father and husband had gone. Had he been kidnapped? Had he lost his mind? Nobody had the answers. The police were contacted. The intelligence community was called in.

"The *rabbanim* in Europe want Rav Refael Levin to do the *goral haGra*," this person told me. "Can you please arrange it?"

I promised to see what I could do.

Rav Refael agreed that this was a situation that warranted using the *goral haGra*.

"You need to spiritually prepare yourself before you do the *goral*," Rav Rafael explained to me. "Come see me in Beis Aryeh later today."

When we were finally assembled in his office, with his father's *Tanach* opened before him, Rav Refael uttered the words, "*Hashem menas chelki v'chosi attah tomich gorali* — Hashem is my allotted portion and my share; You guide my destiny" (*Tehillim* 16:5), with reverence and awe as an introduction to the *goral*. He then asked the question we were attempting to answer.

Rav Refael did the first opening of the *Tanach*, after which he asked me to turn the pages for him as he guided me expertly through the procedure after frequent consultation with a list located at the beginning of the *Tanach*.

"Open up the *Tanach*."

"Where to?"

"Anywhere."

I followed his instructions.

(Author's note: I am specifically leaving out a number of steps in the procedure. The *goral haGra* is not to be tried at home!)

"Count x number of lines."

I counted that number of lines.

"Now count x number of *pesukim*."

I counted that number of *pesukim*.

"What's the final letter in the *pasuk*?"

I told him.

"Now look for the next *pasuk* that begins with that letter."

I followed his instructions meticulously, turning pages and searching for the letter. Eventually I reached a *pasuk* that started with the letter we needed. It was a verse detailing Hashem's nine *middos harachamim* (traits of mercy), as opposed to the verse naming the 13 *middos harachamim*. I had no idea what the *pasuk* was trying to convey.

"What is the *goral* telling us?"

"I know how to carry out the procedure," he replied, "but I don't always know how to interpret the *goral*'s response. In this particular case, I recommend that we turn to the *mekubalim* of Yerushalayim for help."

"Where does one find the *mekubalim* of Yerushalayim?"

"Yeshivas Sha'ar HaShamayim. Go to the yeshivah and discuss the matter with the *mekubalim* in the *beis medrash*. Then return here and tell me what they think."

◆ ◆ ◆

Yeshivas Sha'ar HaShamayim was a mere 10-minute walk away, located on Rashi Street, close to the *shuk*. This was my first introduction to the enticing world of Jerusalem's mystical set. I walked around the *beis medrash* for a few minutes, until I recognized Rav Yitzchok Schwadron, the son of Rav Sholom Schwadron, *zt"l*. I shared with him the reason I was there: I'd just arrived straight from doing the *goral haGra* with Rav Refael Levin.

Rav Yitzchok became very excited — after all, you don't hear of such happenings every day — and he advised me to head straight over to one of Sha'ar HaShamayim's *maggidei shiur* to ask his advice on how to interpret the matter.

The *maggid shiur* heard me out. Then he asked me a few questions.

"If you had been shown the *pasuk* discussing the 13 attributes of mercy, it would have been a clear indication of pure *rachamim*," the *maggid shiur* then explained, "but the *Zohar* relates to the nine attributes of mercy as a mixture of both *din*, judgment, and *rachamim*, mercy." He paused.

"Tell me something," he said after a moment, "is this man a *ba'al teshuvah*?"

"Yes," I replied.

"What probably happened here," he said, "is that this man suddenly developed second thoughts about leading a religious life and decided on the spur of the moment to give it all up and return to his previous nonreligious existence."

He must have registered the look of chagrin on my face, because he continued speaking with a smile. "And the fact that the *pasuk* is alluding to measures of mercy is an indication that he will hopefully return within a short time."

At his suggestion, I conferred with a number of the other *mekubalim*, and the general consensus was that the *pasuk* wasn't giving us a picture of sufficient clarity and that we should go back and do the *goral* again.

I returned to Rav Refael, who was very perturbed about repeating the *goral*.

"What do you mean? You can't do that..."

"Please," I begged him, "the family is suffering terribly. You sent me to Yeshivas Sha'ar HaShamayim, and they're the ones who think you should repeat the *goral*. Please help them out!"

Rav Refael didn't want to repeat the *goral*, but his heart was too soft to deny the family's pain, and he heeded the *mekubalim*'s request. This time the *goral* calibrated a completely different result. Our end result fell out in the *parashah* of that week, the number of the final *perek* was the actual day of the week when the incident occurred, and the *pasuk* itself read, "A man will return to his homestead and to his family," a crystal-clear reference to the present situation, along with what seemed like the promise of a happy ending.

I then relayed the message that the family should expect an imminent return, and, indeed, the man returned to his family a few days later. Upon hearing the good news, I returned to Yeshivas Sha'ar HaShamayim to inform the *mekubalim*, who appreciated my taking the time to update them and who wanted to know what had happened.

I explained to them that the first *maggid shiur* had been correct in his assessment. The man had been dragged down temporarily by the *yetzer hara*, which convinced him to throw everything away and go enjoy whatever enticements the world has to offer. The man had allowed himself to be convinced, but after a few days of living his former lifestyle, he had come to his senses and realized that this was most definitely not the way he wanted to spend the remainder of his life — and he had returned.

This was the first of many times that I saw the *goral* in action, though I never ceased to be amazed by the *goral*'s uncanny ability to pinpoint the exact *pasuk* that we needed to see.

◆ ◆ ◆

Interestingly, the origins of the *goral haGra* were recorded long before the Gra's appearance in Jewish history. Even the many *sefarim* written about the Gaon do not give a clear reason why this particular *goral* is attributed to him. What is clear, however, is that the *goral* is a tool that has been known to *gedolim* for generations. It is very useful in situations where regular *da'as Torah* do not have a clear answer for the supplicant.

There have, of course, been divergent feelings toward using the *goral* among the *gedolim,* with some for and some against, but there are recorded instances of both the Brisker Rav and Rav Aharon Kotler using the *goral* on different occasions. It was especially important during wartime, when people needed to know whether to leave their homes or to remain where they were, and there are entire chapters in *sefarim* relating numerous stories of *gedolim* who used the *goral* to clarify issues that had been previously unclear.

◆ ◆ ◆

During my years learning in the Mir, a *bachur* disappeared. It happened during the summer *bein hazemanim*. A *bachur* had gone on his own to the Judean Desert to hike and enjoy the beauty and solitude of nature. Shortly after he arrived there, he vanished. The police were contacted and a search began. After a few days had passed and the police were no closer to arriving at an explanation, Rav Refael was approached and asked to perform the *goral haGra* on behalf of the family. Not surprisingly, he agreed.

When the family contacted him for the result, Rav Refael refused to tell them what *pasuk* the *goral* had led him to, merely instructing them to daven. Afterward, when the police discovered the boy's body, Rav Refael told me that from what he'd seen in the *goral*, he had known that the boy was no longer alive.

When I asked him why he hadn't shared this information with the family, he explained that he followed his father's methodology when it came to these types of situations. Even though he'd received a clear answer by using the *goral*, the *mesorah* he adhered to in cases like these was to hope and pray that things might change, as *Chazal* tell us, "*Afilu cherev chadah...* — We are not supposed to give up hope even when a sharp sword lies on a person's neck." (*Berachos* 10a).

◆ ◆ ◆

Rav Refael told me the story of a *bachur* who came to see him. He was in the midst of a *shidduch* at the time, and the relationship was progressing and becoming stronger. There was one problem. He was concerned by the fact that he didn't feel sufficiently attracted to her, and he wanted to know whether he should continue to pursue the relationship. The *bachur* asked Rav Refael to perform the *goral haGra* for direction.

"On one condition," said Rav Refael to the boy. "You must promise to abide by the *goral's* response. This is not a joke. If you commission the *goral* to do a job for you, you have to agree to accept the answer and follow it."

The boy agreed. Rav Refael then performed the *goral*, which came out to the verse "*Ayin tachas ayin shein tachas shein* — An eye for an eye, a tooth for a tooth."

Rav Refael explained that the verse "an eye for an eye" alluded to the fact that the boy wasn't anything out of the ordinary with regard to looks, and the couple fit one another perfectly.

"The *goral* is telling you that things are very equal here," he told the boy.

The boy accepted the answer and the *shidduch* was finalized.

◆ ◆ ◆

A woman called from America. A *shidduch* had been suggested for her daughter with a boy in Eretz Yisrael. If her daughter traveled to Eretz Yisrael, she would miss work, and airline tickets at the time were about $1700. Should her daughter drop everything, spend the money, and invest so much time and energy into this *shidduch*?

I suggested that it might be a good idea to do the *goral HaGra* in this situation. Rav Refael Levin had passed away, but his brother, Rav Simcha Levin, was in his upper 80's. He was carrying on the family tradition of using the *goral* to determine answers to thorny personal questions. Unsurprisingly, she requested that I go ahead with the *goral* if possible.

I had a close relationship with Rav Simcha, so I went in to see him with my request, and he agreed to carry out the *goral* for this girl. With me looking on, and lending a hand whenever help was needed, Rav Simcha performed the ancient mystery solver, and we watched as the *goral* led us to a *pasuk* that left no margin for error: "*V'kamta v'alisa el hamakom asher yivchar Hashem* — And you will get up and go to the place chosen by Hashem."

There wasn't any question after that. The girl flew to Eretz Yisrael, the two met, and they were engaged a short while later. For me personally, it had been a truly amazing experience.

Together with Rav Simcha Levin

◆ ◆ ◆

There are many technical challenges in performing a *goral haGra*, and due to the precise nature of the *goral* and the need to pinpoint details, it can be difficult for an older person with failing vision or trembling hands to carry out. One cannot miss a step along the way. There are many pages to be counted and one cannot miss a page. Its need for utter accuracy is daunting and challenging even for someone in perfect physical shape.

That is why Rav Simcha has come to rely on my assistance in performing the *goral* with ever-increasing frequency. Helping him in his *avodas hakodesh* is a privilege I cherish and treasure.

◆ ◆ ◆

I knew a *bachur* who had been learning seriously in Eretz Yisrael for an extended period. He had been going out on *shidduchim* for years, with no results. Beginning to lose hope at his disappointing lack of progress, the *bachur* began toying with the idea of returning to his native South Africa to continue dating there. He wanted desperately to get married, yet he didn't want to leave Eretz Yisrael.

Rav Simcha agreed to do the *goral* for him. The verse the *goral* came out to included the words *"v'ha'aretz asher Hashem Elokecha nosein lecha nachalah l'rishtah* — and the land that Hashem, your G-d, gives you as a portion of inheritance."

The *pasuk*, of course, is referring to Eretz Yisrael. Rav Simcha told him that without question the *goral* was instructing him to remain right where he was.

◆ ◆ ◆

Usually people listen to whatever the *goral haGra* spells out for them. Once in a while, however, there are individuals who break the code of honor that's demanded from someone who willingly submits himself to be adjudicated by the *goral*. This is such an incident.

Two individuals decided to form a partnership in the field of real estate. Instead of looking at properties in the more congested areas of Yerushalayim and Tel Aviv, or other more centrally located real-estate opportunities, the two of them traveled up north, to the upper and lower regions of the Galilee. While in the city of Teveriah, one of the team found a property he considered a very worthy investment opportunity, and he made the decision to close the deal. The second partner also found the property promising, but for whatever reason they weren't able to come to a final decision.

In the end, they had the *goral haGra* performed (it wasn't done by Rav Refael or Rav Simcha). The verse they were led to spoke of portions of inheritance in *Klal Yisrael* with words along the lines of "And this portion went to So-and-so," making it pretty obvious that the property they were considering was ideal for them.

Despite having instructions explicitly spelled out to them by the *goral*, they chose to ignore its advice and not to purchase the property.

It so happened that the money the partners were going to use for their investments had been left by them for safekeeping in an established free-loan *gemach* in Yerushalayim. A short time after they had sought out advice from the *goral* — advice they hadn't followed — the *gemach* found itself embroiled in a set of highly unusual circumstances that left it unable to return the funds to the depositors.

When I heard the tragic tale, all I could think of was the fact that if they had listened to the *goral* and followed its advice, they would have pulled out in time. The story confirmed what I had already known. Nobody is forced to perform the *goral haGra*. But if someone chooses to do so, he must bear in mind how serious a commitment it is and that he is not free to ignore its advice or recommendations.

There were more stories over the years, with the *goral haGra* consistently addressing every issue head-on and precisely to the point. Besides serving as a tremendous manifestation of the hand of Hashem in our world, it was also a catalyst to my becoming close to both Rav Refael Levin and his brother Rav Simcha: two relationships that have enriched my life immeasurably.

Encounters with

Rav
Yitzchok Nosson
Kupershtok

זצ"ל

Rav Yitzchok Nosson Kupershtok at our *vort*

He walked the streets of Yerushalayim in the middle of the night, long white beard tucked neatly into his overcoat, angelic face shining with an otherworldly glow. He carried the tools he needed to remove the city's mezuzahs from their concrete encasements so that he could check them. All of Yerushalayim slept as the tzaddik of Batei Broide carried out his holy task in solitude and with no desire for praise or remuneration of any kind.

His only goal — to fulfill ratzon Hashem.

In this, he succeeded admirably.

He belonged to Yerushalayim and Yerushalayim to him. In essence, they were really one.

Rav Yitzchok Nosson Kupershtok

Part A

D r. and Mrs. Stein* were neighbors of ours in Brooklyn when I was growing up. They were childless, and a few years into their marriage, they became short-term foster parents of a child from the Ohel organization. The boy's name was Yanky Block,* and he was a sweet child who suffered from spina bifida.

His parents resided in a town that was not equipped to deal with the magnitude of Yanky's medical issues — which were severe and daunting even if you lived near the best hospital in the country, but which would be compounded by many degrees in a place that had never encountered these particular symptoms before. In the end, after much agonizing and the seeking of counsel from their family rav, the Block family was advised to give Yanky up for adoption.

I would never have even known about Yanky at all, or that he had lived for a while as a ward of the Stein family when he was very young, were it not for the fact that his adoptive family, who lived in Cleveland and who would bring Yanky to see the Steins every so often, came to visit Dr. and Mrs. Stein one year on Shavuos. Yanky needed a study partner with whom to learn that Shavuos night, and Dr. Stein asked me to volunteer. I did and we studied all that night at Yeshivas Torah Vodaath.

Yanky was a sweet kid, and I ended up learning with him once or twice more over the visit. We developed a limited relationship — both of us were about 12 years old with approaching bar mitzvahs and we had a few other things in common — but I never dreamed that it would progress any farther. Shavuos came to an end, and Yanky disappeared from my life and traveled back to Cleveland with his adoptive parents. I said good-bye and thought nothing more of the matter.

◆ ◆ ◆

Years passed. I was learning in Telshe Yeshivah in Cleveland when I decided that the time had arrived for me to get a driver's license. I'd had just a few driving lessons and was going for the test without very much experience. I had a permit and I studied, but I still wasn't really confident in my familiarity with the state of Ohio's driving laws.

Since I was concerned that my lack of driving experience would hinder my efforts, I decided to take a *kabbalah* on myself that related to driving, with the hope that this merit would stand me in good stead when it came to the test.

My *kabbalah* was a simple one. I basically promised Hashem that if I received my license, I would do my best to perform *chesed* with my driving — maybe visit a nearby nursing home on Friday afternoon or something similar — to ensure that the license possessed a spiritual component and purpose.

One of the children who lived with his family on the Telshe Yeshivah campus heard me discussing my upcoming driving test and the *kabbalah* I had undertaken with a friend. He in turn repeated what he'd heard to his father, Rav Anshel Hellman, the *mashgiach* of the Telshe *yeshivah ketanah*.

A few days later, I was approached by Rav Anshel himself. We had never spoken before, but he didn't let the fact that we didn't know each other get in the way.

"Are you Binyomin?" he asked, introducing himself to me.

"Yes, Rav Hellman," I replied, curious as to what the *mashgiach* of the high school could possibly want from me.

"I heard that you made a *kabbalah* regarding your upcoming driving test. Is that true?"

"Yes."

"Well, did you pass your test? Did you get the license?"

"*Baruch Hashem*, I did."

"So I assume that you are looking for meritorious ways of fulfilling your *kabbalah*. Am I right?"

He was right.

"I have a possible *chesed* project for you."

I waited eagerly to hear more.

"There's a boy living not far from the yeshivah who needs your help. He's about 16 or 17 years old and suffers from spina bifida. He's paralyzed from the waist down and is in a wheelchair. He can move his arms, his brain works perfectly, but his legs don't move."

When I heard the name of his illness, it rang a chord in my mind. Spina bifida. Where had I heard that before?

"This boy had been adopted," Rav Hellman went on, "but it didn't work out, and the boy has moved out of their home and into a supervised apartment. Now he barely leaves the place and just spends his days sunk in his depression, just staring at the four walls."

"I assume that this means he's not doing well?"

"That would be a huge understatement. He's living by himself and almost never has any visitors. He's extremely lonely. It's no life for a young boy!"

"How do you know about this boy?" I asked him.

"Rebbetzin Landau, who's involved with the Bikur Cholim here in Cleveland, told me all about this boy and how he needs some serious help, before it's too late."

I suddenly realized where I knew the words "spina bifida" from. The years fell away, and I recalled that Shavuos night and the 12-year-old boy in the wheelchair. I did vaguely recall someone mentioning Cleveland, but still, what were the chances of a reunion?

"Tell me, Rav Hellman," I said, "is this boy's name Yanky Block by any chance?"

He nodded, surprised that I knew who he was talking about. When I explained, we saw the whole interchange as completely *min haShamayim*. From the fact that his son had overheard my conversation to the fact that he had repeated my *kabbalah* to his father, who had actually taken the time to find me despite the fact that we didn't know each other, and who now wanted me to renew a relationship with someone I had known back in my childhood; it was all very much a script that had been written in Heaven.

"Rav Hellman," I told the *mashgiach*, "it will be my pleasure to get involved and renew my *kesher* with Yanky."

◆ ◆ ◆

I drove over to see him. A heartbreaking scene met my eyes. Here was a boy who was my age, living in an apartment all by himself, with the barest of human contact. I can't even describe what a sad existence it was. I introduced myself, and Yanky was overjoyed that I had come. To my surprise, he remembered me very well from the two times we had learned together, and he welcomed me into his life with open arms.

Thus began a brand-new, challenging, yet rewarding chapter in my life. Yanky didn't even own a stereo, which would have at least granted him access to the pleasure of music. I described the situation to the boys back in Telshe. Within a short time they had chipped in to purchase a top-of-the-line stereo for him, and I brought him music tapes to listen to (people still listened to audio cassettes back then).

In addition to visiting him at home, I would drive over to his apartment and bring him back with me to the yeshivah for

Shabbos. Sometimes he'd come to the yeshivah for a *shiur* or two, other times for a longer visit, but no matter the occasion, the visits served as a catalyst to cheer him up and bring joy and hope into what was essentially a life devoid of all luster and color.

Eventually, Yanky progressed to a point where he was sufficiently stable to return to the home of his adoptive parents. Though he had been in a terrible state of mind when we were first reunited, the learning he'd started doing and his ongoing exposure to the yeshivah and to numerous *bachurim* had done wonders for him, and his entire mind-set had undergone a radical shift.

From time to time I used to imagine helping Yanky reunite with his biological parents. Here was a young man who did not at all remember his parents. He knew that they were chassidim — though he was not at all like them, having been raised by people who were Modern Orthodox — and he harbored an anger toward them that bubbled quietly on a constant simmer. He felt abandoned by those who were meant to care for him and had instead given him up because they'd found it too difficult to deal with his physical handicaps. It was hard to imagine that Yanky would ever agree to meet with the people who had "cast him away."

◆ ◆ ◆

Reb Uri Lehrer was a *tzaddik* of a Yid who lived on the yeshivah campus. Although not officially on the administration of Telshe, he was part and parcel of the yeshivah and highly respected by one and all. One day I received a message that Reb Uri wanted to see me. When we were face-to-face, Reb Uri gave me a smile and said, "I heard that you have a lot to do with Yanky Block. Is that true?"

I nodded. "Yes, I met him years ago, and we've recently rekindled our relationship."

His eyes were excited now.

"You may know Yanky for many years," he said, "but I've just heard some news about Yanky Block that will come as a wonderful surprise to you."

I was understandably curious.

"Your friend Yanky is a descendant of Rav Akiva Eiger and the Chasam Sofer. I know his parents, and I can tell you that these are wonderful people. *Ba'alei chesed*. People with *mesirus nefesh* for *Yiddishkeit*. People who have raised a beautiful family. But deep inside their hearts there is a hole, a void, an empty spot that's filled with love for a child they have never really met, yet whom they love more than life itself. Binyomin, we have no choice. We have to reunite Yanky and his parents!"

I listened to Reb Uri, but I wasn't exactly sure how to handle his passionate dream. Any time I had suggested a reconciliation between Yanky and his parents, I had been treated to a frosty silence followed by angry rants of how he never wanted to see or meet the people who had abandoned him to his fate. Simply speaking, I wasn't sure if there was any hope or way of dealing with the intense resentment and anger that he felt toward his parents.

But Reb Uri, no doubt correctly interpreting the look of doubt on my face, said, "The first thing we have to do is to get you on the phone with Yanky's mother and father."

Reb Uri made the call, and when Yanky's father answered the phone and found himself discussing the well-being of his long-lost son, he dropped the phone from overwhelming emotion. Yanky's parents hadn't known what was going on with their son all these years, and here was a chance to finally receive a front-row seat into what had until now been a closed performance.

Through the agencies, they had arranged for him to receive his tefillin at his bar mitzvah four years before, but that had been their sole involvement.

As we spoke, I could sense the waves of happiness exuding through the phone wires. They hadn't known if their son was mentally healthy or whether there was any real happiness in his life, nor if he was even religious — and here they were, discovering that he was being looked after and that he was not only *frum*, but also had friends in Telshe Yeshivah who took an interest in him and cared for him and blessed him with the gift of friendship when he needed it most. We spoke for a few minutes, and they asked if I would consider driving out to meet them in their home.

I agreed. How could I turn them down?

I can only imagine how strange my coming to visit this family must have seemed to the younger children, who had never even heard about an older brother and had no inkling of the gaping void in the parents' souls. Even the older children only vaguely recalled their mother going to the hospital to have a baby and returning home empty-handed. News of an unknown brother was something they could barely manage to wrap their minds around.

◆ ◆ ◆

When Pesach arrived that year, I returned to Brooklyn for *Yom Tov*, but I arranged for Yanky to spend Seder night with a local Cleveland family.

The father of this particular family was famous for his collection of Haggadahs. Some people collect pens, others stamps. This individual collected Haggadahs. He purchased every Haggadah that came on the market. It was his thing.

After Pesach, they called me to talk about the Seder.

"Binyomin," they said, "you'll never guess what happened at the Seder!"

"Tell me!"

"You know how we own literally hundreds of Haggadahs, right?"

"Yes."

"Well, at the beginning of the Seder everyone chooses which Haggadah he wants to use that year. There was Yanky and there were hundreds of Haggadahs to choose from. Which Haggadah do you think he picked?"

"How should I know?"

"Binyomin, Yanky chose the Haggadah of the Chasam Sofer. Out of hundreds of Haggadahs."

I had to agree: it was a fascinating bit of *hashgachah*, considering the fact that Yanky was still in the dark regarding his lineage and the reality that he was a direct descendant of the Chasam Sofer.

◆ ◆ ◆

Reunions with long-estranged family don't just happen from one second to the next. They take time and careful planning, and so it was here. It was a while before my actual visit to Yanky's parents' home took place, because Reb Uri and I agreed that it would have to wait until *bein hazemanim,* which would commence in a few weeks' time.

I ended up meeting Yanky's family during Pesach vacation, and I found myself impressed by what I saw. If I had entered their home with preconceived notions about parents who abandoned their hapless baby to the rigors of the orphanage, my opinion of Yanky's parents changed within moments of our meeting. These were special people, that was obvious. It was also obvious that they would have taken him home with them if there had been any way in the world for them to do so.

It was after meeting his family that I came to the realization that I had to make restoring Yanky to his family a priority.

And that's what I did.

◆ ◆ ◆

Across the street from the Telshe campus, there is a beautiful park complete with majestic trees, well-tended flower beds, and a vast lake that beckons to people and invites shared confidences. I pushed Yanky's wheelchair over the narrow footpath, past people relaxing with friends and others tossing a Frisbee to and fro. Finally, we came to a halt. I sat down on a bench and turned his wheelchair in my direction so we could have a real conversation. We conversed for a few minutes, and then I broached the subject ever so gently.

"Yanky," I said, "do you ever think about meeting your real parents? Do you ever imagine a reunion?"

His answer came shooting back at me swiftly and brutally.

"No. I never want to see them. They abandoned me. I have no interest in ever meeting them!"

He didn't even want to talk about it. But I didn't give up and kept on raising the idea. It took a long while, but eventually he began warming to the concept of getting to know his family.

After some time I was introduced to one of his older brothers, who became the first person in the family to meet with Yanky. The timing was actually perfect, because I was poised to leave Telshe at that point and move on to yeshivah in Eretz Yisrael. Yanky had met numerous Telshe *talmidim*, and they had become his friends and were more than happy to bring him to *shiurim* and to the *beis medrash*, so I was able to bid him farewell with a light heart and the knowledge that a family reconciliation was in the works.

By the time I left the yeshivah, Yanky was already in touch with several members of his family, and that in turn led to the greatest moment of all: his reunion with his parents. They had been eagerly awaiting this moment, but had handled it with care and allowed things to develop naturally.

In the end, Yanky was reinstated into his large, warm, and loving family. It wasn't long before Yanky bid Cleveland farewell for good and moved to an assisted-living facility not far from his parents' home. He also became a chassid like his parents and grew *peyos* and a beard.

◆ ◆ ◆

I had always known that Yanky was afraid that he'd never be given the opportunity to marry. His state of health was extremely precarious, and it seemed unlikely that he'd ever be given the chance. But his connection and relationship to the yeshivah and the fact that he'd been reunited with his birth family gave Yanky a new zest for life and changed him into a positive person with a mature outlook, one who had become capable of marriage and all it entailed.

When he finally married, it was a gigantic wedding, attended by thousands of people, including many famous singers and many of the friends he had acquired along his route from that lonely and depressing apartment in Cleveland to the outgoing, radiant mentsch he'd become. His wife is also partially paralyzed, and they live together in the assisted-living facility. She has children from a previous marriage, and Yanky treats them like his own children.

I visit Yanky and his wife from time to time, and when I greet the smiling man with the curly *peyos* and cheerful demeanor, I can't help but recall the terribly lonesome and lost teenager I had known. His siblings developed a warm relationship with their brother and visit him so often it's almost impossible to find the couple alone. They are popular, busy, and living a productive life.

Yanky's story is one of those instances where I sometimes feel like pinching myself to see if it's true or just in my imagination.

Throughout the months that I looked after Yanky and devoted myself to his happiness, Reb Uri would tell me the same line every time we met. He knew how much time I was spending with Yanky, and he wanted me to understand the merit of my actions.

"Binyomin," he'd say to me every time our paths crossed, "you should know that Rav Akiva Eiger and the Chasam Sofer are going to repay you for your actions and *mesirus nefesh* for their great-grandson's well-being."

Reb Uri must have repeated this line to me a hundred times. I was fortunate enough to see how his "promise" came to fruition.

◆ ◆ ◆

There was a fine Jew by the name of Dr. Winters* who used to daven at Telshe Yeshivah every Shabbos. Dr. and Mrs. Winters were fascinating people, and they would invite *bachurim* from Telshe to their home for the Shabbos meals. Though I had known the doctor for two years, I had never gone to his home for a *seudah*.

Yanky was my guest at the yeshivah for my final Shabbos in Telshe. For whatever reason, Dr. Winters decided to invite both Yanky and myself to their home for a meal that Shabbos. After davening Shabbos morning, I pushed Yanky through the campus in his wheelchair to the Winters's home.

Dr. and Mrs. Winters welcomed us, and after sitting down at the dining-room table, I glanced at their wall and found myself staring at an intriguing collection of *gedolim* pictures. I recognized the majority of them. I saw Rav Shach leaning over his Gemara and Rav Shlomo Zalman smiling at the camera. But there was one picture of a man — a *tzaddik* with a long white beard (you could see he was a *tzaddik*; his *hadras panim* was awesome) — whom I didn't recognize. I had never seen this man before, and my curiosity was aroused.

"Dr. Winters," I asked my host, "who is the *tzaddik* in this picture?"

"Binyomin," he replied, "that's a story."

◆ ◆ ◆

"Of course, you know Rabbi Brog," Dr. Winters began his tale. "He's the son-in-law of Rav Baruch Sorotzkin (the late *Rosh Yeshivah* of Telshe) and the grandson of Rav Avigdor Miller."

I did know of Rav Brog. At the time he was an *avreich* learning in a *beis medrash* in Cleveland.

"Rabbi Brog was the man who told me about the hidden *tzaddik* whose picture is hanging on my dining-room wall."

My interest took a quantum leap forward. "What do you mean 'hidden *tzaddik*'?"

"Exactly what I said. He's a man living in Yerushalayim who spends his days and nights completely immersed in Torah and *yiras Shamayim*. He has managed to remain almost completely anonymous in the outside world, although he is well known to the circle of *tzaddikim* in Yerushalayim. In fact, he is very much one of them."

"What's his name?"

"Rav Yitzchok Nosson Kupershtok."

"I've never heard of him."

"There's no reason you should have."

"Where's he from?"

"He's lived his entire life in Yerushalayim: the classic Yerushalmi Yid."

"Where did he learn?"

"Rabbi Brog mentioned that he was a *talmid* of the Tchebiner Rav. He also said that Rav Kupershtok is an exceptional *talmid chacham* and extremely poor. I believe he used the term *'ani marud,'* a penniless man — penniless, even by the standards of Yerushalayim of 40 years ago, when it was not uncommon for 10 apartments to share one outdoor bathroom."

"Did he ever work? Was he a *rosh yeshivah* somewhere?"

"Rabbi Brog said that he never held an official position anywhere, but simply sits and learns Torah day and night with phenomenal diligence. The Kupershtoks have raised a beautiful family with sons and sons-in-law who hold prominent positions in the Torah world, and in all that time, Rav Kupershtok has never ceased learning.

"Rabbi Brog told me that his father, who is a rav in Brooklyn, had a congregant who apparently was related to Rav Kupershtok. This man wouldn't stop pestering the rav to tell his son, who was then learning in Yerushalayim, to drop in on his relative, who lived near the yeshivah. He finally instructed his son to go, and so the *yeshivah bachur* went off on a mission to find the elusive Rav Kupershtok.

"He began by asking some of the Yerushalmi Jews he encountered in the *shtiebel* and the neighborhood. Their reaction was always the same.

"'Why do you need Rav Kupershtok?'

"He understood that this man was either very strange or very special, because people were responding in a way that he had not anticipated. Eventually he received directions to the Kupershtok home in Batei Broide, one of the older Jerusalem neighborhoods.

"Batei Broide was constructed in the fashion of the Yerushalmi neighborhoods of yesteryear, with rows of houses built around a courtyard and stairs leading up to the second level. The *bachur* ascended the rickety staircase, walked through the outside hallway, and knocked on the simple wooden door. When he was admitted to the Kupershtok home — a tiny, spotlessly clean apartment with the barest of necessities — he found himself face-to-face with a distinguished-looking Yid with a long white beard, sitting at his dining-room table, poring over a pile of *sefarim*.

"Rav Kupershtok is taciturn by nature, and it is almost impossible to discuss anything other than learning with him. Torah is his lifelong ambition and only major interest. The *bachur* found himself shmoozing with the Rebbetzin, who was far more talkative than her husband. One thing led to another, and soon she confided that they were about to marry off a child and had absolutely no way of paying for all the expenses that were about to be thrust upon them.

" 'Does the Rav ever travel to America?' the *bachur* asked.

" 'My husband never even considered such a thing,' she said. 'He would never go collecting for money. He learns. That's what he knows how to do. But if we don't come up with the money for our share in the apartment, the *shidduch* may very well fall through.'

"Rabbi Brog felt for her.

" 'I have a brother in the Mir Yeshivah in Brooklyn,' he told the Rebbetzin. 'Let me give him a call and see what we can do for you.'

"The young man wasted no time. He contacted his father and brother and told them about the hidden *tzaddik* whom he'd just discovered. He explained that the family was about to marry off a child and had no way in the world of meeting their financial obligations. Would the Brog family be able to help raise some capital?

"One of the Brog brothers went around the Mir in Brooklyn, and every person gave a dollar — that was the accepted donation back then — until he collected a total of about $300. Three hundred dollars was all very well and good, but it was not nearly enough money to allow the Kupershtoks to move ahead with the *shidduch*.

"A few days later, a couple entered the Mir Yeshivah and asked someone to please find the boy who had been collecting for the poor family from Yerushalayim. The *bachur* went off in search of his friend and brought him over to the couple.

" 'We heard that you are collecting funds for a special *tzaddik* from Yerushalayim.'

" 'That's right," he said. 'They're marrying off a child.'

" 'That's what we heard. We are very interested in helping out. We were never blessed with children of our own, and we want to fund this wedding. Can you find out how much money is needed?'

"It wasn't long before he returned to them with a number. Without further ado, the husband removed a checkbook from his pocket and wrote out a check for the full amount. It was a very large check, especially by Yerushalayim standards. The check made its way overseas to Yerushalayim, where it was handed to Rabbi Brog's son, who made his way to Batei Broide, check in hand. He was sure that its arrival would cause the normally serious *talmid chacham* to break into song and dance. After all, here he was receiving all the money he needed, without having to leave his home, shul, or *sefarim*. It was a miracle!

"He laid the check down before the *tzaddik*, expecting to see a smile spread across his face. Rav Kupershtok's reaction was completely unexpected.

"'Are the people who gave you this check *shomer Shabbos*?'

"The implications were clear. If the money came from a kosher source, he'd accept it, but if the people who had given it were not religious and the money had been earned on Shabbos, then Rav Kupershtok wanted no part of it. Never mind the fact that the check had flown directly to his dining-room table from America. Never mind the fact that he had no other way of paying for the wedding. If the money was tainted with *chillul Shabbos*, he wouldn't give it another glance.

"Rabbi Brog's son returned to yeshivah and after making a few phone calls was able to ascertain that the donors were in fact religious people and the money was kosher. And he was left with the feeling that he had just come in contact with one of the most amazing people he had ever met."

After hearing this story from Dr. Winters on my final Shabbos in Telshe, I made what would be a life-changing decision to track down Rav Kupershtok and develop a relationship with him upon my arrival in Eretz Yisrael.

◆ ◆ ◆

It was still summertime when I arrived in Eretz Yisrael. After taking a *farher* from Rav Nosson Tzvi Finkel, the *Rosh Yeshivah* of the Mir, and settling into my apartment, I headed out to the streets of Yerushalayim. I felt a sense of destiny, a feeling that I was on a quest to uncover greatness, and that the address lay within the hands of a certain holy Jew residing in the ancient apartment complex of Batei Broide.

I made my way through the bustling streets of Yerushalayim, following the directions I'd been given, until I passed through the entranceway of Batei Broide and into another world.

Established in 1902 with a donation from one Rabbi Yaakov Yosef Broide of Warsaw, Batei Broide was named in his honor and intended as a housing complex for the wise men of Jerusalem's Ashkenazi community, who studied Torah all day. Though it was located in the city's center and by rights should have been upgraded years ago, the Batei Broide courtyard still looked virtually the same as it did 100 years ago. Little girls with braids and tights played games with one another, while little boys with long *peyos* and suspenders holding up their pants congregated outside the nearby shul. It was a scene out of Yerushalayim of a century ago.

I climbed the staircase to the second-story level and made my way past door after door, scrutinizing every one to see if they read "Kupershtok" on the nameplate. When I reached the Kupershtok apartment, I found the Rebbetzin sitting outside on the tiny porch saying *Tehillim*.

"Excuse me," I said, "I'm looking for Rav Yitzchok Nosson Kupershtok. Is he here now?"

"I'm sorry," she replied. "He's out learning now."

To say I was disappointed would be an understatement.

"When will he be home?"

"I don't know. He's out learning now."

This scene replayed itself time and again over the next few weeks, as I tried my best to track down the elusive *tzaddik* whom I longed to meet. The Rebbetzin soon came to recognize the American boy who put in an appearance at least once or twice a week, and I could see that she felt really bad at having to inform me yet again that her husband wasn't home. She couldn't even tell me where to go.

"I know he's out learning, but I don't know which *beis medrash*, and I don't know when he's going to return home. I'm really sorry."

And I'd have to leave empty-handed yet again. I could see that she felt terrible, but there was nothing she could do for me. It was just not happening.

◆ ◆ ◆

Rav Yitzchok Nosson in his *succah*; notice the decorations, all handmade by Rav Yitzchok Nosson himself

After giving the matter of Rav Yitzchok Nosson Kupershtok much thought, I came up with a plan. With the *Yom Tov* of Succos rapidly approaching, I knew that this was the ideal time to catch Rav Kupershtok. Succos time in Yerushalayim is a magnificent time of year, and it is celebrated by the average Yerushalmi Yid with every fiber of his being. It is also a time when most Yerushalmi Yidden are home, learning and living in their *succahs*. I knew that my chances of meeting him had increased 100 percent.

On the first day of *Chol Hamo'ed Succos*, I left Beis Yisrael and headed over to Batei Broide, filled with tense anticipation.

I found Rav Kupershtok learning in his *succah*, just as I'd anticipated. He glanced up at me, this American *bachur* who kept coming back, and I felt something stirring inside me, for he had the most incredible countenance. It was the *hadras panim* I'd seen in his picture, but magnified a thousandfold. His face literally shone with holiness and purity. It was like seeing an angel in the flesh.

He invited me to sit at the table. I took a seat, filled with a happiness that can't even be described at finally meeting this holy Yid. It was almost a feeling of nostalgia, as if I knew that I would be replaying our first meeting over and over again in the days to come.

"This is the American *bachur* who keeps coming to see you," his wife said by way of introduction.

He looked at me, meeting my eyes with his powerful gaze, and he opened his mouth to speak. I expected him to question me, to ask me why I had chosen him, to ask me why I kept on coming back, but as I said, Rav Yitzchok Nosson was never one for idle conversation. Instead, the first words that came out of his mouth were "*Es iz du a teshuvah in Chasam Sofer. . .* There's a halachic responsum in the Chasam Sofer. . ." And right after that, he continued our discussion by supporting his position with the words of Rav Akiva Eiger.

It struck me with tremendous force: Reb Uri had promised me so many times that the Chasam Sofer and Rav Akiva Eiger would pay me back for my dedication to their descendant, and here it was happening. I only knew about Rav Yitzchok Nosson because I had accompanied Yanky Block to the Winters's home for a Shabbos meal. There I had seen Rav Yitzchok Nosson's picture and learned of the holy Jew from Jerusalem, and, in fact, the first words I heard him speak were regards: warm regards from the Chasam Sofer and Rav Akiva Eiger! I saw tremendous *hashgachah* in the whole story.

◆ ◆ ◆

Rav Yitzchok Nosson was completely Torah. There wasn't much you could talk to him about other than Torah. But eventually, after I'd come to see him quite a few times and we'd talked in learning and gotten to know each other, the relationship began to blossom into an unlikely friendship; this despite the disparity in our ages and backgrounds, and the fact that he was very much a solitary person. In the end, our relationship flourished until it took on a life of its own.

The friendship between the young American *bachur* and the elderly Yerushalmi *tzaddik* became so strong that his children would come to see me as the person closest to their father in the world, to the point that whenever there were things they wanted or needed their father to do, they'd ask me to speak to him and convince him of the justness of their cause. Though Rav Yitzchok Nosson passed away in 2011, whenever I come to visit the Rebbetzin, she tells anyone in the vicinity, "This *yungerman* was more to us than a son."

As for me, I remember her sitting there with her *Tehillim*, once again telling the persistent American *bachur* that her husband wasn't home, and I smile.

Rav Yitzchok Nosson Kupershtok

Part B

I t is virtually impossible to accurately describe who Rav Yitzchok Nosson Kupershtok was and how he lived his life, but I'll try. It's a story that must be told, so that *Klal Yisrael* will know of the jewel that lived — seldom noticed — among them.

Rav Yitzchok Nosson lived his holy life shunning the limelight in a calculated way. Yet despite his aversion to fame and honor, the Brisker Rav had already begun sending people to him for *berachos* by the time he was in his 30's.

"Go to Rav Yitzchok Nosson," he'd tell people who came to him. "His *berachos* make an impression on Heaven."

The Steipler, I was told, did the same.

Though he craved a life of anonymous service of Hashem while adhering to the most modest of profiles, Rav Yitzchok Nosson was known to the great men of Israel, who thought highly of their younger colleague and made no secret of their respect.

Rav Yitzchok Nosson at his regular spot at Kever Rachel

For many years Rav Yitzchok Nosson traveled to Kever Rachel every Friday, where he recited the entire *sefer Tehillim*, pouring out his heart to his Maker in a voice choked by sobs. When I accompanied him there, I witnessed the tears streaming down his face as he read the beloved words, line by line. His davening was such that the Steipler commented, "*HaKadosh Baruch Hu* Himself sits and listens to Rav Yitzchok Nosson's *tefillos* by Mama Rochel."

◆　◆　◆

Rav Yitzchok Nosson came of age in a Yerushalayim where abject poverty was the norm. He studied Torah with incredible diligence notwithstanding his lack of food and money. Rav Simcha Zissel Broide, *zt"l*, the *Rosh Yeshivah* of Chevron, would tell people, "If you want to see one of the 36 hidden *tzaddikim* of our generation, go and visit Rav Yitzchok Nosson."

It wasn't so much that Rav Yitzchok Nosson was hidden from the leaders of the generation. They knew who he was. But the average Jew of his generation, both in Israel and abroad, had never even heard of him — and that was exactly the way he wanted it.

He was in his mid-70's when we first met, and I was immediately struck by his innate and unusual level of modesty. He wanted to hide his greatness, and he succeeded in doing so to a great degree. His relatives knew who he was, as did his close neighbors. But other than this relatively small number of people, he remained unknown.

His diligence was awesome, as were many other details of his life to which few were privy. After his passing, countless stories were told about him. It was at the *shivah* that someone told me that any time Rav Yitzchok Nosson learned of a mitzvah that was being neglected, he would take it upon himself to glorify that mitzvah in the most *mehudar* (beautiful) way possible.

For example, many of the older neighborhoods of Yerushalayim have walls around them. Neighborhoods such as Meah Shearim, Sha'arei Chesed, Nachlaot, Batei Broide, and Batei Ungarin are surrounded by thick walls, designed in past generations to keep marauders from pillaging the hapless inhabitants within. One enters their narrow streets through a *sha'ar*, a gate built into the wall. Who was taking care of the mezuzahs on these gates, checking them on a regular basis to make sure that they were kosher and in usable condition? The answer: Nobody.

Rav Yitzchok Nosson learned of the dereliction and took matters into his own hands. In the middle of the night, he'd remove the mezuzahs from the walls and check them. If there were any problems and a mezuzah needed to be replaced, he'd replace it using his own money with the most *mehudar* mezuzah available. No one funded his initiatives. He did this in dozens of places, for 50 years.

The executive director of one Yerushalayim *cheder* related to the Kupershtok family that Rav Yitzchok Nosson used to bring him a huge bag of freshly baked pitas every day.

"I asked him why," said the director, "to which your father replied that sometimes children forget to bring lunch from home. If they won't eat, they won't have strength to learn. This way anyone who is missing lunch will be able to eat something, and I will have a portion in their Torah study."

He was a product of Yerushalayim's finest Torah institutions, a student of Rav Isser Zalman Meltzer and the Tchebiner Rav, a man who studied day and night with supreme diligence, yet who found the time to carry out endless acts of selflessness without anyone finding out.

◆ ◆ ◆

Rav Yitzchok Nosson was always concerned about whether I had enough to eat in yeshivah. I'd visit him mainly on Shabbos, and during one visit, he mentioned that there was going to be a *hachnasas sefer Torah* in Batei Broide in a few days' time. He invited me to attend, and I accepted his invitation without hesitation. After all, a *hachnasas sefer Torah* in a neighborhood like Batei Broide meant spending time in the august presence of the cream

Rav Yitzchok Nosson writing a letter in the *sefer Torah* during the *hachnasas sefer Torah* in Batei Broide

of Yerushalayim's *tzaddikim* and wasn't an experience to miss.

My first stop was at the house where the *sofer* was writing the remaining letters in the *sefer Torah*. The room was filled with Torah scholars of note. Rav Yitzchok Nosson arranged that I receive a letter in the Torah and stood there beaming by my side.

After the writing ceremony had been concluded and they danced the new *sefer Torah* into the Batei Broide shul, everyone headed in the direction of a local hall for the *seudah*. Rav Yitzchok Nosson directed me through the streets of Nachlaot and into the hall, where he seated me, much to my discomfort, at the head table on the dais, alongside Rav Yisrael Yaakov Fisher, *zt"l*, and many other elders of Yerushalayim.

Rav Yitzchok Nosson sat down beside me and introduced me to the rest of the gathering, who all wanted to know who I was. No doubt they were wondering why their friend had seated a mere *bachur* side by side with the leaders of Yerushalayim.

The food was served, and while Rav Yitzchok Nosson didn't take anything for himself, he served me with alacrity, filling my plate with everything on the table, urging me to eat my fill. I couldn't figure out what was going on. Eventually I realized that bringing me to the *hachnasas sefer Torah* had all been part of his plan to make sure I ate a decent meal.

◆ ◆ ◆

Though Rav Yitzchok Nosson was not well known, here and there people did come to see him and ask him for *berachos*. Once, when I was at his house, he showed me a note that a girl had left asking him for a *berachah* for *shidduchim*. Rav Yitzchok Nosson told me how impressed he was by this girl based on the type of things she had written. Her *yiras Shamayim* was clearly evident in her note, and he showed me her name, wondering if I knew what seminary she attended.

I recognized her family name, and after a little investigation on my part I was able to track her down. The next time I visited, I told him where she was and her seminary's location, not comprehending why he needed this information.

Later on I found out the whole story.

She had come to his home for a *berachah*, only to be informed by the Rebbetzin that her husband was out learning. Undaunted, she'd left the note that had so impressed Rav Yitzchok Nosson with its sincerity. For Rav Yitzchok Nosson, the story was only beginning. He was sorry that she had not found him at home, and he feared that she would be upset at having missed her opportunity. So he asked me to find out what seminary she attended, because he'd decided to go down to her school and personally give her a *berachah*!

When I heard this story, I knew beyond a shadow of a doubt that this girl had just been the recipient of an extraordinary blessing. Wanting to verify my feelings, I touched base with the people who had helped me track her down and learned that she was the first girl in her class to become a *kallah*. I wasn't surprised. Such a *berachah* from a *tzaddik* like Rav Yitzchok Nosson could not possibly be ignored in Heaven. To me the outcome had been obvious.

◆ ◆ ◆

Rav Yitzchok Nosson was the type of person who didn't only sympathize when someone else was suffering; he did his utmost to alleviate the other's hardship. When one of my friends from the Mir got engaged to the daughter of a Yerushalmi family, I attended the *vort*, and while there, I got into a conversation with his future father-in-law.

Through the course of the conversation, it became clear to me that the man didn't appreciate what a special son-in-law he'd acquired. I was pained by our exchange, knowing as I did the *chasan's* high-caliber qualities in all areas. I would have spoken up myself in his defense, but he would have perceived my words as just that — a defense — and they would have meant little to him. This bothered me, but I wasn't sure what to do about it.

The next time I went to visit Rav Yitzchok Nosson, this incident came up in our conversation. Rav Yitzchok Nosson knew the father, as he did almost every Yerushalmi Yid, but he didn't react

With Rav Yitzchok Nosson at a *simchah*

to my words. Two minutes later we were talking about something else.

Months passed and the day of the *chasunah* arrived. I entered the hall and found, to my astonishment, Rav Yitzchok Nosson sitting and learning at one of the tables. Knowing that his connection to the *kallah*'s family was tenuous at best, I asked Rav Yitzchok Nosson why he was there.

"You mentioned that the girl's father doesn't fully appreciate what a fine son-in-law he's getting," he responded. "I came to tell him what a wonderful *shidduch* he made!"

◆ ◆ ◆

Nissan 1999. Pesach was on the way. The streets of Yerushalayim, usually so full of American yeshivah students and seminary girls, cleared out as nearly everyone returned home for *Yom Tov*. Only a handful of *bachurim* remained behind. I stayed in yeshivah for Pesach that year for a number of reasons. My parents didn't have the money to pay for the airfare, and even more importantly, I wanted to experience Pesach in Yerushalayim, a time when the city reverted back to its pure Yerushalmi roots.

While I was visiting Rav Yitzchok Nosson one afternoon during *Chol Hamo'ed*, he began questioning me once again about my eating habits and whether there was sufficient food to eat in the yeshivah. Without thinking too much about it, I admitted that the food situation was a little weak right then.

Face filled with concern over my "plight," Rav Yitzchok Nosson rose, went over to his closets, and, over my strenuous protests, emptied out their contents into bags for me to take back with me to yeshivah. Bananas, nuts, Pesach cookies, grape juice… whatever he could find was stuffed into two bulging shopping bags for the "hungry" *bachur*.

"Take this with you," he insisted, "so that you'll have what to eat in yeshivah!"

"There are grocery stores and places to purchase food," I shot back. "I can't take this."

With Rav Yitzchok Nosson, however, there was no arguing. He ignored my refusals and forced me to take his bags of groceries back with me. Though I was chagrined beyond belief that I was compelled to accept his food (I knew how little money the Kupershtoks had and what a sacrifice this was for them), I couldn't deny that a small part of me was gratified by his love and caring for me.

Before I left, he called up his son-in-law Rav Aharon Fisher, the son of Rav Yisrael Yaakov Fisher — today the Rav of Zichron Moshe — and asked him if I could eat at their home for the final *Yom Tov* meals. I then returned to yeshivah, *Yom Tov* invitation secured, feeling both uncomfortable by his present and filled with love for this holy man.

"What's this?" my roommates wanted to know when I entered the dorm, lugging the two bulging bags. I explained what happened and how this Yerushalmi Yid felt an acute responsibility for an American *bachur* who was hungry and who wouldn't allow me to leave without emptying his shelves. Who does things like this? Who empties his closets when he himself is so destitute?

Pesach food never tasted so good.

I presented myself at Rav Aharon Fisher's home on the seventh day of Pesach, where I enjoyed both the Yerushalmi conversation and the *Yom Tov* fare. As the meal wound its way to its conclusion, we *bentched* and I thanked my hosts. I was about to leave, when Mrs. Fisher approached me holding a pan in her hands containing an entire cake, which she had baked especially for me to take back to yeshivah.

"I have to thank you," she said. "My father never asks his children to do anything for him. It was very strange," she continued. "My father called me up and asked if I could bake a cake for him. I was taken aback. He had never asked me to bake him anything ever before. I asked him why he wanted the cake, but he wouldn't say. Then, on *erev Yom Tov*, he called me back and told me that the cake was for the *bachur* he was sending to eat at our home. You have no idea how happy I was to be given the opportunity to do something for my father, and it was all because of you!"

◆ ◆ ◆

I tried to daven *Kabbalas Shabbos* and *Ma'ariv* with Rav Yitzchok Nosson every week. During the short interval of time before *Ma'ariv* began, he'd relate some of the *chiddushim* that he'd come up with during the past week. I found him to be a person who was always, always, thinking in learning, no matter where he was or what he was doing.

As a *talmid* of Rav Isser Zalman Meltzer and Yeshivas Etz Chaim, he naturally gravitated toward the study halls of his youth and spent the majority of his time learning in the Etz Chaim library. In his youth, he was usually the last one to leave the yeshivah building.

Etz Chaim was situated on Jaffa Road, vulnerable and unprotected, and at the time that Rav Yitzchok Nosson was a boy learning at Etz Chaim the security situation vis-a-vis the Arab residents was volatile and unpredictable. Rav Isser Zalman feared for Rav Yitzchok Nosson's safety. After considering the matter, Rav Isser Zalman presented his student with a key to a particular section of the Etz Chaim *otzer hasefarim*, a room in the yeshivah that was kept locked at all times due to the fact that it housed the personal library of Rav Chaim Berlin, *zt"l*, which contained hundreds of rare and extremely valuable *sefarim* and artifacts.

Only one other person had the key to that part of the library, and no one else was allowed entrance, making it the perfect place for Rav Yitzchok Nosson to spend his nights poring over his beloved *sefarim* for hours at a time.

If he wasn't at Yeshivas Etz Chaim, he was in the locked library of Yeshivas Tchebin, learning undisturbed and in silent solitude. Even after he'd finished his learning *seder* and left, he'd mumble words of Torah to himself when he walked in the street: a prime example of a person constantly engaged in Torah study.

When I'd accompany groups of people to his home for *berachos*, his wife would do the entertaining while he sat at the head of the table without saying much. All the while, I'd see his lips moving as he learned and learned, interrupting himself to give the people his *berachah* and immediately returning to where he'd left off when the visit had been concluded to everyone's satisfaction.

Rav Chaim Brim, *zt"l*, had been his study partner in their youth, and when I once mentioned Rav Yitzchok Nosson's name to him, Rav Chaim looked me in the eye and said the following memorable words:

"I can personally testify that in the last 30 years, Rav Yitzchok Nosson hasn't walked four *amos* without Torah —" Then, correcting himself, he added, "And not four *amos* without a *chiddush* in Torah."

Rav Chaim had not been exaggerating in the slightest. When I'd visit Rav Yitzchok Nosson on Friday night, he'd tell me a question that had occurred to him. By the time I returned on *motza'ei Shabbos*, he'd have already developed three different approaches to answer it. His was a mind that never stopped toiling in Torah, and he never ceased to amaze me with his wisdom, brilliance, and sheer diligence.

◆ ◆ ◆

Rav Yitzchok Nosson exhibited extraordinary care and concern for the people around him. At one point during the year, I was poised to finish *maseches Nedarim*. I decided to stay up all night with a *chavrusa* and complete the last few *dafim* at Rav Yitzchok Nosson's shul in Batei Broide, planning to make the *siyum* after davening the next morning.

It was the perfect place for an all-night learning marathon: quiet, peaceful, and off the beaten track, where we'd be able to learn undisturbed for hours on end. Plus, it contained true *kedushah*. I called Rav Yitzchok Nosson, who had a key to the building, explained my plan, and asked him to please leave the door open for me that evening.

I met my *chavrusa* at the Batei Broide shul at midnight, expecting to find an open door and an empty shul. To my chagrin, Rav Yitzchok Nosson was waiting for us. Not content with leaving the door open, he'd been worried that we wouldn't be able to figure out how to turn on the heat or lights, that we wouldn't have something to drink, that we wouldn't be comfortable in every way. So he stayed up to make sure that everything was taken care of.

We learned through the night, making the *siyum* as the sun rose above Yerushalayim, and after davening I began setting out plates with cakes and cookies for the members of the *minyan* to enjoy. To my surprise and slight consternation (at having caused him so much work), Rav Yitzchok Nosson came to *Shacharis* with his own plates of fresh baked goods and drinks for the assembled.

After the *siyum* had concluded and everyone had left, Rav Yitzchok Nosson told me that although he'd wanted to invite us home to his house for breakfast, his Rebbetzin was still asleep and it wasn't possible. Therefore he'd arranged for us to eat breakfast at the home of Rav Moshe Salant, a famous Yerushalmi elder and the son of Rav Yosef Salant, the author of *Be'er Yosef*. Through Rav Yitzchok Nosson's breakfast arrangement, I would come to develop a relationship with Rav Moshe Salant, but on that morning my *chavrusa* and I followed this stranger through the Yerushalayim alleyways until we arrived at his home, where he bade us to wait for him until he returned from the store.

We were happy to do so.

Rav Moshe returned having literally purchased everything remotely related to breakfast that the grocery offered for sale. Cottage cheese, smooth white cheese, plain and flavored yogurts… It was obvious that this was not the usual breakfast fare in the Salant household, but Rav Yitzchok Nosson had made the request and Rav Moshe Salant had hurried to accede.

At the end of the day it became clear that one couldn't just ask Rav Yitzchok Nosson to leave on a light in a shul or to keep the door unlocked. For Rav Yitzchok Nosson, every person was a world unto himself and worthy of being treated as if he were the most important person in the universe.

◆　◆　◆

When one of my grandfathers came on a visit to Eretz Yisrael, and I mentioned that I wanted to set up a meeting between the two of them, Rav Yitzchok Nosson refused to allow my *zeide* to come see him at his home. He insisted that he would come to the hotel instead.

"But my *zeide* wants to come see you," I told him emphatically, almost plaintively. "He's the guest coming from the States and wants to meet you at your home!"

"Your *zeide* is a *chashuve Yid*, and I will meet him at his hotel," came the laconic response, completely unfazed by my entreaties. It was decided. There was nothing to discuss.

On another occasion, a famous *maggid shiur* with whom I was well acquainted wanted to go see Rav Yitzchok Nosson for a *berachah* and asked me when would be a good time for them to meet. When Rav Yitzchok Nosson heard that this man intended to come to his home, he was horrified by the very idea.

"He wants to come to me?" he asked me incredulously. "*Chas v'shalom*. It's out of the question. It would be a lack of *kavod haTorah!*"

"But he wants to come to you," I reiterated.

My words fell on deaf ears. There was no way that he was going to allow such a *marbitz Torah* to expend so much effort to come see him. It was out of the question.

When Rav Chaim Stein, the *Rosh Yeshivah* of Telshe, visited Eretz Yisrael, he asked me to arrange a meeting for him with Rav Yitzchok Nosson. Following my instructions, I relayed his request to Rav Yitzchok Nosson. His response was predictable.

"*Nein! Chas v'shalom* that a *rosh yeshivah* should come to me. Find out where he is and I will go to him!"

In the end, I accompanied Rav Yitzchok Nosson to his visit with Rav Stein in Mattersdorf. No matter that Rav Yitzchok Nosson had written many *sefarim* and was a respected *talmid chacham* by the most exacting Yerushalmi standards. His humility was so ingrained that it was almost abhorrent in his eyes for someone great in Torah to come see him.

After all, he was just a "simple Jew."

Rav Yitzchok Nosson Kupershtok

Part C

R av Yitzchok Nosson published his first *sefer* when he was in his mid-30's. It was a treatise on the subject of using electricity produced by Jewish people on Shabbos in Eretz Yisrael.

A comprehensive *sefer* on a vital topic, it was widely celebrated in the yeshivah world. Rav Yitzchok Nosson devoted eight years toward writing the *sefer*, traveling to Bnei Brak on a number of occasions to confer with the Chazon Ish throughout. Not content with writing about a topic while equipped with only a rudimentary and theoretical understanding of its applications, Rav Yitzchok Nosson went so far as to actually visit Israel's Chevrat Chashmal, its electric company, where he saw firsthand how electricity is produced. The end result was his *sefer*, *Me'oros Nosson*, where he concluded that it is forbidden to use electricity produced by Jews on Shabbos.

When he was finished writing, Rav Yitzchok Nosson brought the *sefer* to his Rebbe, the Tchebiner Rav, for perusal and a letter of approbation. The Tchebiner Rav had been one of those who did rely on the assorted *heterim* that existed when it came to electricity, and he did not use a generator on Shabbos. It took the Tchebiner Rav quite a while to give Rav Yitzchok Nosson a *haskamah* for the *sefer*, and when he finally did, he said that it was a "costly" *haskamah* on his part.

"I reviewed the *sefer*," he explained, "and found it to be correct on every level. But to write a letter of approbation for this work would mean that I concur with the author's judgment, and if that were the case, how could I satisfy myself with relying on my previous leniencies and continue to use Israeli-produced electricity? I therefore had to switch over to a battery myself — an expensive proposition, making this *haskamah* quite a costly one for me!"

Rav Isser Zalman Meltzer also stopped using electricity produced by Israel's electric company on Shabbos at least partially due to the influence of Rav Yitzchok Nosson's *sefer*.

◆　◆　◆

Many authors try their utmost to actively push their *sefarim*. It's understandable: people want others to learn their work. Rav Yitzchok Nosson operated differently. On the occasions when visitors came to his home, events would usually play out the same way. Within moments of arrival, the guests would find themselves engrossed in Torah conversation. At times Rav Yitzchok Nosson would quote something from one of the three halachic works that he had written, following up his quote by showing his visitors the exact wording inside. The visitor would then ask to purchase the *sefer*.

If the person had not expressly come to purchase the *sefer*, but had only found out about it in the course of their conversation, Rav Yitzchok Nosson would give it to them while emphatically refusing any offers of remuneration. When I asked him why did this when the visitors so clearly wanted to purchase his *sefarim*, he explained to me that the Gemara discusses the concept of *kisufa:* where a person may feel forced to buy the *sefer* because he pities the author. He therefore refused to accept their money under any circumstances, notwithstanding the fact that he was penniless and the person begging to buy the *sefer* was a wealthy man. It made no difference to him; he wouldn't sell it, he would give it away. And he did. Again and again.

This is not to say that it was impossible to arrange some assistance for the Kupershtok family. There were ways. At times I managed to slip the Rebbetzin some money for *hachnasas kallah*. If a wealthy person insisted on giving them some money toward the wedding of a child or grandchild, they'd accept. But they never looked for it; they never, ever asked for financial assistance, and you had to work hard to convince them to accept the help.

◆ ◆ ◆

On one occasion I told Rav Yitzchok Nosson about a Yid named Reb Uri who used to sit beside the door of the Mir Yeshivah's main *beis medrash*. He was a widower who had lived a truly fascinating life. I told Rav Yitzchok Nosson how Reb Uri invited *bachurim* over to his home for Shabbos meals and how I had been one of those fortunate enough to have been granted the experience.

"How does this Yid support himself?" Rav Yitzchok Nosson wanted to know. I could see that he felt real concern for Reb Uri, though they had never met. "Purchasing enough food for *bachurim* must cost him a lot of money."

I said I didn't know, and Rav Yitzchok Nosson didn't pursue the matter.

It so happened that Reb Uri was an expert on Yerushalayim and the living legends who populated its tiny roads, courtyards, and alleyways. He knew all their names and was familiar with family histories and lore. When someone mentioned a Yerushalmi name to Reb Uri, he considered it a personal challenge to be able to respond with a host of information on that person's background, lineage, and life. Knowing this, I once asked him if he knew Rav Yitzchok Nosson.

"Of course I know Rav Yitzchok Nosson. He came to visit me in my home!"

This was a surprise. "When was that?"

"He came over one evening and said, 'Reb Uri, I hear that you have *bachurim* over at your home on Shabbos for meals. How do you have the necessary funds to afford this?'

"When I admitted that I didn't really have enough money for everything that I needed, he handed me some money. He returned again on Purim with *matanos l'evyonim*, which he presented to me for this specific purpose."

It was exactly what I would have expected from Rav Yitzchok Nosson. He had asked me about Reb Uri's financial situation, while never saying a word about his plans. Unbelievable: here was Rav Yitzchok Nosson racing through the streets of Yerushalayim handing out *matanos l'evyonim* when by all accounts he should have been the one on the receiving end.

Until this day I wonder where Rav Yitzchok Nosson got the money he needed to carry out his phenomenal life of *chesed*. How was such an exquisitely poor man like Rav Yitzchok Nosson able to accomplish so very much? I have no explanation, other than to say that Hashem sends the necessary funding to those who know how to use it.

◆ ◆ ◆

When most people think of the words "*Zeh Keli v'anveihu* — This is my G-d and I will glorify Him," they think that means buying a silver menorah. Rav Yitzchok Nosson didn't possess the money to purchase objets d'art, but he did have two hands, and these he used to glorify Hashem. He purchased a slab of wood, drilled holes into it, and filled them with crystal cups for a beautifully designed and original menorah. It was the most breathtaking menorah I ever saw, designed out of simple materials that barely cost money, using only the raw talent that he'd been born with — and his burning love for the mitzvah.

Before Chanukah Rav Yitzchok Nosson would experiment with every type of olive oil available, attempting to discover which lasted the longest and burned the most evenly. He did the same with materials of all kinds, as he deliberated how best to construct the handmade wicks he was going to use for his menorah.

It didn't stop there. His *succah* was decorated with original ornaments of all kinds that enhanced its magnificent appearance, every one of them crafted by his own hands.

The *aron kodesh* in the Batei Broide shul is very old and very beautiful. Every beam is painted another color; there are murals, bells, and tiny hanging lights — all designed by Rav Yitzchok Nosson, the work done in the middle of the night when no one else was around. He'd paint and draw and hammer, exemplifying the words of *"zeh Keli"* with his very own hands, in the most simple and authentic meaning possible. If anyone finds the idea of an elderly, white-bearded *tzaddik* with a paintbrush in his hands somewhat incongruous, to me it is a vision of extraordinary beauty and charm.

◆ ◆ ◆

One of the men learning with me in *kollel* had been married for 10 years without a child. I could tell that he was feeling desperate, and I wanted to help him out.

"I know a Yerushalmi *tzaddik* whose *berachos* possess tremendous power for salvation."

I saw his face perk up in hopeful interest.

"They are especially potent when it comes to people with infertility issues."

Excitement blazed from his eyes.

It was true. Rav Yitzchok Nosson himself had been born through a miracle. His parents lived in the "Strauss Courtyard" — right outside Jaffa Gate and the Old City walls, a neighborhood known today as Musrara — in a compound filled with *ba'alei mussar* of the finest vintage. The courtyard was the kind of place where the *shamash* made the rounds from house to house in the predawn hours, banging on the windows with a stick and calling out in Yiddish, "Wake up! Wake up to serve the Creator!" Strauss Chatzer was truly *Yerushalayim shel Ma'alah*.

His father, Rav Yehudah Yosef, had been married for many years and hadn't been blessed with children. He divorced his wife, married another woman, and still didn't merit offspring. Rav Yitzchok Nosson's father was 67 years old on the Purim that a *minyan* of *tzaddikim* from the Strauss Courtyard locked the doors of their shul and convened as a *beis din shel matah* (an earthly *beis din*), with the goal of decreeing that Heaven should bless Rav Yehudah Yosef with a son.

Nine months later, Rav Yitzchok Nosson was born.

It's possible that the story of his miraculous birth had an everlasting impact on him, because when it came to blessing childless couples, his *berachos* were extremely powerful and successful. My friend jumped at the opportunity to receive a *berachah* from Rav Yitzchok Nosson, and nine months later, his wife gave birth to twins. Naturally, the brand-new father wanted to repay Rav Yitzchok Nosson by offering him the role of *sandak*. I encouraged him to visit Rav Yitzchok Nosson with his offer, never dreaming that he would be turned down. But he was, politely but firmly.

"I will speak with him," I promised my friend. I was confident that I could persuade him to accept the honor. But no matter what I said or how I pressed, Rav Yitzchok Nosson refused. I had hit a wall of steel and couldn't understand why.

One day he called me to explain his reasons.

"Reb Binyomin," he said, "let me tell you why I can't serve as *sandak*. If I'm the *sandak* at this *bris*, people will see me. They will wonder who the stranger is. They will ask if I'm the grandfather. They will be told that I am not the grandfather. 'Who is he?' they will want to know. 'He is the man who blessed them with children,' they will be told. And then, Binyomin, tomorrow there will be lines of people waiting outside my door for *berachos*, and that's not for me. It's not who I am, it's not the role I am ready to accept upon myself. And that's why I cannot serve as *sandak*."

◆ ◆ ◆

While I was a *talmid* there, Rav Asher Arieli delivered his famous Gemara *shiur* in the Mir bomb shelter from 6 to 7 o'clock every evening. One night I emerged from the concrete-enforced cellar to the upstairs hallway, only to find Rav Yitzchok Nosson standing in the doorway waiting for me. I was shocked to see him there. For Rav Yitzchok Nosson to have come to the Mir meant a walk of close to half an hour. Something must be wrong.

As soon as he began speaking to me, I could tell that he was completely beside himself.

"What happened?"

He explained. An American *bachur* from one of the finest yeshivos in the city had called when he was out learning. His wife answered the phone. The *bachur* explained that he wanted to come to the Kupershtok family for a meal on Shabbos if possible. The Rebbetzin apologized, but explained that it wasn't possible. The fact was, she wasn't up to it. She suffered from diabetes, among other ailments. Just cooking for the two of them was almost beyond her capabilities at that point, and if an American boy was coming to their house, they'd feel obligated to prepare way in excess of their normal Friday-night meal. She'd told all this to her husband, who was devastated by the idea of a hungry *bachur* with no place to go for his Shabbos *seudah*.

"Please find out who this *bachur* is, Binyomin, and tell him that we will take care of him," he begged me. "I feel so bad — A *bachur* with no place to go — We'll work something out — find him a place to go — speak to the *mishpachah* —"

"Rebbe," I said, trying to comfort him, "you don't have to worry about him. There is no end to the open houses all over Yerushalayim that host *bachurim* every Shabbos. There's no such thing as a *bachur* not having food to eat and a place at a Shabbos table."

"How do you know?" he asked me. "Maybe this boy truly doesn't have where to go!"

"I'm telling you, he called your house because he wanted the opportunity to spend time with a special Yerushalmi Yid, not because he needs a place to eat the *seudah*."

Rav Yitzchok Nosson would not be comforted or convinced.

"Binyomin," he entreated me, "please do me a favor and go to his yeshivah. Find the *bachur* and reassure him that we will take care of him. Will you do this for me?"

Again I tried to convince Rav Yitzchok Nosson that there was absolutely nothing to worry about; *bachurim* called up people all the time because they wanted to experience the authentic Yerushalmi experience. But Rav Yitzchok Nosson just kept begging me to locate the *bachur*.

In the end I had no choice. Simply speaking, I feared for Rav Yitzchok Nosson's health. I left the Mir and headed to the boy's yeshivah. It took me 15 minutes to track him down. When I finally found him, I drew him to the side of the room and related the entire story.

"They never have *bachurim* over at their home," I told him. "The Rebbetzin isn't well. She's barely able to take care of the two of them."

He was devastated by the havoc that he'd caused to Rav Yitzchok Nosson's peace of mind. Now it was his turn to plead with me to relay the message that although he truly appreciated the gracious offer, he had already managed to find another place to go. I called Rav Yitzchok Nosson. Relayed the message. Heard the palpable note of relief in his voice. He thanked me from the bottom of his heart.

I returned to the Mir marveling at the concern this *tzaddik* possessed for every member of *Klal Yisrael*, and how he couldn't rest as long as he pictured a hungry and lonely *bachur* in need of a meal.

◆ ◆ ◆

As a *bachur* I used to receive phone calls from desperate Yidden around the world. They called me because they were searching for miracles and salvation, and they'd heard that I had access to men like Rav Yitzchok Nosson, Rav Refael Levin, and Rav Chaim Kanievsky. They called me, a young *bachur*, because they didn't know where to turn. And when I answered, they begged me to go to the *gedolim* I knew and ask them for a *berachah*. Though I had never dreamed that this would be the outcome of my relationship with these great men, I considered it my mission to help as best I could.

One evening my phone rang at about 7 o'clock, the screen flashing an international number. I could almost feel the emergency before I even picked up.

"Hello?"

"Is this Binyomin?"

"Speaking."

They introduced themselves, told me that they were facing an incredibly difficult situation, one that needed a miracle.

"What happened?"

They explained that their daughter was supposed to get married that very evening, but that the *chasan* had called a few hours earlier saying that he wanted to call off the wedding.

"We don't know what to do. People will be arriving to the wedding hall in a few hours from all over. We need direction — *berachos* — a miracle — Please help!"

They were begging me, crying to me over the phone. Night had already fallen in Yerushalayim, but it was still daytime in America and they were beseeching me to save them. I promised to do what I could. With no choice, I made my way over to Batei Broide to knock on Rav Yitzchok Nosson's door. When he opened up, he was surprised to see me standing there.

"Binyomin, what happened?"

I explained the situation. "Everyone there is going out of their minds with worry!"

"Tomorrow is the *yahrtzeit* of the Ohr HaChaim HaKadosh," Rav Yitzchok Nosson replied in his calm, soothing voice. "Call the *kallah*'s family immediately and tell them to light a candle *l'ilui nishmas* the Ohr HaChaim and to learn from his *sefer*. I'm going to go to the Ohr HaChaim's *kever* to daven. Tell them that it's all going to work itself out in the merit of the Ohr HaChaim."

I was shocked by his confidence. For all practical purposes, Rav Yitzchok Nosson had just given me a promise that the wedding would take place on time! And, indeed, they called me back a few hours later from America to inform me with tremendous gratitude that the wedding was back on. The *chasan's rosh yeshivah* had gotten involved and managed to convince him that he was making the mistake of his life.

The wedding did take place that evening, and the couple are happily married until this very day, with the *chasan* never knowing how Rav Yitzchok Nosson Kupershtok of Yerushalayim had promised that everything was going to be O.K. and how he had gone running to the *kever* of the Ohr HaChaim to drench his tomb with tears and pray that there should be a satisfactory end to this story, though he had never met the people involved and had no clue who they were. It was sufficient for him that they were Yidden who needed help.

They needed help and he was there to provide it.

◆ ◆ ◆

The relationship I shared with Rav Yitzchok Nosson extended to include additional members of my family as well. My father-in-law, for example — a genuine *talmid chacham* and *marbitz Torah* — met Rav Yitzchok Nosson and was fascinated by his wisdom, humility, and brilliance. He was also amazed that he had never met or heard of him, despite the fact that my in-laws resided on the border of Nachlaot and Rav Yitzchok Nosson in Batei Broide, just a short distance away.

At one point, my father-in-law had a growth that needed to be surgically removed. He was operated on at Hadassah Ein Kerem, where everything proceeded without a hitch. He was recovering in his hospital room when his first visitor walked into the room. It was Rav Yitzchok Nosson. When I showed up a few short hours after the surgery, I was informed by my father-in-law with a twinkle in his eye that our good friend Rav Yitzchok Nosson had beat me to it and had already put in an appearance.

◆ ◆ ◆

I had been married for a few years when I began studying with another young man my own age in a local *kollel* in Beit

Shemesh. I enjoyed learning with him and found his mind sharp and filled with a broad range of knowledge. There was just one problem, and that was his attitude. He'd enter the room with a scowl on his face and reply to my questions and friendly overtures with monosyllables. Something was eating him up inside.

I could tell that he was a very private person and that it would be difficult for him to open up to someone else. On the other hand, his problems were destroying him.

"Look," I finally said to him one day, "something is really bothering you. You come in here every day looking as if the world is coming to an end. What's on your mind?"

It was hard for him, but eventually he forced himself to confide in me.

"You can never understand what I'm going through."

"What do you mean?"

"Our lives are completely different."

"How so?"

"When you come home in the afternoon or at night, you walk through the door into a warm house. There are children playing and babies crying. Life is happening."

"And by you?"

"By me? It's exactly the opposite. My wife and I have been married for years without kids. She works long hours every day, and when I enter my house all I hear is silence. Solitude. Loneliness."

I heard him out. Gave him my shoulder to lean on. Let him cry out his soul. When he finished talking, I looked him in the eye.

"Listen to me. There's a *tzaddik* in Yerushalayim whom I know very well. His name is Rav Yitzchok Nosson Kupershtok. He's a miracle worker. I am going to bring you and your wife to him for a *berachah*. Today."

He agreed immediately. Didn't question me. Didn't scoff. Merely ran out to get his wife. We took a bus to Yerushalayim a short while later. Soon enough we were sitting around the simple wooden table in the Kupershtoks' tiny apartment: Rav Yitzchok Nosson and his Rebbetzin, the couple and me.

The room was filled with an air of expectancy. I introduced everyone, and a minute later my friend had begun pouring out his heart to the elderly *tzaddik* with the lustrous beard and shining face. It was so hard for them. The social pressures, the dashed hopes, it was just too much — Tears streamed down both their faces as they cried out the pain of a childless life.

Rav Yitzchok Nosson listened to everything they had to say with a river of tears flowing down his cheeks and into his soft white beard. The Rebbetzin cried along with him. It was a moment of pure, tear-filled closeness. Things ran their course. Half an hour later we rose to leave. I could sense that their hearts were lighter already. As they turned to go, the Rebbetzin spoke up in authoritative tones.

"You have nothing to worry about. *Mir haben shoin poi'el yeshuah geven* — we've already achieved a salvation."

Where he was taciturn, she was outspoken. Yet she was able to speak for him. Rav Yitzchok Nosson respected his wife immensely and would answer *amen* to her *berachos* with deep conviction, obviously considering her a truly righteous woman.

The Rebbetzin knew what she was talking about: nine months later, my friend and his wife had a baby boy. Since then, the previously childless couple has been blessed with quite a few more children. Once the gates of tears opened up, they remained open.

As for me, I will never forget that night of tears, the power they signified and the absolute feeling of empathy that abounded in the Kupershtok gateway to Heaven.

◆ ◆ ◆

When Rav Shlomo Zalman Auerbach's Rebbetzin passed away, the *posek hador* made the following incredible statement at her funeral: He would not ask *mechilah* from his wife, he said, because he hadn't hurt her feelings or caused her pain in the 50 years they'd been married.

This statement engendered a huge (and well-deserved) stir at the time.

Rav Yitzchok Nosson passed away before his Rebbetzin; she is still alive, *ad meah v'esrim*, and any time anyone comes to see her, the conversation rapidly moves to her departed husband and the esteem and respect she felt and continues to feel for his memory.

"We were married for 70 years," she always tells her guests, "and in all that time, my husband never once, not once, caused me any pain!"

◆ ◆ ◆

Rav Simcha Zissel Broide, the late *Rosh Yeshivah* of Chevron, was Rav Yitzchok Nosson's childhood friend, both of them having grown up together in the Strauss Courtyard across from Jaffa Gate. At Rav Simcha Zissel's *levayah,* as Rav Yitzchok Nosson walked alongside the procession of mourners, I fell into step beside him. At one point we happened upon one of the distinctive blue vans of the Yerushalayim *chevrah kaddisha.* The driver caught a glimpse of Rav Yitzchok Nosson and asked him to join them on the drive to Har HaZeisim.

Rav Yitzchok Nosson, however, wouldn't dream of boarding the van and leaving me behind. Despite the fact that there really wasn't room for additional passengers, Rav Yitzchok Nosson boarded the van while pulling me up along with him to take a seat among the *chevrah kaddisha.*

"Can I please have a drink?" he asked one of the *chevrah kaddisha* members.

They were more than happy to oblige.

"Of course, Rav Yitzchok Nosson."

One of them poured him a drink, honored at having been granted the unique opportunity of serving one of Yerushalayim's holiest inhabitants. Rav Yitzchok Nosson thanked him profusely and then handed me the cup.

◆ ◆ ◆

Like many *gedolim* of the previous generation, Rav Yitzchok Nosson was never one for pictures. Uncannily, in the beginning of our relationship, whenever I tried to take a picture of him, not knowing that he had an aversion to being photographed, something always went wrong.

Every time I'd develop a roll of film (remember those?), the pictures of Rav Yitzchok Nosson were consistently problematic. Sometimes there'd be two of him in the same picture. Other times, one photo was superimposed on top of another.

It was only once we'd grown closer and he actually gave me permission to take pictures of him that they began coming out clear and beautiful.

An example of the photos of Rav Yitzchok Nosson that didn't come out as planned, until permission was granted

♦ ♦ ♦

Though many people in Eretz Yisrael are engaged in an ongoing war against the relentless onslaught of Jerusalem pigeons and doves, Rav Yitzchok Nosson sprinkled rice outside his apartment for them, attuned as always to the needs of every creature, following the example of "*V'rachamav al kol ma'asav* — Hashem has mercy on all His creations" (as the Arizal comments, we should take a lesson from this verse that we, too, should show compassion for Hashem's creatures). If he ever had to be away for a few days, he'd make sure to purchase sufficient rice for the duration of his trip and bring it to a designated "rice sprinkler" who'd take over for him while he was away.

Those trips were rare occasions. Normally, one could see Rav Yitzchok Nosson going about his daily routine, sprinkling rice for the birds, while murmuring under his breath, "He has mercy on all His creations — He has mercy on all His creations —"

◆ ◆ ◆

Growing up in the Yerushalayim of 90 years ago, Rav Yitzchok Nosson was surrounded by *gedolim* and men of exalted moral rectitude who guarded the gates of the Holy City with a fierce determination to keep the foreign culture of the outside world at bay. As a youngster, he once participated in a demonstration protesting the establishment of a certain school, then opposed by the leaders of the Yishuv. Sixty years later, Rav Yitzchok Nosson approached the executive director of the institution to beg his forgiveness if he had caused him to feel slighted by his actions on that long-forgotten day.

Long forgotten by everyone else maybe, but not by Rav Yitzchok Nosson, who couldn't bear the thought that there might be someone alive who bore even the slightest grudge against him in his heart.

◆ ◆ ◆

Rav Shlomo Zalman Auerbach, *zt"l*, was once leaving the Kosel when he caught sight of Rav Yitzchok Nosson Kupershtok. Upon seeing Rav Yitzchok Nosson, Rav Shlomo Zalman turned to his companion and said, "*V'chi chiddush hu sheha'olam kayam? V'chi chiddush hu shehachamah zorachas?* Is it a *chiddush* that the world exists or that the sun shines — if Rav Yitzchok Nosson lives among us?"

◆ ◆ ◆

Rav Avraham Genuchovski, another of the original *talmidim* of the Tchebiner Rav, was an outstanding *talmid chacham* and *tzaddik*. He was also one of Rav Yitzchok Nosson's closest friends and contemporaries. He was asked to speak at Rav Yitzchok Nosson's funeral and did so — from the heart — relating a number of incidents that made an impression on him and that he felt characterized Rav Yitzchok Nosson and his approach toward *avodas Hashem*.

He related how he was once approached by someone he knew from the neighborhood who requested financial assistance in the form of a loan. Not being able to help the man, he decided to turn to Rav Yitzchok Nosson for advice.

"Come to my house in the afternoon and I'll see what I can do," Rav Yitzchok Nosson told the individual seeking the loan.

When the supplicant arrived at his home a few hours later, Rav Yitzchok Nosson handed him a significant sum of money, which he had personally borrowed on behalf of his visitor. The lender had been prepared to trust Rav Yitzchok Nosson, who was willing to put himself on the line for a fellow Yid. And so, when the borrower entered his house for what he imagined would be a brainstorming session, he was surprised to find the money already waiting for him.

◆ ◆ ◆

Rav Yitzchok Nosson was a frequent visitor to *kivrei tzaddikim*. He'd visit the Ohr HaChaim's *kever* on his *yahrtzeit* for hours, and he would go up to Meron for an entire week before Lag BaOmer. This was a perfect opportunity for him to spend time davening for all the people who needed salvation, and he utilized it to its maximum. I actually spent time with him in Meron, sharing the tiny room that he had access to in the upper levels of the building, watching him swaying over his *Tehillim* and Gemara, learning and davening under the benevolent gaze of Rabbi Shimon and his son, Rabbi Elazar.

Rav Yitzchok Nosson donated a *ner tamid*, a perpetual oil lamp, for many *kevarim*. He did this at Me'aras HaMachpeilah in Chevron, providing a local Jew with sufficient oil to last a few months and restocking when it ran out. He did this at *kevarim* throughout the country as well. Any time I'd visit a *kever*, I'd keep a sharp lookout for one of his oil lamps, and since I recognized his artistic style, I was able to spot them. And they were all over.

He provided the shul in Meron with a special lamp that burned for 25 years. The wick was made with lead, and it never burned out. It was a massive cup, and his delegate would fill it with a two-week supply of oil at a time.

Rav Yitzchok Nosson passed away on a Friday night. On that same night, for the first time in a quarter of a century, that oil lamp finally burnt out. His son got a phone call from Meron on *motza'ei Shabbos* informing him that for the first time in 25 years there seemed to be something wrong with the wick.

"There's nothing wrong with the wick," his son replied. "It's just that its owner has passed away."

That wasn't all. On that memorable Friday night, a light went out in the home of Rav Yitzchok Nosson's daughter where he was living at the time and in the homes of three additional children.

◆ ◆ ◆

In the traditional homes of Yerushalayim, there's an accepted practice that continues until this very day, whereby all children and grandchildren gather at their grandparents' home on *motza'ei Shabbos*. I have a memory of one particular *motza'ei Shabbos* that I will never forget. Rav Yitzchok Nosson sat in regal splendor at the head of the table in his tiny apartment, with the entire Kupershtok family assembled around him like the offshoots of a bountiful olive tree. Somehow, miraculously, there was room for everyone.

It was during that gathering that I was asked to tell how a *bachur* from America like myself ever came to know of Rav Yitzchok Nosson Kupershtok in the first place. There must have been 30 Yerushalmi Yidden sitting or standing in that tiny room in Batei Broide as I shared a story that began in Brooklyn, continued in Telshe Yeshivah in Cleveland, and culminated in one of the most beautiful relationships of my life in Yerushalayim of old. The daughters-in-law wiped tears from their eyes, and it was a very emotional evening for all present as I explained the background of our relationship in my broken Yiddish and Hebrew.

The powerful connection between Rav Yitzchok Nosson and myself only intensified over the years and lasted until his final day on earth. The family told me many times that they considered me their father's closest friend. So much so that they requested that I eulogize Rav Yitzchok Nosson at his funeral in Batei Broide.

I had been standing in the midst of the distinguished crowd, shoulder to shoulder with many of the *roshei yeshivah* and *gedolim* of our day, when one of the family asked me to speak. I refused. Who was I, after all, to speak in such august company?

But knowing the Kupershtok family, I figured that they wouldn't take my refusal sitting down. And, in fact, I was half-way out the door when I heard my name being announced over the loudspeaker.

I had no choice. I had been called up.

And so it came to be, in a way that could have only been scripted by *Shamayim*, that a virtually anonymous American *yungerman* stood up in the most Yerushalmi of shuls, at the same *bimah* where *gedolei hador* had eulogized one of the lions of their *chaburah*, and spoke from his heart about a person who had had an incredible impact on his life.

Family members with tears in their eyes told me later that my *hesped* had touched them deeply, filled as it was with personal stories about Rav Yitzchok Nosson: stories, anecdotes, and practices of the deceased that even his own grandchildren hadn't known about their patriarch.

As I stood there, surrounded by *gedolei Yisrael*, and reminisced about my connection to one of the greatest (albeit virtually unknown) among them, I couldn't help but recall how I had been promised "that the Chasam Sofer and Rav Akiva Eiger would repay me for the care and love I had shown their grandson."

If my relationship with Rav Yitzchok Nosson Kupershtok was repayment for my good deeds back at Telshe, I knew that I had merited payment far beyond anything I had ever done for a sad and lonely handicapped Jewish boy.

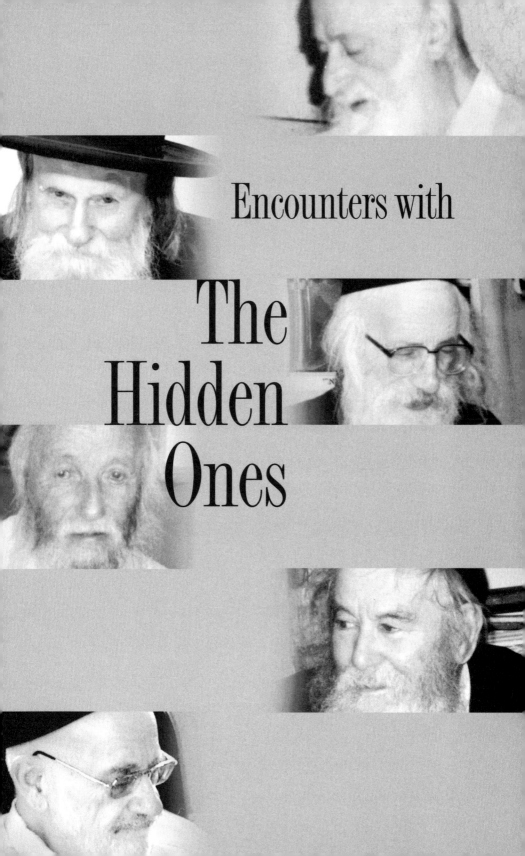

Encounters with

The Hidden Ones

There are men who are the secret guardians of the Jewish people. Men who refuse to surrender to the temptations of life in the modern world. Men who wouldn't dream of lowering their standards the slightest bit.

They are the hidden tzaddikim.

The Hidden Ones
PART A

Rav Nachman Dubinki
Rav Velvel Eisenbach

A s a *bachur* in America, when studying the halachos of *Tikkun Chatzos* in *Shulchan Aruch*, I had wondered whether there were still any people in the world who actually felt the pain of the *Shechinah* enough to make this halachah a part of their lives. Once I made it across the ocean from the campus of Telshe in Cleveland to the Mir Yeshivah in Yerushalayim, I was eager to try and find those who felt the destruction of the Beis HaMikdash keenly enough to bemoan its loss on a nightly basis.

During the course of my investigation, I was informed by a number of elderly Yerushalmi Yidden that there was a *tzaddik* who lived in Batei Nathan, a courtyard in Meah Shearim, by the name of Rav Nachman Dubinki. He was the the man I sought.

When I came to Eretz Yisrael, Rav Nachman was already extremely old, and in fact he passed away a few years ago. Rav Nachman lived on the building's first floor, and I was told by those in the know to make my way to his home at around midnight, during the hour of *chatzos*, and look through the window for a glimpse of his *avodah*.

I walked through the alleyways of Meah Shearim on that fateful night. All was still, and a feeling of peace permeated the atmosphere. The storefronts were closed and gated, and the windows of the homes were dark. Here and there a chassid dressed in Yerushalmi garb passed me, intent on his face, purpose to his gait. Soon enough I reached Rav Nachman's home and glanced into the window that abutted the street. Inside I saw a man with a shining light emanating from his face. I saw a man whose entire life had been one of service to his Creator, a man who lived to exalt the One Above in any way he could.

After seeing that holy countenance only once, I knew that I wanted to be close to this man and would do what I could to bridge the age and culture gap that lay between us.

At the home of Rav Nachman Dubinki

Rav Nachman's apartment was a throwback to the kind of homes Yidden lived in a century ago: a few sticks of furniture, some dim lightbulbs, and bathroom facilities located outside in a makeshift enclosure. No telephone, fax machine, or computer; it was as if time had stood still, and you were entering the Yerushalayim of the British Mandate, perhaps even of the Ottoman Empire.

His rickety bed had three legs; the fourth leg was broken and the bed propped up by tiles. The home was shabby even by Yerushalayim standards, devoid of light and material goods, but sustained and illuminated by the inner satisfaction of its inhabitant. By the time I met him, Rav Nachman must have been close to 90. His wife had already passed away, and his children were elderly themselves. Yet he was always *b'simchah*, always smiling and filled with *joie de vivre:* a combination of true exultation of spirit and a tremendous desire to serve Hashem.

This is not to say that he had an easy life. Not at all. Rav Nachman had lived through the years in Yerushalayim when almost every family had lost children to the stormy winds of secularism, and the Dubinki family had not emerged unscathed. I never found out how badly he was hurt by the "novel" ideas emerging from Europe that left the Yishuv bereft and forlorn; I only know that he had been scarred. And yet, despite the decades of hardships and a lifetime of austerity, despite the fact that he could barely walk and had to be wheeled everywhere in a wheelchair, Rav Nachman was possessed of a soul that soared joyously in the realms of the highest devotion to the *Ribbono shel Olam*.

In much the same way that the Chafetz Chaim was constantly awaiting the arrival of Mashiach, so it was with Rav Nachman Dubinki. He kept a brand-new *shtreimel* on top of his closet to be donned when Mashiach arrived. Mashiach's imminence was a simple fact of life to him. Whenever someone entered the room and sat at his table, Rav Nachman's standard conversation opener was to remind his visitor that Mashiach was coming any day and that our redemption from *galus* was at hand. He'd then begin describing our 2,000 years of exile, the unbearable suffering, the trials and tribulations, and how we were all waiting with such anticipation for the day when everyone would finally understand Who was King of the universe.

He'd quote the *Zohar* with relish, using rich, descriptive vocabulary as he explained how apartments were going to fall down from the sky and how challahs would begin growing on trees with the advent of Mashiach.

As he spoke, I'd look around the room and watch as Rav Nachman drew his listeners into his world. Suddenly his visitors were feeling a tremendous anticipation for Mashiach, because they had been granted a window into the soul of a person who yearned for his arrival with every one of his senses.

Once, a group of boys I had taught the previous year returned to Eretz Yisrael for a short visit. We got together and I escorted them through the streets of Meah Shearim and over to the home of Rav Nachman Dubinki, hoping they'd receive a little inspiration. Of course, within minutes of their entering his home, Rav Nachman embarked on his favorite theme: the coming of Mashiach. His eyes gleamed, his lips smiled, his entire being was caught up in the beautiful day after... He looked like an angel as he painted the sweetest picture in the world.

The boys were so convinced by his words, so sure were they that Mashiach would be there on the morrow, that they toyed very strongly with the idea of canceling their tickets. How could they leave Eretz Yisrael just as Mashiach was arriving?

And if you asked, "Tell me, Rav Nachman, why do you want Mashiach to come so badly?" he'd reply, "What do you mean? When Mashiach comes, we'll be able to run through the streets to learn, and there won't be any immodesty, and Yerushalayim will be a city of purity. *Oy*, how good it will be when Mashiach finally comes."

He repeated his message time and again, sitting in the same seat, with the same brilliant smile, while undergoing and experiencing the same *yissurim*. Nothing could mar his belief in Mashiach's imminent arrival and *Klal Yisrael*'s redemption. He was in the hospital and out of the hospital, but no matter what happened to him, or the level of excruciating pain he was in, he still radiated the same intense happiness and satisfaction with the *Ribbono shel Olam* and His world, always with incredible joy and always sitting and waiting for Mashiach to arrive.

Rav Nachman was once describing how wonderful it was going to be when Mashiach came. "We'll be able to run with our legs to go learn Torah."

One of the people listening interjected, "Rav Nachman, you'll be able to throw away your walker!"

Rav Nachman became visibly nervous at the speaker's words. "*Nein, nein, nein*," he responded forcefully. "The walker isn't mine, it belongs to Yad Sarah [an organization that provides medical equipment]. We can't throw it away! We have to give it back!"

His innocence and purity was simply the sweetest thing you could imagine.

◆ ◆ ◆

Rav Nachman never spent a night out of Yerushalayim. Though he lived for close to one hundred years, he was fiercely insistent on never sleeping anywhere else. On the rare occasions that he visited Me'aras HaMachpeilah in Chevron, it was only after making 100 percent sure that he'd be able to return by evening. In this Rav Nachman was the quintessential Yerushalmi Jew: a man who held Yerushalayim sacred in its essence and who treasured the privilege of just being able to reside in the heavenly city, while filled with the secure knowledge that Mashiach was coming, perhaps the next day.

Who can forget his reply when people beseeched him for a blessing?

"Why do you need my *berachah*?" he'd question them in wonderment. "Mashiach is coming today! You're going to receive everything you need! Just hold on a little bit longer!"

It was *emunah peshutah* — simple, solid belief — at its very best.

◆ ◆ ◆

Then there was Rav Velvel Eisenbach, *zt"l*. He, too, passed away around the 100-year mark, having lived a fruitful life by the most exacting Yerushalmi standards. Though physically a tiny person and in his upper 90's, Rav Velvel possessed the stamina, internal strength, and mental discipline of a serious *yeshivah bachur* and committed himself to learning sessions around the clock.

Rav Velvel's day commenced at 2 in the morning at the Kosel with the recitation of the entire *sefer Tehillim*. He'd return home after davening, eat breakfast, then go and learn a regular morning *seder* at one of the Yerushalmi *kollelim*, which he followed with a second *seder*. It was clear that Rav Velvel lived his life with the words and message of "*Shivisi Hashem...*" emblazoned on his heart and soul.

I used to bring groups of *bachurim* to Rav Velvel as well. They connected to his unassuming manner and were enthralled by his diligent approach to life and the fact that he was so, so busy with learning at an age when the vast majority of people want nothing more than to sit back, read the paper, and drink a cup of coffee.

On one such visit, while climbing the steep staircase to Rav Velvel's austere apartment in Batei Ungarin with a group of American kids, we passed his neighbor, a Yerushalmi woman. She took one look at the exuberant group and apparently was disturbed because she knew Rav Velvel had nothing in his pantry to offer his visitors. American tourists were arriving at his home, and one was supposed to put out some refreshments — and there would be nothing to serve. The neighbor ran home to put together a plate of refreshments. She did it rapidly and made her way a few minutes later to Rav Velvel's home.

Of course, Rav Velvel couldn't refuse her offering (just try and refuse a Yerushalmi mama), and no doubt a part of him was relieved at being able to offer the simple plate of cut-up fruit to his guests: apples, dates, and nuts assembled with efficiency and good taste.

"*Nu*," Rav Velvel commanded his guests, "make a *berachah* on the fruits of Eretz Yisrael!"

At the home of Rav Velvel Eisenbach

The group were quick to follow his command, the platter of fruits mostly demolished within mere seconds of being passed around. Everyone made loud *berachos* and everyone answered "*amen*," and Rav Velvel was happy. When it was time to leave, the plate was empty save for a few pieces of fruit.

As we made our collective way down the staircase of Batei Ungarin, my eye was drawn to the sight of a diminutive figure leaving his home, holding a plate on which rested two lonely pieces of apple, the remains of his neighbor's *chesed*. It was Rav Velvel on his way to return the plate. Though most people would have assumed that the woman meant for all the fruit to be eaten and would have no doubt consumed the remaining pieces themselves, Rav Velvel wasted no time in returning the apples. They were not his; they had been presented to him for a specific purpose, and now they had to be returned.

The memory of the nearly 100-year-old wizened *tzaddik*, plate in hand, will remain with me for the rest of my life. If I could paint the scene on a canvas, I would title it "Yerushalmi *tzaddik* and fruit."

What absolutely endearing people populated those century-old homes!

◆ ◆ ◆

When a guest would enter Rav Velvel's home, he was expected to kiss the mezuzah. If someone passed through the doorway without paying the mezuzah homage, a loud shout would emerge from his small throat: "*S'iz duh a mezuzah!*" The person would have to retrace his steps and kiss the mezuzah, and then he could be welcomed into Rav Velvel's poverty-stricken, spiritually wealthy abode. Once a person experienced that shout, he would never forget to kiss Rav Velvel's mezuzah again.

His children told me that when Rav Velvel was a young man, he supported himself by teaching *Chumash* to the local children. "The holy Rav Shloimke of Zhvill used to come and stand by the door to listen to our father teaching *Chumash* to the little *kinderlach*."

Rav Velvel had a regimented discipline when it came to his learning. He had a daily session in *Chovos HaLevavos*, *Shas Bavli* and *Yerushalmi*, and *Chumash* and *Rabbeinu Bachya*, among countless other *sedarim*. He was one of the only people still living who had begun studying *daf yomi* from the first cycle instituted by Rav Meir Shapiro, until he passed away, covering *Shas* this way some 11 times.

On one particular day, an emergency arose and Rav Velvel didn't manage to learn the day's *daf*. He went to sleep knowing that he would have to learn two *dapim* on the morrow. He'd been asleep for a short while when his father appeared to him in a dream. Not mincing words, Rav Velvel's father proceeded to give his son a slap across the face while shouting at him, "*Vos shlufsts du?* Why are you sleeping?"

Rav Velvel never missed the *daf*; this had been the first time. But his long-deceased father was not about to allow his beloved son to slack off. There was a *daf* to be learned and no time to waste.

◆ ◆ ◆

Sometimes I'd come visit Rav Velvel at home and find him studying with a grandchild. Rav Velvel would read the verse and his grandson the *Rashi*. On and on. When that *seder* came to an end, another grandchild would arrive to study something else with him. He simply never stopped learning.

During the weeks of *Shovavim* (the six weeks commencing with *Parashas Shemos* and concluding with *Mishpatim*), when saintly Jews the world over impose stringencies on their way of life, Rav Velvel would fast often. If that were not sufficient for a man of such advanced age, he refused to break his fast unless there was a minimum of three men to partake of his meal, which would give him access to a *zimun* for *bentching*. No *zimun*, no meal. End of story.

One Thursday, during the weeks of *Shovavim*, I brought a *bachur* to Rav Velvel's home for a *berachah*. It was already way after sunset when we arrived, and when we walked into his home, we were approached by his much-relieved son, who informed us that his father had been refusing to break his fast because there was no *zimun*.

"Please join us for a *seudah*," he entreated us. "My father hasn't eaten since before sunrise!"

We needed no second invitation.

◆ ◆ ◆

Watching Rav Velvel eat a meal gave insight into the *Chazal* (*Berachos* 64a) that participating in the meal of a *talmid chacham* is like enjoying the *Shechinah*. Rav Velvel would place a piece of parchment before him on the table, on which was inscribed the Name of Hashem, and before every bite, he'd take a moment to gaze at the parchment and utter the words *"heilige Bashefer"* — holy Creator — before actually placing the food in his mouth. Every move was carried out with the awareness of his Creator.

You can read about *"Shivisi Yidden"* of 200 years ago, and here was a man who lived his life with the same behavior and traditions of those long gone, except that he was still alive and well in 2008.

During the meal, I watched as he was served a steaming bowl of soup. Before partaking of the savory soup with its flavorful aroma, Rav Velvel poured himself a cup of soda (one of the unusually flavored drinks produced by Superdrink) and proceeded to spill it into his soup, effectively ruining the flavor. Unable to contain my curiosity, I asked his son about what I'd just witnessed.

"My father eats solely for strength to be able to serve Hashem," his son replied. "He wants no enjoyment from his food. By pouring the soda into his soup, he ensures a meal of sustenance without enjoyment."

I nodded in amazed comprehension.

His son next served him a plate of cut-up almonds. I watched as Rav Velvel took a handful of almonds and began chewing. Noticing me staring at him, Rav Velvel explained to me that almonds were a luxury he'd normally avoid, but the doctor had told him they were healthy for his heart. Of course, there had to be a reason he was allowing himself to partake of such an "earthly delight."

When the brief meal came to its conclusion, Rav Velvel motioned for us to dance around the table, which we did, singing "*Tzaveh Yeshuos Yaakov.*"

"My father is about to retire for the night," explained his son, "since he needs to rise at 2 in the morning. But the Rambam writes that a person is supposed to walk four *amos* after eating and before going to sleep. By dancing around the table, my father knows that he has fulfilled the Rambam's dictum and can retire for the night with an easy mind."

There was a *seder* and reason to every move. Everything was calculated according to the Torah and to what Hashem expected from him.

◆　◆　◆

It was a Thursday night. Before Rav Velvel went to sleep, his son brought a knife sharpener from the closet, and Rav Velvel proceeded to sharpen his knives — exactly as the *Shulchan Aruch* advises. (The *Shulchan Aruch* states that one should sharpen his knives on *erev Shabbos*.) Though many people do not even recall this halachah due to the fact that our knives are already sharp and usually remain that way, Rav Velvel kept the *Shulchan Aruch* as it was written. The halachah of sharpening knives had therefore been assigned a permanent spot in his Thursday-night ritual.

It was the first time in my life that I'd seen anyone being scrupulous in following this practice. The knowledge that there existed Yidden who treasured every word of the *Shulchan Aruch* gave me peace of mind.

◆ ◆ ◆

Every time Rav Velvel came to the end of a page of Gemara, and before continuing on to the next folio, he'd say, " '*V'larasha amar Elokim mah lecha l'saper chukai* — But to the sinner Hashem said, 'To what purpose do you recount My decrees?'(*Tehillim* 50:16)." In Rav Velvel's world, one had to do *teshuvah* before learning: "*Men darf teshuvah tun* — One has to repent." And Rav Velvel proceeded to do *teshuvah* — sincerely, wholeheartedly — before proceeding. I later discovered that the Ketzos HaChoshen acted in precisely the same manner while learning.

Rav Velvel lived in Batei Ungarin, in close proximity to the Toldos Aharon *beis medrash*. His son told me that the Toldos Aharon Rebbe once asked Rav Velvel why he never joined them for a *tisch*.

"You'd give me honor," Rav Velvel replied.

There would be no attending public events if it meant him being whisked up to the head table.

The Hidden Ones
PART B

Rav Zundel Kroizer

I met Rav Zundel Kroizer, *zt"l*, by virtue of the fact that he and Rav Yitzchok Nosson Kupershtok were neighbors in Batei Broide and were the closest of friends. Rav Zundel had written *sefarim* on the entire *Shas* and all of *Chumash*. He was a Yid who had attained great levels of holiness. Rav Moshe Salant, *shlita*, personally attested to me that Rav Zundel never once spoke *devarim beteilim* — never once wasted his words — in 80 years!

"How do I know this?" continued Rav Moshe Salant with a twinkle in his eye.

"Rav Zundel," he explained, "doesn't have many friends. There's a reason for that. It's because it's extremely difficult — almost impossible really — to be friends with someone who sits and learns from day to night and whose soul is entirely consumed with the study of Torah. He's one of the *masmidei hador*, one of the most diligent individuals of the generation!

"However," continued Rav Moshe, "every person needs some kind of friendship. It's a human need. So who are Rav Zundel's friends? The people he grew up with, people like myself. I've known him for 80 years, and in all that time I never heard him engage in *devarim beteilim*. And if I, who knew him so well, never heard any wasted words emanating from that holy mouth — well, then, who did?"

◆ ◆ ◆

For much of the period that I studied in the Mir Yeshivah, I learned with the *Rosh Yeshivah*, Rav Nosson Tzvi Finkel, *zt"l*. One day, when I came over to learn, I was carrying a *sefer* that had been written by Rav Zundel Kroizer. Rav Nosson Tzvi opened the *sefer* to take a look at it and soon began reading the inscription that Rav Zundel had personally penned to me in the *sefer*'s front page.

"Binyomin," he said to me, interest filling his voice, "how did you come to be acquainted with Rav Zundel?"

"I visit him from time to time, and we talk in learning."

Rav Nosson Tzvi leaned back in his chair and said, "My father-in-law, Rav Beinish, arranged a learning session between Rav Zundel and myself many years ago. We used to learn for 50 minutes at a time. In those 50 minutes we covered five *blatt* of Gemara, *Rashi*, and *Tosafos*."

The next time I visited Rav Zundel I couldn't help mentioning my priceless new information.

"Rav Nosson Tzvi told me that you used to learn with him many years ago."

"What?" he exclaimed in response. "Rav Nosson Tzvi isn't ashamed to admit that he learned with such a simpleton?"

Rav Zundel couldn't understand how such a famous *Rosh Yeshivah* as Rav Nosson Tzvi would admit to learning with such a lowly personage like himself. I could only smile in response.

◆ ◆ ◆

At the *vort* of Rav Zundel Kroizer's grandson

Until his recent *petirah*, Rav Zundel and I shared a very close connection. I used to speak to him on a regular basis, usually to share a Torah thought, though sometimes to ask his advice. Our relationship was something that I cherished and treasured.

Rav Zundel Kroizer and Rav Yitzchok Nosson Kupershtok davened in the same shul in Batei Broide. One of the most fascinating sights in the world was seeing the two of them sitting side by side on the same bench and davening to Hashem. Both of them were tall men, both of them with long white beards, and both of them possessed incredible *hadras panim* — a special glow that shone from their faces.

On Friday nights both of them davened an extra-long *Shemoneh Esrei*, which caused them to miss reciting "*VaYechulu*" with the rest of the congregation. I'd watch the two of them finish davening, take their three steps back, and then come together to recite "*VaYechulu*." The commentaries say that when two people recite "*VaYechulu*" together, it's as if they are bearing witness to the creation of heaven and earth. Looking at the two of them, I could not imagine two more fitting witnesses joining together to present testimony on the creation of the world. What a sight that was!

◆ ◆ ◆

Rav Zundel didn't host *bachurim* in his home for Shabbos meals, but he did invite all the *bachurim* who davened at the shul in Batei Broide home for a simple *kiddush* after davening. During this *kiddush* Rav Zundel gave us permission to ask him any questions we had on any area in Torah. For the group of boys from Brisk and Mir, it was amazing to see his complete mastery of the entire Torah.

Boys asked him questions from *Zevachim* and *Menachos*, *Bava Kamma* and *Bava Basra*. You didn't have to explain or provide him with an explanation. No matter what *sugya* you brought up, he was familiar with it and knew what you were going to ask before the words exited your mouth.

The poverty in his home was astounding. Rav Zundel didn't even own a complete *Shas*; instead, there were numerous volumes, all from different sets, scattered around his home. Despite the fact that he didn't own the *sefarim* possessed by every Jewish home, Rav Zundel had managed to acquire a level and caliber of learning that was a throwback to previous generations.

◆ ◆ ◆

"My grandmother used to wash the family's clothing by hand, like all the Yerushalmi women of Meah Shearim," Rav Zundel's granddaughter related. "At some point, washing machines started becoming commonplace in Eretz Yisrael, revolutionizing people's approach to washing clothes. Even the staunchest Yerushalmim, with their deeply ingrained mistrust of anything new, found themselves impressed by the concept of not having to wash clothing by hand. My grandparents had no available funds for such luxuries, but they saved up for a long time and eventually were able to purchase a washing machine.

"The washing machine arrived, and my grandmother enjoyed it immensely. But then one day, she happened to glance at the bookcase and noticed the row of mismatched *sefarim* standing there. Then and there my grandmother made the decision to sell her washing machine and buy her husband a complete *Shas* — which she did, notwithstanding that she now had to revert to washing their clothing by hand in the freezing Yerushalayim winters."

Though only a number of volumes remained from that original *Shas* sponsored by the Rebbetzin's *mesirus nefesh* for her husband's learning, I suddenly understood what life had meant for the wives of these great men, and how they had been willing to do anything they could to spur their husbands on to the levels of greatness they knew them to be capable of.

◆ ◆ ◆

At one point Rav Zundel ran a check-cashing *gemach*. People brought him their checks, which he exchanged for cash. He provided this service for a limited amount of time on a daily basis.

Batei Broide is located on the border of the Machaneh Yehudah section of Jerusalem, a neighborhood that at the time was replete with unsavory characters. Somehow, a few of the neigh-

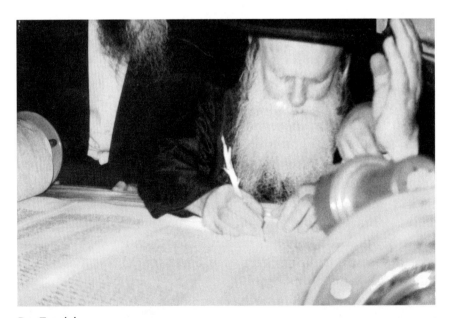

Rav Zundel

borhood thieves found out that Rav Zundel kept a substantial amount of cash in his home, and they began keeping an eye on him. It didn't take them long to learn his schedule and to know that he left his home every night at 2 in the morning to go to the *mikveh* and then to learn.

One night, as Rav Zundel was exiting his apartment, he was accosted by a few members of the gang. The thieves, knowing that he lived alone, pushed him back into the apartment and forced him to open the safe, which they emptied of all valuables. They then left the house after warning him against trying to follow them.

You'd think that a person would be downhearted after such an experience, but Rav Zundel told one of his companions that he'd just completed writing a Torah work on the topic of trust in Hashem (I have a copy of his *sefer*) and it was clear to him that Hashem had presented him with this challenge to see if he was really serious regarding the concepts he'd written about. *Hishtadlus?* He put up bars on his windows. *Bitachon?* He kept his equanimity and his quiet good cheer despite the frightening encounter.

◆ ◆ ◆

When a daughter of one of Rav Zundel's neighbors from Batei Broide became engaged, there was a matter of disagreement between her and the *chasan* as to where the young couple would live. The girl wanted to move into the courtyard where her parents lived and where she'd grown up, but the *chasan* was adamant about living in Meah Shearim, due to Batei Broide's close proximity to Agrippas Street and the *shuk* and the spiritual challenges that living there would entail. Unable to come to an agreement on the issue, the couple decided to go ask Rav Zundel's opinion.

Rav Zundel listened carefully, nodding his head when the *kallah* told him how important it was for her to reside close to her parents and family. But his brow furrowed and there was puzzlement in his gaze when the *chasan* presented his side, explaining how the area's lack of modesty was a deterrent for him.

"There's too much *peritzus* near Batei Broide," the young man explained.

"*Peritzus?*" said Rav Zundel. "*Ich hob kein mol nisht gezein kein peritzus!* I have never witnessed immodesty near Batei Broide!"

The fact is, Batei Broide does lie adjacent to the marketplace, and the level of modesty is none too great. Not only that, but the entire area borders the section of downtown Jerusalem known to one and all as "town," not the most savory part of the city. Yet Rav Zundel Kroizer, whose mind was constantly engaged in Torah learning and who didn't look beyond his *dalet amos*, was honestly able to look people in the eye and say with complete innocence that he'd lived in the area for 80 years and had never once seen anything he shouldn't have. This was a level of holiness that is virtually impossible to find, yet I saw it time and again among the holy men of Yerushalayim.

Their innocence, purity, and angelic ways, their sizzling spirituality and absolute love for their Creator left me spellbound and yearning to follow in their ways.

What magnificent human beings they were and are!

◆ ◆ ◆

Despite being a man who never wasted time, Rav Zundel was extremely cognizant of everyone he met and did his best to make each one feel good. He did this with a smile, a warm word, and a wonderful sense of humor. I came to understand how important this was for him when I realized that Rav Zundel had taught himself how to sign his initials in English.

I'd watch the American Yidden enter his home and ask to purchase a copy of one or two of his *sefarim*. In almost every scenario, they'd ask him to inscribe them as well. With a modest smile and a twinkle in his eye, Rav Zundel would scrawl "Z K" for his appreciative audience, who couldn't get over the fact that this elderly Yid from the Yerushalayim of a century before knew how to sign his initials in English. It made people laugh, made them feel good, and this in turn pleased Rav Zundel no end.

◆ ◆ ◆

Knowing that Rav Zundel rose at 2 in the morning, rain or shine, summer or winter, to spend the rest of the night involved in *avodas Hashem*, I knew that he'd be up and available for at least a short window of time at about 8 in the morning. It was the perfect opportunity to call him when I had a question on something I was learning.

One morning I called him right about 8 o'clock.

"Ah, Reb Binyomin," he said with pleasure when he recognized my voice, "what can I do for you?"

"Actually," I replied, "I had a question to ask you on the Gemara that I'm about to teach my *shiur* later this morning."

"Look at the difference between you and me," he responded. "While I'm in the middle of eating breakfast, you're busying yourself with *Shas*!"

Never mind the fact that he'd been up since the middle of the night and was well into his daily learning. Here was a chance for him to make me feel good, and he grasped it with both hands. Seriousness in learning and sweetness in life; that was Rav Zundel.

◆ ◆ ◆

Rav Zundel didn't attend weddings. His day was set up in such a way that weddings didn't fit in. After *Ma'ariv*, he ate supper and then retired for the night in order to rise at 2 a.m. for the *mikveh* and learning. Consequently, weddings were out of the question. The longest he ever stayed at a wedding, even for his own grandchildren, was until the end of the *chuppah*. Afterward, with mazel tovs handed out like fine wine, Rav Zundel was gone.

Rav Zundel didn't attend our wedding. I didn't expect him to. But in the middle of the *chasunah*, someone handed me a letter that he'd written especially to me, wishing me all manner of *berachos* on my special day. Once again, it wasn't expected or necessary, but for Rav Zundel "small" gestures such as these were a normal mode of expression.

◆ ◆ ◆

For the first 10 years that I knew Rav Zundel, it was virtually impossible to get him to give a *berachah*. I don't know if this was due to his innate modesty, or, as someone who knew him well once told me, "Rav Zundel knows that he possesses an uncommon power to bless people yet hesitates to do so, since it's difficult to know whether the recipient is deserving."

Whether this was the actual reason was debatable, since Rav Zundel never explained himself to me, but knowing the reality and that he shied away from granting *berachos*, I made sure to only bring people to talk in learning with him, but never for *berachos*. It was a delicate situation, and I didn't want people to feel that there was something wrong with them, that they were undeserving for some unknown reason, or that his refusal to bless them was in any way personal, since it wasn't.

And then I came across a very beautiful concept that Rav Chaim Kanievsky discusses in his *sefer Taama D'Kra*. He quotes from the *pesukim* in *Chumash* where Yaakov Avinu refused to allow Esav's angel to return to Heaven before giving him a *berachah*. Rav Chaim was puzzled by this action on Yaakov Avinu's part.

"We know," he writes, "that one is not supposed to ask an angel for a blessing! In fact, it is brought down in the name of the Vilna Gaon that we should leave out the third stanza of *Shalom Aleichem*, 'Barchuni L'Shalom,' since we are asking the angels to bless us — and not Hashem. Since when," asked Rav Chaim, "do we daven to angels and not to the *Ribbono shel Olam*?

"The difference in this case," answers Rav Chaim, "was that the angel had caused Yaakov harm. The spiritual pain that he'd given him during their battle allowed Yaakov to demand payment from the angel before letting him return to Heaven. The angel owed a *berachah* to Yaakov: plain and simple.

"When a *tzaddik* owes someone a *berachah*," Rav Chaim concludes, "the *berachah* is extremely potent and valuable and is usually fulfilled."

After reading Rav Chaim's words, I came to the conclusion that this was the way to go. In order to receive Rav Zundel's *berachah*, it had to come from a place of *hakaras hatov* on his part for the person he was blessing. And, in fact, my feelings on the matter were proven to be true.

♦ ♦ ♦

Many years before, Rav Zundel had worked as a *melamed* for a family in Bnei Brak. All week long he stayed in their home, only returning to Yerushalayim for Shabbos. In due course, the relationship came to an end, but Rav Zundel's sense of gratitude to the family knew no bounds and remained in his heart.

Any time a member of the family needed a *berachah* for anything important, they would have their grandfather (Rav Zundel's erstwhile employer) pick up the phone and give him a call, after which he'd bless them.

"Time after time," one of the family members told me, eyes shining with sincerity, "Rav Zundel's *berachos* came true for us!"

Where there's a will, there's a way, and now I had finally figured out how to obtain one of Rav Zundel's coveted *berachos*. The next time I was approached by someone who wanted me to take him to Rav Zundel for a *berachah*, I explained that Rav Zundel didn't give *berachos* to people as a matter of principle, but I did have a way that he might be able to get him to change his policy.

The man was intrigued. "How so?"

"I happen to know that one of Rav Zundel's grandchildren is experiencing some pretty serious challenges in a certain area right now and that Rav Zundel is very worried about him. If you are willing to give the necessary funds to help the family take care of their child, I think we may be able to go to Rav Zundel with a request for a *berachah* out of *hakaras hatov*."

The man agreed to foot the bill, to the family's (and Rav Zundel's) immense relief.

A short while later, the benefactor arrived in Israel. I took him to meet Rav Zundel, where I introduced him as the man who had provided the vital assistance for the *mishpachah*. Rav Zundel blessed him powerfully and with no hesitation. Two months later, the man's 27-year-old daughter, who had been in *shidduchim* for quite a few years, got engaged.

This is a very important point and I can't stress it enough. When you go to visit a *gadol*, if there is anything that you can do for the *gadol* that will make him want to bless you out of *hakaras hatov,* — you should jump at the opportunity. Rav Chaim states clearly that a *berachah* given from a heart filled with thankfulness is way more effective. I saw this with Rav Zundel time and again.

The Hidden Ones
PART C

Rav Mordechai Aharon Scheinberger
Rav Meir Shachor

zaddikim, angelic though their behavior may be, are also human, and, like all humans, they enjoy spending their time with like-minded people; in their case, with individuals who devote their lives to the undeviating service of Hashem. Being on close terms with Rav Nachman Dubinki and davening in his *vasikin minyan* helped me get to know his *chaveirim*. Meeting Rav Velvel and spending time in his company afforded me the unique opportunity to meet his circle of friends. "*Chavra, chavra is lei.* Every person has a friend." And so I came to meet Rav Mordechai Aharon Scheinberger, *shlita*.

Another lofty inhabitant of the Batei Ungarin neighborhood, Rav Mordechai Aharon is a walking *sefer Torah* and as unassuming as a person could be. He holds no official position; no title adorns his name. He simply sits and learns from morning until night.

You can ask Rav Mordechai Aharon a question on any section of the Torah you want. He will never tell you, "It's a Gemara on this page." That isn't his way. Instead, Rav Mordechai Aharon will rise from his chair and remove the *sefer* from the shelf, intent on showing you the source inside. It matters not whether the topic is to be found in the Gemara, Mishnah, *Zohar*, or *Chasam Sofer*. He will open the *sefer*, usually only a few pages away from the exact spot that you need.

Rav Mordechai Aharon's knowledge is of an encyclopedic nature. In fact, someone told me that he once approached one of the greatest *gedolim* of our age with a question and was told — astonishingly — that he didn't know the answer! A while later, the man asked Rav Mordechai Aharon the same question and was given a source to look up. After looking up and studying the source, the man returned to the *gadol* to inform him of the answer to the question.

Visiting with Rav Mordechai Aharon in his *succah*

The *gadol* glanced at him with his penetrating eyes and spoke, *"Bist geven by Reb Mordechai Aharon'n?* Have you been to see Rav Mordechai Aharon?"

Even that world-famous *masmid* and leader made it crystal clear that when it comes to Torah knowledge, Rav Mordechai Aharon stands at the top of the pyramid.

◆ ◆ ◆

I have known Rav Mordechai Aharon for many years and can personally attest to the fact that he has suffered much in his years on earth. Yet I never caught him with a frown on his face or exhibiting even the slightest hint of sadness. No matter what — and at times his challenges really were almost insurmountable — Rav Mordechai Aharon never lost his smile.

While escorting a famous rav from the States to the homes of some of "my" Yerushalmi *tzaddikim*, the rav turned to me and said, "You know something, Reb Binyomin? I know people back home who are literally living in mansions, and they aren't happy people. And then I come to see these *heilige* Yidden of Yerushalayim. They are living in shacks, and the genuine *simchas hachaim* they possess is unbelievable!"

◆ ◆ ◆

I came to visit Rav Mordechai Aharon one afternoon during *Chol Hamo'ed Succos*. First we schmoozed a little bit, and then I asked him something in learning.

"A *rega*, a second," he said to me. "*Men darf unton de kapote* — I have to put on a *kapote*."

There was no talking in learning without his outer garment.

◆ ◆ ◆

Whenever people came to see him for *berachos*, he'd escort them to the door when it was time to leave. One night I arrived at his home with a visitor. It was a real winter night in Yerushalayim, with a chilly wind and frigid rain pouring down from a cloud-filled sky. On this particular evening, Rav Mordechai Aharon didn't content himself with walking us to the door. Instead, he escorted us into the outer hallway and all the way to the stairs.

As we walked toward the staircase, he uttered the verse "*Ki malachav yetzaveh lach lishmorcha b'chol derachecha* — He will charge His angels for you to protect you in all of your travels" (*Tehillim* 91:11). And then he said the words again.

At the time I didn't really grasp the import of his words. After all, Rav Mordechai Aharon always escorted his guests and gave them *berachos*, but part of my brain did register that he had chosen to escort us farther than he normally would, and that he'd repeated his *berachah* twice. Still, I didn't make anything of it, merely taking his leave and venturing forth to brave the forceful brunt of the Yerushalayim rain.

From Batei Ungarin, we traveled on to Bnei Brak. As we drove, the rain poured down in torrents, the windshield wipers working overtime to clear the window from the never-ending stream. All of a sudden we heard a huge explosion. The car shook from the impact. Not knowing what had just occurred, we pulled over to the side of the road and upon inspection realized that we had suffered a major blowout, powerful enough to completely shred the tire.

On the positive side, the blowout happened just as we were turning onto the exit leading into Bnei Brak, giving us a place to stop and deal with the situation. Five minutes earlier and we'd have been stranded in the middle of an extremely busy stretch of highway with no place to stop and no way to deal with our emergency. More than that, we had been driving fairly quickly. A blowout like we had puts a car in danger and can easily cause a driver to lose control of his vehicle. I didn't even want to imagine how things could have turned out if they'd gone even just a little differently.

Though we had no way of knowing whether Rav Mordechai Aharon had foreseen what was coming, I couldn't discount the sheer timing of his double *berachah* and extended taking of leave. After all, he'd never done or said anything like that before.

All in all, it was a pretty amazing experience.

Coincidence?

Didn't seem that way at the time.

♦ ♦ ♦

Rav Mordechai Aharon shared the following incident with me.

When Rav Elyashiv was nearing the end of his life and the doctors had already given up hope, Rav Mordechai Aharon was approached by a certain individual who wanted to know whether from a halachic perspective one was supposed to pray for a person who had one foot in the *Olam HaEmes*.

"I had the same *she'eilah* a while back," Rav Mordechai Aharon told the man. "My father was lying in the hospital bed. The doctors had all but given up hope for a recovery. It seemed to me that at that point there was no reason to daven for him any longer. And so I stopped. With the best of intentions. It was a wasted prayer.

"Two nights later I had a dream, in which my father appeared to me. 'Why aren't you davening for me any longer?' he demanded.

" 'The doctors said that you're no longer here,' I replied, 'and that you've already moved on in everything but body. I thought that there was no reason to daven any longer.'

" 'You see that I know what's happening around me,' came my father's response. 'You see that I know.'

"That dream taught me a lesson I never forgot. To cease davening for a person, even when he is 'gone,' even when there's no chance or purpose, cannot be an option."

In the end, Rav Elyashiv had a number of amazing recoveries before he was ultimately *niftar*. Who can judge how vital those prayers were when it came to keeping him here with us in this world?

♦ ♦ ♦

Rav Nachman Dubinki and Rav Mordechai Aharon Scheinberger were *chaveirim*. Their *neshamos* were united and bound up with the love true Torah scholars possess for one another.

Ten years before Rav Nachman passed away, he approached Rav Mordechai Aharon with a request.

Rav Mordechai Aharon reassured his friend that he would do anything for him.

"In that case," said Rav Nachman, "I would like to give you a certain amount of money for you to distribute to the poor at my *levayah*."

The request hit Rav Mordechai Aharon like a pile of bricks falling off a high building. After all, who likes to hear talk about a "*Yedid Nefesh*" leaving this world for the next? And besides, how did Rav Nachman know that his turn to leave was going to come before Rav Mordechai Aharon's? Still, this was his request.

It wasn't often that Rav Nachman asked anything of anyone and Rav Mordechai Aharon did not feel capable of turning him down. He accepted the proffered bundle of money, stowing it away in a safe place for the next 10 years. And yes, Rav Nachman did end up passing away first, and Rav Mordechai kept his promise to distribute the money.

How did Rav Nachman know that his time would come first? There is no way to answer.

◆ ◆ ◆

While Tel Aviv boasts that it is the city that never sleeps, many sections of Yerushalayim are fairly quiet at a relatively early hour. For the most part, Yerushalayim is not a party town. But though there may not be much going on that can be termed "nightlife," there's an entirely different type of nightlife happening beneath the surface and out of view. My eyes were opened to this undeniably attractive benefit to living in the Holy City on the night that I spent in the shul in Batei Broide prior to celebrating a *siyum* the following morning.

I'll never forget that night.

It was 3:30 in the morning. My *chavrusa* and I were firmly entrenched in the final *daf* of the *masechta*, when all of a sudden the doors leading into the shul swung open and a tiny man came striding inside, huffing with exertion. He was elderly and

Rav Meir Shachor at the
entrance to his home

walked with a limp, but he moved with undeniable *zerizus* and
fluidity. He climbed onto the benches and began adjusting the
curtains. He then moved to the back of the room and started fid-
dling around with the ancient oven used to heat up the shul. He
lit the candles by the *amud* and opened the *aron kodesh* to check
on the *sifrei Torah* inside.

He did everything with quick, practiced movements, paying us
no heed as he went about his regular routine. When he finished,
he sat down at one of the tables, opened a Gemara, and commenced
with his own learning. He studied with an almost childish sweetness, with a *niggun*, like a young boy's first taste of Torah. When
he finished learning, it was still half an hour before the first person
would be arriving for *neitz*. He opened up his siddur and started
from the beginning. *Modeh Ani...Pitum HaKetores*...everything
with a tune, with a *niggun*, with such an easy, pleasant manner.

Who is this Yid? I wondered.

Later on I asked Rav Yitzchok Nosson's Rebbetzin about the tiny man with the boundless energy.

"Ah, you mean Rav Meir Shachor. He's a *tzaddik*, and the son of a *tzaddik*."

Once I heard the name, I had to know a little bit more about him. It turned out that Rav Meir Shachor resided in Shikun HaRabbanim, a somewhat famous residential neighborhood one block from the Jerusalem Central Bus Station. From his home to Batei Broide was a good 15- to 20-minute walk, especially for a man of Rav Meir's advanced age. Yet every morning he'd walk to the shul in the dead of night — winter or summer, it mattered not — to make sure that everything was ready for the morning regulars who depended on him to open the shul for them.

Here he was, a man who rose in the middle of the night to serve his Creator — who learned and davened and sang like a saint — and he was so quiet that hardly anyone outside his own circle had ever heard of him.

After he finished his morning *avodah* at the shul in Batei Broide, he'd continue his day with a *seder* at Etz Chaim and another *seder* at Yeshivas Sha'ar HaShamayim with the *mekubalim* of Yerushalayim. Back-to-back learning sessions, just like a young man of 30!

I began bringing people to Rav Meir for *berachos*, and he handed them out like candy — along with a *vort* or a beautiful Torah thought. The more I found out about him, the more I understood the greatness hidden within this extraordinary individual. He was a man who had never hurt another person. He never said a bad word about anyone or fought with another human being.

There are *tzaddikim* and leaders with huge courts and *gabbaim* galore who are visited by hundreds of people daily. Then there are the hidden *tzaddikim*: men of advanced age keeping impossible daily schedules and filling their every moment with *avodas Hashem*. They are mostly unknown to anyone outside their immediate neighborhood. How interesting it is that these two worlds of *gedolim* are operating side by side.

Rav Michel Shurkin, a noted *talmid chacham*, related a story about Rav Moshe Feinstein, *zt"l*, in one of his *sefarim*. There was an elderly Yid living on the Lower East Side, Rav Yaakov Safsel, who was known as the Visker Ilui. When he passed away, Rav Moshe eulogized him at his funeral.

"There are two types of *gedolim*," Rav Moshe said. "The first is constantly in the spotlight, known to one and all. His opinion is sought after and everyone knows who he is. The second kind of *gadol* is like the Visker Ilui: sitting in an old-age home, forgotten by the world, with no one knowing who he was despite the fact that he knew all of Torah!

"Who does the *Ribbono shel Olam* treasure more?" Rav Moshe asked the people at the funeral. "The well-known leader and the famous *tzaddik*, right?

"The truth is," concluded Rav Moshe, "that it's not that way at all. Hashem prefers the unknown *tzaddik*, the person whom nobody knows, the hidden man of glory. '*El zeh abit el ani u'nicheih ruach v'chareid al devari* — It is to this that I look: to the poor and broken-spirited one who is zealous regarding My word' (*Yeshayahu* 66:2)."

The *tzaddikim* of Yerushalayim personified this. They walked the streets, and no one gave them a second glance. Men who held the entire Torah on their fingertips, men who loved their fellow Jew and only had words of warmth for friend and stranger alike. I observed and followed them, I studied them, and it was clear to me that these men of the "Sacred Society" were beloved by Heaven.

◆ ◆ ◆

Rav Meir lived on the third floor of his building. One day he fell and had to live in a rehabilitation center for a few months, where he underwent physical therapy and was retaught how to walk. I went to visit him at the center, and I wondered what he was going to do when he was allowed to return home. How was this tiny powerhouse of spirit going to run up and down three flights of stairs to catch his *minyanim*?

It wasn't as if he could just move to a lower apartment, because Shikun HaRabbanim is a neighborhood where homes are handed down from one generation to the next and seldom put on the market. The chance of Rav Meir being able to purchase an apartment on a lower floor was virtually nil.

But in a fascinating twist of *hashgachah*, the moment Rav Meir was released from the rehabilitation center an apartment became available on the lowest floor, one building over from where he lived, and he moved right in.

◆ ◆ ◆

Many times I brought people to Rav Meir for *berachos* for all sorts of challenges. I cannot tell you how many times the supplicants felt that there had been a layer of *ruach hakodesh* present in his blessing. Rav Meir didn't just give a *berachah*. He'd always compose a *mashal*, a parable to go with the blessing, and in those parables the people would see themselves in a way that was uncanny.

Once I took a friend of mine to see Rav Meir. His wife was about to give birth and he wanted a *berachah* for "a *leidah kalah*," an easy birth. Rav Meir began to bless him, but unlike his normal blessings, on this particular occasion it took him 10 minutes to get it out. It was extremely unusual.

"A man walks into a fruit store and wants to purchase a kilo of oranges," he would say. "The man behind the counter, however, hands him more than he needs. So you should receive even more than you need..." That was his normal method and procedure.

On this day, however, Rav Meir started with one parable and then moved on to another one. Then another. While usually satisfied with his first *mashal*, that day he kept on stopping and starting another one. I couldn't understand what was happening. So many *meshalim*, but no actual *berachah*! Finally, after about 10 minutes, he succeeded in formulating a *berachah* that he found satisfactory.

My friend's wife gave birth a few days later. He called me first thing in the morning.

"Binyomin," he exclaimed in a voice filled with emotion, "you can't imagine the danger she was in! She was bleeding uncontrollably, and the doctors didn't know what to do. It was an emergency situation, touch and go in a way that had us thinking the worst! Binyomin, the fact that she's alive right now is a miracle!"

Then he paused.

"Binyomin, do you recall how we went to Rav Meir Shachor for a *berachah* and how long it took him to find the right words for us? How he kept on rephrasing the *berachah* and trying to do it better and more effectively? There is no doubt in my mind that Rav Meir was privy to some hidden information and was pulling strings for us all through the *berachah* that never ended. Binyomin, those 10 minutes were the most well-spent 10 minutes of my life!"

So humble, so simple, so unfailingly gracious, so righteous, and yet unknown and hidden, living his life like a servant of Hashem. That was Rav Meir Shachor, may his merit protect us, a charter member in good standing of Yerushalayim's "Holy Society of *Tzaddikim*."

The Hidden Ones
Part D

Rav Yitzchok Zilber

During one of my visits to Rav Chaim Sarna, *zt"l*, the esteemed *Rosh Yeshivah* of Chevron Yeshivah, there was a knock on the door. Standing on the doorstep was Rav Yitzchok Zilber.

Many of Yerushalayim's most outstanding residents claimed that Rav Yitzchok Zilber was one of the 36 hidden *tzaddikim* of the generation. Rav Beinish Finkel said it about him, and Rav Elyashiv concurred.

Rav Yitzchok spent many years of his life under Communist rule in Russia. KGB. Siberia. Midnight knocks on the door. He never once was *mechallel Shabbos*, notwithstanding the insane pressure of his society. Some dubbed him the Chafetz Chaim of Russian Jewry.

I'd heard about Rav Yitzchok while still learning in America, and it turned out that he was a first cousin of my grandfather. I took that bit of news as an invitation to develop a relationship with the master of *mesirus nefesh*.

The most famous story that everyone used to tell about Rav Yitzchok took place directly after he arrived in Eretz Yisrael, after finally being allowed to leave the Soviet Union. One of Rav Yitzchok's first stops upon reaching Israeli shores was Yeshivas Mir, where he presented his 15-year-old son to the *Rosh Yeshivah*, Rav Chaim Shmulevitz, *zt"l*, and asked that he be accepted as a member of the student body.

One detail worth mentioning: his son was wearing a pair of shorts at the time.

Rav Chaim's sharp gaze took in the young boy, still nowhere near ready to learn in the Mir. And the shorts! His mode of dress was clearly not appropriate for a *yeshivah bachur*, and Rav Chaim felt that he had no choice but to turn down the Russian father's request.

Rav Yitzchok began to cry.

"What could we do? It was so hard — I did my best — I managed to learn with him the three *Bava*s —"

"The three *Bava*s?" wondered Rav Chaim. "*Bava Kamma, Metzia,* and *Basra*?"

Rav Yitzchok nodded.

Rav Chaim tested the boy. He knew all three *masechta*s backward and forward! Rav Chaim broke down in tears. He rose, went into the Mir Yeshivah study hall, and gave a sharp rap on the *bimah*. The room grew silent. He then delivered a blistering *mussar shmuess* about how this 15-year-old boy's achievements in Torah created an awesome obligation on every *ben Torah* alive.

"If this youngster could master three of the longest and most arduous *masechta*s in *Shas* while living under the dark cloud of the KGB and the threat of being deported to Siberia, then what are we going to say in our defense when the time comes for us to stand before Hashem?"

That 15-year-old boy in shorts grew up to become Rav Bentzion Zilber, a venerable member of Yerushalayim's society of *talmidei chachamim*.

◆ ◆ ◆

Rav Yitzchok took the responsibility for Israel's Russian Jews onto his broad shoulders. *Brisos, kiddushin, agunos*...he was constantly busy trying to fan the flames of religion among his brethren. He did all this in a very quiet yet effective way. Rav Chaim Sarna's Rebbetzin was involved in similar projects, and Rav Yitzchok would come to consult with her from time to time, and that's why he had arrived at the Sarna home that day.

As Rav Yitzchok was concluding his conversation with the Rebbetzin, Rav Chaim turned to me and said, "I'm going to show you something."

I waited to see what Rav Chaim had in mind. Calling Rav Yitzchok over to his side, he began whispering into his ear. Immediately, Rav Yitzchok rose and told Rav Chaim in abrupt tones that he had to leave.

After the door closed, Rav Chaim said to me, "Do you want to know what I told him?"

I nodded.

"I began discussing one of the *chesed* operations that he controls. Rav Yitzchok refuses to talk about himself and the amazing work he does. The moment I mentioned anything that smacked even faintly of praise, he was up and out the door!

"The fact that Rav Yitzchok is one of the thirty-six hidden *tzaddikim* is not even a question," said Rav Chaim decisively. "The only question is whether the remaining thirty-five are on the same level as he is."

◆ ◆ ◆

One of the things I enjoy most of all is when I have the opportunity to introduce two of the *tzaddikim* I know to each other. Rav Dovid Barkin, my rebbi at Telshe, sent me to learn under the tutelage of Rav Asher Arieli in the Mir. Though he had sent numerous *bachurim* to Rav Asher's *shiur* over the years, the two had never met. It was my pleasure to introduce them to each other. Here, too, I had the privilege of introducing Rav Yitzchok Zilber to Rav Yitzchok Nosson Kupershtok at the *bris* of one of our sons.

Rav Yitzchok Zilber meeting Rav Yitzchok Nosson Kupershtok
at our son's *bris*

I named this son after my grandfather and honored Rav
Yitzchok Zilber with *krias hashem*, with the privilege of announc-
ing the name of the newborn, since he was my grandfather's first
cousin. When the time came for Rav Yitzchok to announce the
baby's name, he recited the relatively lengthy text preceding the
announcement of the name by heart with astounding fluidity.
After the ceremony's conclusion, Rav Yitzchok Nosson turned to
Rav Yitzchok and said, "I've never seen anyone recite the *nusach*
of *krias hashem* by heart before."

"I wasn't by one *bris* and not by 100 *brisos*," Rav Yitzchok
explained. "I officiated at over 10,000 *brisos*."

In Russia, behind the scenes, while hiding from the KGB, in
the basements and cellars, Rav Yitzchok was the one arranging
everything. Yes, you could believe that he knew the *nusach* by
heart!

◆ ◆ ◆

"Your *zeide*," Rav Yitzchok said to me on more than one occasion, "possesses a one-of-a-kind *zehirus* (scrupulous carefulness) when it comes to heeding the laws of *lashon hara*."

I didn't know what he meant by that or even how he would have come to know such a thing. True, they were cousins, and they had even met on a few occasions, but while my *zeide* lived in the States, Rav Yitzchok had been in Russia and later Israel. Yet he discoursed on my grandfather's meticulousness in matters pertaining to *shemiras halashon* with such confidence!

On one of my grandfather's visits to Eretz Yisrael, Rav Yitzchok arranged to bring several of his children and grandchildren to meet him. "I want you all to meet an *ehrliche Yid*," Rav Yitzchok explained to his family. "There aren't that many left in the world. He is one of a handful."

I was taken aback by this strong statement. I was surprised and a little curious by what he meant.

In much the same way that Rav Chaim Sarna had wanted to show me who Rav Yitzchok was, so did Rav Yitzchok want to show who my grandfather was. The entire group sat in the hotel room shmoozing and enjoying one another's company, when Rav Yitzchok turned to his children and gave them a meaningful glance. I realized he was hinting to them that he was about to show them what my *zeide* and his "*ehrlichkeit*" were all about.

I watched the two elderly cousins engaging in warm conversation. Suddenly, out of the blue, Rav Yitzchok asked my *zeide* about a certain relative of theirs. My *zeide* had been having a good time up until then. His face had been shining with friendliness and the pleasure of spending time with his old friend and cousin. Yet the moment he heard Rav Yitzchok's question, he became completely serious. The change in atmosphere was something to see. He slapped the table with his hand and asked his cousin, "*Hertz zich ein* — listen to me, Rav Yitzchok. Is there any *to'eles* (reason) for this conversation?"

Rav Yitzchok turned to his family, a huge smile plastered across his face as he proved his point about my grandfather —

his gleeful expression speaking volumes without his even saying a word.

My grandfather had no idea what was happening, but Rav Yitzchok was showing his family and me how even when two cousins who almost never had the opportunity to get together, and were finally meeting after all this time, even then, in the midst of their heart-to-heart conversations, if someone started discussing someone else with the *possibility* that the conversation might possibly lead to *lashon hara*, my *zeide* reacted like a man who'd just realized he was walking in a minefield.

It was then that I understood exactly what Rav Yitzchok meant when he called my grandfather an *ehrliche Yid* of the type that didn't exist anymore.

◆ ◆ ◆

When my grandfather passed away, Rav Yitzchok was recovering from open-heart surgery. He eulogized my grandfather — the funeral was in Sanhedria, not far from his home — but no one expected him to come be *menachem avel* at the *shivah* in Bayit Vegan. And yet Rav Yitzchok arrived, a man in his 80's, heart surgery or no heart surgery, and he shlepped his ravaged body up three flights of stairs because the building was old and had no elevator. Three flights couldn't stop the man who had walked three or four miles through the Siberian tundra to catch a *minyan*.

He took a seat before my uncle. They looked at each other.

"Just promise me one thing." He was still out of breath from his arduous climb up the stairs.

"Anything," my uncle replied.

"Don't tell my son that I was here."

◆ ◆ ◆

One day I came over to visit Rav Yitzchok when he was already very old and sick. My heart went out to see him lying on the couch, coughing, hacking, gasping, every breath coming with excruciating effort and pain.

At the home of Rav Yitzchok Zilber

There was a Russian man seated across from Rav Yitzchok, and the two of them were conversing half in Russian, half in Yiddish. From what I understood, the man's wife was sick, and Rav Yitzchok was asking him whether he had called a certain doctor or not.

The man shook his head in the negative.

Rav Yitzchok pulled himself off the couch. It took him a long time, even with the help of those in the room. Grunting and groaning, he eventually managed to rise to his feet, body still heaving from his wracking coughs. He then walked over to the phone hanging on the wall and called the doctor himself.

Not enough that he was so sick, not enough that this man had somehow managed to get in to see him when he could barely move. Not enough that he should care enough to inquire about the man's wife's health and recommend a doctor. But that he should rise in his condition to make the appointment himself — that was something I had never seen in my life.

❖ ❖ ❖

For a while I learned in a *kollel* in Yerushalayim that had opened up not long before and was still not registered with the government office that provided funding to yeshivos. There was really no reason for the funding's delay; it was pure bureaucracy and nothing to be overly excited about. The problem lay in the fact that the yeshivah was operating on the assumption that the money would be coming soon. Without the funding, it was all over, and they were rapidly reaching a point of no return. If the funding didn't arrive momentarily, the entire institution was going to disintegrate.

It had reached a point where the secretary's primary task was to get up in the morning and go to try and find out what new delays were in the works for that day. All the papers were in order. All the procedures had been followed. Everything was ready for a bank transfer: a bank transfer that just wasn't arriving.

I could see that the *Rosh Yeshivah* was suffering immensely from the pressure and the mounting debt, which was approaching $100,000. I gave the matter some thought and eventually I hit upon a plan.

"Rav Yitzchok Zilber is my cousin and we have a relationship —"

"Go on," he prodded me.

"Anyway, Rav Yitzchok is one of the nicest people I know and helps anyone who comes to see him if he can. One of Rav Yitzchok's sons-in-law is an influential person in government circles. It might be a good idea to ask him to intercede for you with the people who hold the strings. Let's go talk to him and tell him that the yeshivah's entire existence is currently in danger. I'm sure he'll be willing to help us as much as possible."

We set up a date for the meeting.

To my immense surprise, the *Rosh Yeshivah* got into the car with a few of his younger children in tow. I didn't understand why he was bringing little kids to a crucial meeting, but I said nothing. We arrived at Rav Yitzchok's house, and when we knocked on the door, Rav Yitzchok said, "Are you here with a car?"

We nodded.

"Perfect."

We looked at each other in surprise.

"Today is my wife's *yahrtzeit*, and I need to get to Har HaMenuchos right about now. It would be a big help if we could all go there together."

An unexpected request, but maybe it was all for the good. This way, we would have Rav Yitzchok all to ourselves, a captive audience, as it were, until we arrived at the cemetery. It would give the *Rosh Yeshivah* plenty of time to explain his predicament. But the second he entered the car, Rav Yitzchok told us his wife's name and said, "This drive will give us the perfect amount of time to learn *mishnayos* for my wife's memory." He then proceeded to launch into *mishnah* after *mishnah*, all recited by heart, giving us no chance to plead our cause.

We pulled up at the cemetery, and suddenly I realized that if we were there for his wife's *yahrtzeit*, it was safe to assume that his son-in-law would be there, too.

He was.

I stood there, racking my brain, trying to figure out what course of action to take. There was no time to discuss the matter with Rav Yitzchok. He didn't even know that we were hoping for some intervention with his son-in-law. What to do?

As if all this wasn't sufficient, the *Rosh Yeshivah*'s children began acting up, as little kids do. Oblivious to their father's pressures at the *kollel*, they were horsing around and fighting with one another, and it reached the point where they began disturbing the crowd as they recited *Tehillim* for the *nifteres*.

As soon as the group concluded their *Tehillim*, I decided to approach the son-in-law. True, we had never met and didn't know each other at all, but he was standing right beside Rav Yitzchok and I figured, *This is it. Our big chance.*

The *Rosh Yeshivah* and I approached and asked him if we could have five minutes of his time. He graciously agreed. The *Rosh Yeshivah* launched into a description of the seriousness of his situation. The rabbi politician listened, or tried to, because the *Rosh Yeshivah*'s kids had run out of patience at that point, and their crying and general antics were completely out of hand — all this as their father stood there, begging and crying for the very existence of his yeshivah!

The children were pulling at their father's arm and trying to shlep him out of the cemetery and over to the car. "Abba, come already! Abba, come already!" They wanted to leave and they wanted to leave now, and there was nothing to discuss.

Rav Yitzchok's son-in-law saw what was going on. He took in the father's stressed look, the pressure on his face, and the children pulling on his arms without letup.

"Tell me quickly," he said with great kindness. "What is it that you need?"

The *Rosh Yeshivah* went straight to the point. Told him the issue. The son-in-law listened. Nodded his head. The fact that the children were there clearly made him feel sympathy for the poor harried *Rosh Yeshivah* and inevitably more open to helping him with all the considerable tools at his disposal. In the end, a conversation that could have taken an hour with no guaranteed results took five minutes.

"I'll be at the office tomorrow. I'll speak to them."

Everyone shook hands all around. Two weeks later, the yeshivah received the money. The yeshivah was saved, and the *hashgachah* we witnessed that day remains embedded in my memory.

The Hidden Ones

PART E

Rav Sraya Diblitzky

B nei Brak is a city congested with both vehicular and foot traffic. Having originally come into being as a small agricultural village over 100 years ago, many of its streets are not equipped to handle an influx of cars. Yet the city's main thoroughfares have adapted to modern-day life and are filled with the perpetual motion and commotion of hundreds of buses and cars throughout the day.

Busiest among them is Rabbi Akiva Street, home to hundreds of businesses of all kinds. But come Shabbos, the turbulent and exhaust-filled street closes down to traffic and is instead crowded with hundreds of people tranquilly strolling home from shul or on their way to visit friends and family.

Numerous smaller streets branch off of Rabbi Akiva Street, leading to other parts of the city. One of the most famous of all is Yerushalayim Street, where the city's municipality is located and which skirts the boundaries of Ramat Gan.

In the middle of Yerushalayim Street, not far from a beautiful park and Bnei Brak's seat of government, stands the private home of one of Bnei Brak's lesser-known Torah dignitaries: Rav Sraya Diblitzky. Originally constructed by Rav Sraya's father, a wealthy businessman, decades earlier, the house stands alone, apart from the nearby homes and buildings. Rav Sraya spends the majority of his days in his study learning by himself, quiet, unassuming, not making any waves.

Rav Sraya Diblitzky is the author of over 60 *sefarim*, many of them on different areas of halachah. He is also an expert on the *minhagim* and traditions of all Jewish communities worldwide.

Rav Sraya's father had been a very wealthy man back in Riga, the owner of a successful chocolate factory, and he had developed close relationships with the *gedolim* of the day when the family moved to Eretz Yisrael. Rav Sraya was an only child whose natural aptitude for learning had been recognizable from a young age. He was beloved by the Chazon Ish, who even came to visit him when he'd been hospitalized as a child.

Rav Sraya identified no one place as his yeshivah. He'd sat at the feet of the Chazon Ish and other *gedolim* in Bnei Brak, and in Tel Aviv he'd learned for months at "Beis Knesses HaGra," a shul where he gleaned gems of Torah from the *talmidim* of the Vilna Gaon. He'd spent much time in Yerushalayim as well, in close proximity to men such as Rav Yaakov Moshe Charlap and Rav Dovid Baharan: men who were representative of an entire generation of true *ovdei Hashem*. He carefully observed the *tzaddikim* of Sha'arei Chesed and recorded their individual *minhagim*, and he visited the study halls of Kaminetz and Chevron, where he got to know many of today's *rabbanim* and leaders. Eventually he became noted in the fields of *dikduk*, halachah, and Kabbalah, achieving a powerful proficiency in all three.

Most of his *minhagim* are in accordance with the Vilna Gaon, and Rav Sraya is considered by many to be the primary expert on the Gaon's *minhagim* alive today. On the other hand, many of his *minhagim* also come from Sephardic or even Yemenite sources, not to mention a few whose origins lie in the world of Chabad. Rav Sraya does not wear a frock and sports a short beard. While not shunning the spotlight completely, he is more than happy to remain in the shadows learning undisturbed for hours at a time.

His *sefarim* are highly erudite pieces of work and give first-hand testimony to how he has spent the last 80 years of his life. He has written *sefarim* on the laws of mourning, *Tikkun Chatzos, hilchos sheva berachos*, and many other areas of halachah, his focus directed toward the halachos that are lesser known, the goal of his work to bring clarity to obscure and little-known topics. His *sefarim* are complete treatises on individual mitzvos in which he outlines how to perform the mitzvah in the most scrupulous way possible both from a *nigleh*, revealed, and *nistar*, hidden, perspective.

Rav Sraya spends his entire day learning while clad in tallis and tefillin. On the one hand, he is a tremendous *oveid Hashem* in a very intense way and, on the other, very much a person who greets everyone he meets with a smiling, happy face. If there is an inherent contradiction between the two paths, Rav Sraya didn't get the memo.

He is a man who is extremely pressured for time, with *sedarim* arranged around the clock. Yet his internal pressure gauge seemingly turns off when people visit him seeking his advice and sage counsel. With them, Rav Sraya has patience and a true listening ear.

◆ ◆ ◆

After coming across some of Rav Sraya's *haskamos* for assorted *sefarim*, I realized that here was one man I just had to meet. Obtaining his address wasn't difficult as it was printed on the stationery he used when writing his *haskamos*.

The Egged bus dropped me off not far from his home, and I simply knocked on his door and introduced myself. He welcomed me into his life, and from that time onward we developed a rela-

Visiting with Rav Sraya Diblitzky in his *succah*

tionship. Any time I had a question in halachah, Rav Sraya was familiar with the *sugya* and was able to provide a comprehensive response within seconds of hearing the question.

There is a halachah in *Shulchan Aruch* that states (*Orach Chaim* 307) that a person should refrain from discussing mundane matters on Shabbos. This is a level that most of us would feel is almost impossible to achieve. How difficult is it really? Consider the following.

Someone once approached Rav Chaim Kanievsky to ask his advice about a certain difficult challenge he was undergoing.

"I can either give you something easy to do or something difficult."

"Give me the difficult thing," the man said decisively.

"If you want the more difficult *avodah*, accept upon yourself never to discuss weekday matters on Shabbos."

The questioner was taken aback. Was this so difficult a task?

The truth is, any person who has tried to actually fulfill *Chazal's* dictum to speak only holy words throughout the entire Shabbos knows just how challenging it can be.

Rav Sraya meets that challenge. There were times throughout the years, primarily when my wife had recently given birth and was still in the hospital, that I had the opportunity to spend Shabbos with Rav Sraya. It was an incredible experience to watch a person whose entire essence never strayed from words of holiness for more than 25 uninterrupted hours.

Rav Sraya repeatedly points out throughout his *sefarim* that people should take this halachah more seriously, and he includes practical ideas to help people achieve this lofty level. For example, Rav Sraya writes that while he lives alone, which makes it easier for him not to discuss mundane matters on Shabbos, what about people who have guests or family members at their Shabbos table? How are they supposed to manage the conversation?

He concludes that it all depends on how much a person has prepared before the meal. If a person takes the time to prepare interesting Torah ideas appropriate for the crowd at his table, he can ensure that the conversation remains appropriate and enjoyable.

Most of us have grown up with a picture in our minds of the Chafetz Chaim's one-of-a-kind determination to shield his mouth from uttering *lashon hara* of any kind. We have all heard countless stories about his awesome sensitivity to *shemiras halashon*. Yet impressed as we are, it's hard for us to believe that people can actually live this type of life in today's society. It seems like a mission impossible.

Rav Sraya is proof: it's not impossible.

◆ ◆ ◆

We were at the Shabbos table enjoying our *seudah* on a Shabbos that I spent in Rav Sraya's home. He delivers a number of *shiurim* at a nearby yeshivah every Shabbos and usually invites a few of the *bachurim* to his home for one of the meals. One of the guests sitting at the table mentioned the name of a certain person. He didn't say anything negative about that person, merely mentioned a name. Immediately Rav Sraya brought his hand down on the table three or four times, bringing that particular conversation to a halt.

We have all seen how rapidly a conversation may at times transform itself from praising a certain individual to pointing out all their annoying character traits. It happens all the time. But not when there's a firm rule in the house that precludes all discussion of other people.

◆ ◆ ◆

Taciturn by nature, it's almost impossible to have a conversation with Rav Sraya about mundane matters. Though he might relate a story or two in the *succah* during *Chol Hamo'ed*, in general those occasions are few and far between. The fact that he keeps to himself made it extremely difficult for me to get to know him on a deeper level. Yet he intrigued me as a person, and I found myself drawn to try harder. I couldn't help wondering who Rav Sraya was and how I'd be able to discover his essence.

I eventually concluded that it might be best to approach my quest from the direction of Rav Sraya's friends. With persistence comes clarity, and eventually I managed to discover Rav Shmuel, one of his longtime *chavrusa*s, with whom Rav Sraya studied Kabbalah twice a week.

When I met Rav Shmuel, I found myself face-to-face with a *chassidishe* Yid in his mid-40's. The conversation flowed freely between us.

"I always knew that Rav Sraya was a *yachid b'doro*, unique in his generation, when it comes to refraining from *lashon hara*," he told me.

"Please tell me more about him. Stories I never heard."

Rav Shmuel acquiesced.

"One day when I arrived for our learning session, I found Rav Sraya suffering from an illness. Before we opened our *sefarim* and started to learn, Rav Sraya turned and looked me in the eye.

" 'Rav Shmuel?'

" 'Yes?'

" '*Chazal* tell us that when a person isn't feeling well, he should search for the good deeds that he has managed to accomplish and mention their merits aloud.'

"I nodded my head.

" 'Rav Shmuel,' he said to me with extreme seriousness, 'how long have we known each other?'

" 'About eight years,' I replied.

"Tell me then, Rav Shmuel: in the eight years that we have known each other, can you testify that you have never heard me utter a word of *lashon hara*?'

" 'Yes, I can,' I told him emphatically.

"Rav Sraya seemed satisfied by my declaration.

" 'So you can testify about the last eight years, and I can add testimony about the 52 years preceding those, in which I merited to hold myself back from uttering even one word of *lashon hara* in all that time.' "

This was no joking matter. This was Rav Sraya searching for merits to save himself from illness.

How many of us can stand before our Creator and testify that not one word of *lashon hara* crossed our lips in 60 years?

On another occasion I brought a group of people in to see Rav Sraya. These people were extremely meticulous when it came to *shemiras halashon*, and knowing what such information would mean to them, I related Rav Shmuel's story before we went in to see Rav Sraya. Of course, they were astounded. A few minutes into the meeting one of the group raised the topic that was on everyone's mind.

"Rebbi," he began, "we are constantly trying to better ourselves in the area of *shemiras halashon*. We learn the Chafetz Chaim's *sefer* daily and try to incorporate its message into our lives. But we are still human, and we don't always succeed. Rebbi, please tell us, how? How does a person manage to abstain from *lashon hara* for 60 years? We want to know the secret!"

Everyone in the room leaned forward, anticipating Rav Sraya's response. To their surprise, Rav Sraya laughed. Then he grew more serious.

"*Rabbosai*, I want to tell you all something."

They were tense, expectant.

"Not speaking *lashon hara* for 60 years is not the most difficult thing in the world. A person can accept this upon himself and is capable of achieving this feat. The more difficult task, however, is knowing what one is allowed to say at those times when he absolutely must speak. Abstaining from speech is doable. The real problem begins when you have to speak, when halachah obligates you to talk; then you have to really know what you are allowed to say and what not."

With those few sentences, Rav Sraya showed his visitors that even a man such as he — even a man able to testify to 60 *lashon hara*-free years — was still daunted by the myriad complex challenges of *shemiras halashon*.

◆　◆　◆

Knowing that Rav Sraya had written a *sefer* on the topic of *Tikkun Chatzos*, basically a how-to manual of when and how to do it, and that he never missed reciting *Tikkun Chatzos*, no matter what the circumstances — knowing all that, I found myself wanting to see Rav Sraya in action. I wanted to see the master at work. The only question was how to actually accomplish it.

Eventually I came up with a solution.

I arrived in Bnei Brak late one night with an overnight bag and my tallis and tefillin. I alighted at the stop closest to his home and knocked on the familiar door. Rav Sraya was pleasantly surprised to see me and invited me into his home.

Though his wife had passed away years earlier, the house was alive and vibrant with the sounds of Torah. Leading the way into his study, Rav Sraya bade me sit and asked me with concern, "Reb Binyomin, it's already very late. Do you have a bus back to your home at this hour?"

"No," I replied simply. "The last bus to my house left Bnei Brak hours ago."

"Where were you planning on sleeping then?"

"It's not a problem," I explained. "There are any number of *batei medrash* close by where I can go and learn for the rest of the night. If I need to sleep, I can always lay my head down on a *shtender* or something."

I had been hoping for his response, and it came.

"No, no, Reb Binyomin. Of course you can stay in my home tonight."

Rav Sraya accompanied me to one of his many bedrooms and set me up for the night, making sure I was comfortable and had everything I could possibly need.

I wasn't sure of my next move. Though he had written a comprehensive work on the subject of *Tikkun Chatzos* and made no secret of how important a place this mitzvah occupied in his life, I didn't feel comfortable asking him for permission to let me sit in the study with him while he went about his *avodah,* but I hoped that Rav Sraya would leave his door open while he mourned the destruction of the Beis HaMikdash.

To my immense joy and relief, he did.

Not only didn't he close the door, but when he began reciting the words of the *Tikkun,* it was in a very loud voice, giving me the opportunity I so craved.

Rav Sraya was about 80 years old at the time of my late-night visit to his home. I knew that there was a cushionless couch in his study, and that he would take a short rest on its uncomfortable surface before rising at 10 minutes before *chatzos.* I heard him leave the study and make his way to the kitchen, where he poured himself a drink and made a loud *berachah.* Then he returned to his study to commence the *Tikkun Chatzos.*

His *avodah* began with a recitation of the *Tikkun's* introductory chapters of *Tehillim.* He chanted them one by one, slowly, feeling each of the words.

A few chapters of *Zohar* were next on the list, and they were followed by additional *tefillos,* which Rav Sraya uttered word by word with immense concentration. You could hear him savoring every syllable. It went on and on, lasting about an hour and a half. It was incredible to listen to it. Here was an elderly man, and he had taken upon himself the type of *avodas Hashem* that men half his age wouldn't have been able to sustain for more than a few nights. Yet he managed it every night without fail.

But the thing that impressed me most about his *Tikkun Chatzos* was yet to come.

◆ ◆ ◆

Many times when people come to Rav Chaim Kanievsky for a *berachah*, they tell him why they've come and he answers them with "*berachah v'hatzlachah.*" These days he has taken it a step further and shortened what was his standard two-word *berachah* into the one word "*buha,*" which is an abbreviation for "*berachah v'hatzlachah.*"

On one occasion, when Rav Chaim responded to a supplicant with "*berachah v'hatzlachah,*" the man made a face. It was obvious that he was disappointed by Rav Chaim's brevity.

Rav Chaim took note of the man's reaction.

"What's the matter?" he asked him. "*Berachah v'hatzlachah* includes everything you are asking for. It's all-inclusive."

Rav Sraya wasn't even content with "*buha.*" Instead, he'd wait for the person seeking his blessing to tell him what it was that he wanted, and then Rav Sraya would answer "*amen.*" Of course, people would rather hear a lengthy blessing, but Rav Sraya didn't see the point and contented himself with "*Amen,* may your needs be fulfilled."

On the night I merited to witness Rav Sraya's *Tikkun Chatzos,* however, I came to realize that it wasn't as simple as all that. After Rav Sraya finished the *Tikkun,* he ended his evening supplications with a "*Yehi Ratzon*" in which he included "all the people that came over to me today for *berachos,* and those who called on the phone, or people I was told about who are suffering and need a *yeshuah.* All the *tefillos* should be accepted...."

The litany went on and on, and showed me that whereas his answers to the people themselves may have been limited to a one word — "*amen*" — the people whom he blessed never really left his mind, heart, or prayers. While people everywhere were sleeping comfortably in their beds, Rav Sraya was beseeching Hashem for those in need from the depths of his heart.

You should never be disappointed by a *tzaddik's berachah*, because you can never know how much time and energy he will invest in davening for you after you leave. That point was hammered home to me that night, and I never forgot it.

Even Rav Refael Levin, who went out of his way to bless people with long and detailed *berachos*, had another *minhag* that I found out about from people who actually witnessed it. Every morning, when Rav Refael and his Rebbetzin came to open the shul before *vasikin*, they'd approach the *aron kodesh*, open it up, and then the two of them, Rav Refael and his wife, would literally shed tears for all the people who had come to see them for *berachos* and advice on the previous day. Real tears.

People may have thought that Rav Refael forgot about them after they left his home, but that wasn't the case. For Rav Refael and his wife, their efforts for those individuals was just beginning. It meant davening for them at special times — It meant crying for them — It meant that the Levin family would now begin carrying that person in their hearts.

When I left Rav Sraya's home the following morning, my mind was filled with everything I'd heard. Though I had barely slept, I almost danced through the early-morning, still-deserted Bnei Brak streets. When Rav Sraya had graciously invited me into his home for the night, I hadn't known what I was in for. His *avodah* had surpassed my wildest expectations.

Encounters with

Rav
Nosson Tzvi Finkel
זצ"ל

Rav Nosson Tzvi wishes me mazel tov at our wedding

He was the scion of a noble family, yet who would have imagined that the young boy from Chicago would one day take his place as the heir to the Mir dynasty?

A man who suffered great physical hardship with every step he took, Rav Nosson Tzvi showed us the power of absolute determination, unparalleled mesirus nefesh — and extraordinary siyatta d'Shmaya.

The power of devotion and love for Torah.

Rav Nosson Tzvi Finkel

Part A

Under the leadership of Rav Nosson Tzvi Finkel, the Mir Yeshivah underwent exponential growth. He transformed the yeshivah from a one-building institution into what amounts to a university-sized campus, with multiple buildings spread out over a large area: buildings filled with thousands of *bnei Torah*. All those plans were still in their infancy, though, when I arrived, ready to exchange the icy winds of the Telshe campus in freezing Ohio for the sunny warmth of the Beis Yisrael neighborhood of Yerushalayim.

Rav Nosson Tzvi Finkel, *Rosh Yeshivah* of the Mir, welcomed me into his yeshivah with open arms, and, like many other *bachurim*, I ended up learning with him *b'chavrusa*.

◆ ◆ ◆

With the advent of Rosh Chodesh Nissan, the yeshivah cleared out as the student body returned to their homes around the globe.

I, however, was more than content to spend my Pesach in close proximity to the holy Yidden of Yerushalayim.

As an aside, many *bachurim* who come to Eretz Yisrael never have a real opportunity to experience the true essence of Yerushalayim. Throughout the year they are mainly surrounded by others from their native country, and then, as Pesach approaches, they return home. The upshot: they never really see what lies beneath the surface of the Holy City. For the vast majority, learning in Eretz Yisrael is overwhelmingly an English-speaking experience. For the boys who remain behind, however, it is very different, as they are given a bird's-eye view of a lifestyle they've never witnessed before.

It was a wonderful period for me. I was free to spend my day however I saw fit, and I saw fit to spend most of it in the *beis medrash*. In those few weeks I experienced some of the best learning I ever had, feeling the special *siyatta d'Shmaya* that takes hold of a person when he's going above and beyond. I spent a lot of time talking to Rav Asher Arieli in learning, and I was gratified when he responded to some of the *chiddushim* I shared with him by telling me, "Binyomin, this is true *Toras Eretz Yisrael*! You have only merited this type of success because you remained here over *bein hazemanim*."

There were other treasures to be acquired at the same time. One of these was a deeper, closer relationship with Rav Nosson Tzvi. Since there were so few *talmidim* around, I inquired as to whether we could begin learning together, and of course the *Rosh Yeshivah* agreed, finding time for me as he always did for every single one of the thousands of boys in his care.

Learning with Rav Nosson Tzvi was an amazing experience for a number of reasons. Diagnosed with Parkinson's at a young age, even then it was already extremely difficult for the *Rosh Yeshivah* to do anything. It was difficult for him to prepare *shiur*. He was so weak. So, so weak. It was a miracle he could do anything at all!

He'd open up piles of *sefarim* in preparation for the *shiur*. He'd throw a question at me from one source, another question at me from a second source. But everything was scattered, without a common, uniting thread. And I never ceased wondering and worrying how he was going to deliver a proper *shiur* based on the varied ideas that we had covered.

But then he'd stand up at the front of the *beis medrash*, and he'd open his mouth, and out would come such beautiful Torah: a carefully constructed edifice of polished thought that bespoke hours of painstaking preparation. The *siyatta d'Shmaya* was undeniably present.

I don't have to tell you about his *mesirus nefesh,* his personal self-sacrifice. Everyone in the yeshivah witnessed it on a daily basis. I had considered myself shockproof from the efforts the *Rosh Yeshivah* would exert for the sake of Torah, but on the day of his daughter's wedding, when I dropped in to wish him mazel tov and mentioned that he was obviously too busy to learn together later that day, he disagreed with me without hesitation.

"Of course we're learning today, Binyomin!"

"What time should I come over?"

"Twelve o'clock."

"I'll be there."

I arrived at the Finkel home at noon and found Rav Nosson Tzvi dressed in his Shabbos finery and waiting for me at the head of the table. We then learned from the moment I entered the room until it was time for him to leave to the wedding hours later.

◆ ◆ ◆

No doubt there are thousands and thousands of *bnei Torah* who fondly recall making their way past the Mir Yeshivah's main building, across the street beside the small metalwork factory, around the bend, and up the short flight of stairs to the simple apartment of the Finkel family: an apartment that was humble in furnishings and appliances, yet possessed a glow of wealth that could make the richest people gape with envy.

The kitchen sported a small Formica table and a few chairs, a row of plain cabinets, a counter or two, and Rebbetzin Finkel, who had a warm smile and welcoming words for every person who crossed her threshold. The dining room held a couch, a table, some chairs, and bookcases that lined the wall from end to end and from floor to ceiling, all filled with *sefarim* and notebooks and the word of Hashem.

From these modest headquarters, Rav Nosson Tzvi directed an empire that impacted the entire Jewish world with its strength. All done by someone who could barely move.

◆ ◆ ◆

During *bein hazemanim*, the yeshivah went out of its way to provide meals for the boys who stayed in the dorm. It was definitely not something to be taken for granted, and we appreciated the gesture immensely.

On one of the days there wasn't sufficient food for the assembled, and one of the *bachurim* felt justified in complaining about this to Rav Nosson Tzvi.

My personal feeling was that the yeshivah was going above and beyond by providing us with meals in the first place, but this *bachur* seemingly didn't think twice about going in to disturb the *Rosh Yeshivah* with his "major problem."

Rav Nosson Tzvi heard him out patiently. He then reached into his pocket and handed the boy a 200-shekel bill.

"Go buy pizza," he told him.

◆ ◆ ◆

Rav Nosson Tzvi

Rav Nosson Tzvi delivered *shiurim* before the entire yeshivah on a regular basis. It was not easy for him. He was weak and suffering from an illness that would have put far stronger people than he out of commission. Yet he did not allow anything to get in the way of his dedication and devotion to teaching Torah to his *talmidim*.

One *shiur* in particular stands out in my mind due to the fact that a certain *bachur* interrupted the *Rosh Yeshivah* repeatedly with his questions. Were the *Rosh Yeshivah* a man in the prime of health, it might not have been construed as disrespect. But it was impossible not to notice how supremely difficult it was for Rav Nosson Tzvi to give that *shiur*. We could see him grabbing onto his *shtender* and trying to control his movements, while this boy kept asking questions as if oblivious to his agony.

Before you defend the *talmid* by telling me that asking questions is the accepted practice during a *shiur klali*, I will preempt you by stating the same thing. It is acceptable to ask a question in the middle of the *shiur* — if it's a very good question. It is most certainly not an accepted or an acceptable practice for the same boy to interrupt the speaker multiple times in the course of a *shiur*.

I watched their interchange with interest. Many a *Rosh Yeshivah* might have lost their patience with the questioner and silenced him with a biting comment. Rav Nosson Tzvi did nothing of the kind, even as undertones of tension and impatience with the *bachur* began coursing through the assembled, with feelings of "enough is enough," have a little respect!

Rav Nosson Tzvi finally turned his loving gaze upon his errant *talmid* and said with a big smile, "Yisrael Meir,* I see that you have an abundance of Torah to say today. Maybe you'll take over saying a *shiur* when I finish."

He said these words of gentle reproof with a tender smile, leaving the *bachur* with the feeling that the *Rosh Yeshivah* still held him in high regard.

◆　◆　◆

Many days, while we were sitting and learning, someone would enter the apartment requesting to speak with the *Rosh Yeshivah*. Often it would be a Mir *talmid* who had written a *sefer* and had personally come to present Rav Nosson Tzvi with a copy. Rav Nosson Tzvi would reach into his pocket, remove a wad of bills, and hand it to the *talmid* with the warmest of wishes and a genuinely proud smile that spoke volumes. It was his way of validating his student's hard work and accomplishments.

Sometimes it was an elderly Yerushalmi Yid (the yeshivah had quite a few of them among its student body) who'd enter the apartment with a "*shtickel Torah*" that he wanted to share with Rav Nosson Tzvi. The tradition of sharing fine pieces of Torah had been around since the days of Rav Leizer Yudel — the former *Rosh Yeshivah* and Rav Nosson's great-uncle — and Rav Nosson Tzvi continued it with love. He'd listen, comment, enjoy, discuss — and then hand the man some money to show his appreciation.

One time an Israeli *talmid* came to the house to bid the *Rosh Yeshivah* farewell, as he was about to embark on a trip overseas. Rav Nosson Tzvi removed several bills from his pocket and handed it to the boy.

"You're going to *chutz la'aretz*," he told his student. "You should have some money to go shopping."

◆ ◆ ◆

I'd watch him learn until he'd used up every ounce of energy and there was nothing left. He learned until the exhaustion took over and he was forced to rest. We began with him sitting in his chair. When it became harder for him to concentrate, he'd lie down on the couch. The pages of his well-worn Gemara would come out of the binding, and he'd hold them in his hand as he pushed himself to the maximum.

One afternoon, I was reading the Gemara as he followed along inside with his eyes. Suddenly I realized that his fatigue had overcome his resolve and he'd fallen asleep. I stopped reading and waited for him to wake up.

He awoke two minutes later and gave me a look of reproach. "Binyomin," he said to me, "why did you stop reading?"

Never mind the fact that he was operating on empty. He expected me to continue and to never cut him any slack due to his condition.

◆ ◆ ◆

Rav Nosson Tzvi was forced to take numerous medications every day for his various ailments. The medicines couldn't be ingested on an empty stomach. One Shabbos afternoon, as a few *talmidim* sat and learned with him at the dining-room table, the *Rosh Yeshivah* rose, went into the kitchen, and returned with a plate in hand on which he'd placed five or six tablets, a peach, and a piece of cake.

He took his seat, we resumed learning where we'd left off, but then a minute later he rose once more, returned to the kitchen again, and returned with another plate piled with cake, which he placed before us.

It was obvious that he had gotten the cake for himself because he wasn't allowed to take his pills on an empty stomach. But once he had brought cake for himself, there was no way in the world that he'd allow us to sit and learn with him without being provided for as well. The greatness of everything he did and every step he took was compounded by the fact that he was almost incapable of walking in the first place. What would have been a simple task for someone else took him much, much longer. Yet he did these things for his *talmidim* happily, because he loved every one and wanted them to know it.

◆ ◆ ◆

The Mir was ensconced in its original building back then and had just completed a critically needed annex, but the Beis Yisrael neighborhood had yet to undergo any sort of urban renewal program. It was very much a modest and old-fashioned, almost seedy neighborhood, with twisting roads and narrow, rock-strewn paths. The Beis Yisrael sewer system flooded in the harsh Jerusalem winters, and the canvas-roofed additions that many people built onto their tiny homes baked the residents in the summers.

Despite the difficult conditions, the sweet sounds of learning and davening emerged from behind the shabby doors of the yeshivos and shuls that were found on every block. The Jerusalem municipality would eventually devote serious money to repaving its streets and repairing the ancient mess and tangle of pipes lurking beneath the crumbling roads. But all that was in years to come.

The fact that the yeshivah was located in an area that also was home to the lower echelon of society and surrounded by poverty and squalor meant that a fair number of its neighbors were people with "pasts": having done various stretches of time in assorted Israeli prisons.

Though my love for the Mir was absolute, *Shabbos Kodesh* would usually find me making my way through the thoroughfares of the Holy City, walking toward the homes of many of Yerushalayim's luminaries whom I had come to know over the course of time. I usually ate one or both of my Shabbos meals at the homes of *gedolim* like Rav Yitzchok Scheiner, *Rosh Yeshivah* of Kaminetz, or Rav Shmuel Yaakov Bornstein, *Rosh Yeshivah* of Chevron Geulah. Other *seudos* were spent in the august company of Rav Chaim Sarna or Rav Yehudah Dvir, my long-standing Friday-night *chavrusa*.

It was not that I eschewed the yeshivah spirit in any way — there were just too many great men living in Yerushalayim whom I wanted to meet and learn from. The streets of Yerushalayim were literally filled with *tzaddikim*, both of the revealed and hidden varieties, and I was like a child in a candy shop who wanted everything all at once.

One particular Friday night, however, I wasn't feeling well and elected to eat in the yeshivah. I went down to the dining room, found myself a seat in a corner, took a portion of challah and food, and settled down to my solitary meal, determined to eat quickly and retire for the night. I stuck to my plan, finished eating fairly rapidly, *bentched*, and made my way back upstairs toward my dorm room.

As I entered the wing where my room was located, I noticed a strange-looking individual walking quickly down the hallway. Though there was a yarmulke perched on his head, he was wearing jeans and a sport jacket, and it was obvious that he didn't belong in the Mir dorm. However, knowing how many people came and went in the yeshivah, I didn't make anything of it, merely passing him by on the way to my room.

My vague feeling of disquiet intensified, however, when I reached the door to my room, tried the handle, and found that it wouldn't turn. There was something obstructing my entrance on the other side of the door. At once perplexed and uneasy, I looked around the hallway, searching for inspiration as to what was going on. I was at a loss until I happened to glance at the windowpanes located directly over the door, and I saw to my surprise and chagrin that they had been completely removed from their frame!

I immediately realized that my room had been burglarized. Unfortunately, dorm rooms the world over aren't immune to this type of scourge, and at that time the Mir Yeshivah dorm was viewed by the local talent as an easy mark. It was common for dorm rooms to be robbed and for boys to lose their passports, cash, and valuables.

Suddenly everything made sense. The thief had removed the three panels of glass above the door and climbed into the locked room. He then placed a chair beneath the door handle to prevent anyone from surprising him while he was in the room. He stole whatever he wanted, and then left the way he had come.

The moment I realized that my room had been the target of a robbery, my heart skipped a beat. Although I was not a wealthy boy and didn't possess much in the way of money or expensive items, I had been helping Rav Dovid Cohen, *Rosh Yeshivah* of Chevron, sell his *sefer* on *Kesubos* in the Mir and had left the $200 I had been paid for the *sefarim* in my pants pocket — pants that were hanging on one of the open closet doors.

I had heard many times that thieves always head straight for the pants. My unease turned into a deep feeling of anxiety at the knowledge that I might be out $200 of someone else's money, with no way to repay him! It seemed obvious to me that the stranger I had just seen making his diffident way through the Mir dorm was the thief, and that there was no time to lose if I ever wanted to see my valuables again.

I ran down the hallway and out of the dorm into the misty Jerusalem evening, my head swiveling in every direction as I peered through the gloom, trying to identify a hurrying stranger. It took me a second, but I was just in time to see a man walking swiftly down the street. I knew that if I lost sight of him for even a second he would disappear, and I would never find him again.

Time was crucial here. I wasn't sure how to handle the situation. Even if I managed to confront him and he admitted to having taken my things, they were *muktzeh* and there wasn't anything I could do with them. Also, I didn't know if he was armed and dangerous. In the end I decided to at least follow him, hoping he would lead me to his home, which would give me a chance to find him another day.

It didn't take me long to realize that this man lived in the neighborhood. It was clear that he knew his way around as he slinked with practiced ease through the narrow alleyways of Beis Yisrael. I almost lost him a few times, yet somehow I managed to stay on his trail despite the fact that he seemed to be an expert at blending into the shadows. I also noticed that the man had a recognizable limp and took note of his approximate height and build.

At some point it appeared that he had discerned that I was following him and was leading me in circles. Besides, it seemed to me from the way he was swaying from side to side that he was drunk. Eventually, I turned around and went back to yeshivah.

When I was finally able to get back into my room, I was faced with the hardest challenge of *shemiras Shabbos* in my entire life. I desperately wanted to know whether he had taken the money, yet I had to control myself until Shabbos was over. As soon as we made Havdalah I ran to my room, stuck my hand in my pants pocket, and discovered to my immense relief that the money was still there. My shaver was missing, and the thief had taken a bottle

Rav Nosson Tzvi at our *vort*, with Rav Aharon Chadash seated at his right

of cologne that belonged to a French roommate, a pile of loose mezuzah *parashiyos* that another roommate had purchased for a friend, and a number of additional items that had been lying around. Rav Dovid Cohen's money was safe, though, and I was finally able to breathe a deep sigh of relief.

◆ ◆ ◆

On Sunday morning I began working out what to do. I conferred with Rav Aharon Chadash, the Mir *mashgiach*, and when I described the man to as many people as I could, a friend of mine told me excitedly that according to the details I had provided, he could almost picture the man, and there was a good chance he knew who it was.

"He works at a local falafel shop nearby," he told me.

We wasted no time. Five minutes later we were entering the falafel shop, the aroma of hot frying oil and cold chumus assailing our senses. I took one look at the person behind the counter and recognized him immediately. We had found our man.

The moment our eyes met, I knew that just as I recognized him, so he recognized me. Obviously the man wasn't thinking very clearly, because there is no better way to identify yourself as a criminal than to flee the scene upon being spotted — and the second he comprehended who I was and why I had come, he slipped out of the shop and simply vanished.

Now, however, the game was just beginning.

There was a *sefarim* store adjacent to the falafel shop, and we asked the owner where his neighbor lived. He gave us an address, and we decided to head over there, hoping to deal with the situation once and for all.

◆ ◆ ◆

Uneasy about confronting him ourselves, we called the police, who arrived in record time. Together with a number of the strongest boys in the yeshivah, we knocked on the man's door. He opened the door and asked the police what they wanted.

"You were identified as having been roaming the halls of the Mir Yeshivah during a break-in."

"That's nonsense," he exclaimed. "I wasn't even here this Shabbos!"

Clearly the man was prepared to brazen his way out of everything.

One of the guys standing there made the following statement, which totally destroyed his equilibrium: "Rav Kaduri told us that the thief lives in this home!"

I don't know why he said that statement, which wasn't true, but the falafel store owner — who may have been a thief and a felon, but who still possessed a kind of reverence for a Torah great (and, to be honest, who was also not too bright) — responded, "No, the rav means that I used to be a thief. Not anymore!"

With this, by admitting that he had been a thief in the past, the man had just compromised any chance he had of denial. Realizing that he'd slipped up with his last few words, the thief suddenly closed the door in the face of the police, locked it, and wouldn't open up no matter how they banged.

Of course, it wasn't long before the neighbors began congregating, each relating stories of their neighbor the thief. The man didn't seem to have many allies on his home turf. By the time the police managed to get the door open, our quarry was long gone, having apparently installed an escape route in his home in cases of an emergency. He climbed through a ceiling panel and escaped across the rooftops of Beis Yisrael, ending any chances of questioning him further.

A short search through the apartment turned up many of the stolen goods, and the police immediately sat down and wrote out an arrest warrant for the man, detailing the evidence that had been uncovered in his home.

"The second you see this man," they said, "call us, and we will come down to arrest him."

Things calmed down after that, and I began asking around, trying to find out more information about our friendly neighborhood thief. It seemed that the man came from a religious family, but like many people who grow up in poverty-stricken neighborhoods, he fell in with the wrong crowd. He had spent time in prison in the past and had fallen prey to drugs and alcohol abuse. He was one of those people who had slipped through the cracks of society, and the truth is, after I'd learned all about his life, I felt sorry for him.

A short while later one of his brothers, an obviously religious man, came to see me at the Mir.

"I just wanted to talk to you about my brother Menachem," he said.

Then he told me that his brother had been married, had made a stab at leading a decent life, had gotten divorced, and even had daughters who were students at one of the Bais Yaakov schools in the city. Truthfully, it was a tragic story. He begged me to drop the case, promised me that they'd return everything that had been taken, and pleaded with me not to send his brother Menachem back to prison.

"He's trying to lead a decent life," he told me over and over. "Please give him another chance."

I pictured Rav Nosson Tzvi listening to this man. I thought of the *Rosh Yeshivah*'s patience and his merciful attitude toward everyone he came in contact with. Could I, as his *talmid*, send this man to jail?

In the end, I made a few copies of a picture of him that we'd gotten from his apartment and hung them up around the yeshivah with words of warning. I also told a few of the guys who frequented the area that if they saw him in the nearby vicinity, they should give me a call.

One morning my cell rang. I answered.

"Binyomin, I've just seen him around the Mir."

"I'll be over in a second."

I'd been carrying the police arrest warrant in my pocket, putting me in the ultimate position of power vis-à-vis this individual. I made my approach and showed him the warrant.

"Look, Menachem," I said to him, "you're finished. We know where you live, we know that you're the thief, we even found the goods in your apartment. I could have you arrested this second. On the other hand, I was visited by members of your family who pleaded your case. They told me that you are really a good person at heart and promised me that you're going to change."

I looked him straight in the eyes.

"Menachem, if you promise me with all your heart that you're going to do *teshuvah* and turn around your life, I'll give you another chance. But just so you know, I'm going to come around to your store and apartment and check up on you. We live pretty close to each other, and I will be involved in your life."

"That's fine with me," he replied, grateful beyond words that I was willing to throw him a little rope.

"One more thing."

"Anything."

"We are going to become *chavrusas*."

"What?!"

"That's right. We are starting to learn together. Have you ever studied *Mesilas Yesharim*?"

"A little."

"Good, so you're already familiar with it."

From that day on, I became part of his life. I walked over to the store on a regular basis to check that he was opening up on time and living his life like a *mentsch* and making a *parnassah*. He promised me that he was going to stop drinking — the real source of his problems — and followed through by pouring every drop of every last bottle he owned down the sink. For about a year, the two of us learned together on a weekly basis: thief and *yeshivah bachur*, studying the word of Hashem.

Menachem kept his word and stayed off alcohol. He constantly thanked me for giving him the impetus to return to the full Shabbos observance of his younger years. He told me that he saw tremendous blessing in his new life as a result of his newfound return to Torah and mitzvos. In addition, he was finally able to develop a genuine relationship with his two daughters, who were once again able to look their father in the eye without being repulsed by who he was.

Our relationship lasted as long as I remained in the Mir. Once I left, we drifted apart, though I don't go many days without remembering the sweet thief who really wanted to live an honestly Jewish existence, and who showed me in a very real and meaningful way that even a person who has fallen especially low can change, grow, and turn his life around.

♦ ♦ ♦

Rav Nosson Tzvi contributed an incredible amount to my growth as a *ben Torah* and as a human being. He was always there for me, and his warmth and benevolence helped me feel appreciated and valued. I so much wanted to pay him back — even just a little bit — for everything that he'd given me. With this in mind, I figured that when it came time for me to marry, I'd make sure to honor him with *siddur kiddushin*. This would be my way of thanking him for his dedication as a true *mechanech* and role model.

Rav Nosson Tzvi and Rav Yitzchok Nosson Kupershtok at our *vort*

And then I got engaged and all my plans went out the window.

The sheer volume of political correctness that goes into making a Jewish wedding is staggering and can overwhelm even the most astute and socially adept. How much more so when it came to the *chasan* himself, who has no prior experience in these things.

I didn't really care about any of the details. It mattered little what hall the wedding was in or what band we used. I didn't really care if both fathers walked me down or if I was escorted to the *chuppah* by my mother and father, and my wife by her parents. There were only two things that mattered to me. One, that my wife was there. Two, that I could honor Rav Nosson Tzvi with *siddur kiddushin*. It was payback time and I had a debt.

Then the phone rang. America was on the line.

"Binyomin?"

"Yes?"

"We just wanted to go over a few details."

"Go on."

"Okay, for *siddur kiddushin*…"

Wait a second, I'm thinking. *Siddur kiddushin has to go to Rav Nosson Tzvi…*

"…should go to Zeide," they were saying as if it was the most obvious thing in the world.

"But I wanted to give it to the *Rosh Yeshivah*."

"Binyomin," my father said in a tone that brooked no argument, "Zeide does *siddur kiddushin* at every wedding in the family. How do you think he's going to feel if after flying in all the way from the States to be at your wedding, he has to watch someone else do it?"

I had no answer.

Having to inform Rav Nosson Tzvi that he was not in fact going to be honored with *siddur kiddushin* was the most difficult conversation I ever had with him. I walked up the stairs to the simple living room feeling like a prisoner being led to the guillotine. How could this be happening? Here I wanted to honor him so badly, and now I was being forced to withdraw my *hakaras hatov* from him! Every step felt like a mile as my heart thundered in my chest.

Rav Nosson Tzvi was sitting at the dining-room table in his usual seat. He looked up at me when I entered the room, and his warm eyes shone with intelligence and love. I wanted to hug him, not disappoint him. I took a seat beside him — cleared my throat — couldn't meet his gaze.

"What's on your mind, Binyomin?"

"Well, you see, it's like this — Remember when I told the *Rosh Yeshivah* that I wanted him to be the *mesader kiddushin* at the wedding?"

He nodded.

"So my Zeide —"

He cut me off right there. Didn't even allow me to finish the sentence.

"It's his."

That was it. It was his.

Next worry: Would he show up at my wedding even though I had taken *siddur kiddushin* away from him? Could I expect him to? Wasn't it like a slap in the face to a man, to a *tzaddik*, who had given me so much?

In the end, I needn't have worried. Of course he came to share the happiest night of my life, staying for a short time before apologetically explaining that he had to leave, since he had another four weddings of *talmidim* to attend that evening.

I knew that I would never forget those two simple words — "it's his" — and that with those two words, he'd taught me what it meant to give in and how to live life in a way that would only bring one joy and satisfaction. Basically, with those two words — "it's his" — and with his attitude of being *mevater* for another, my rebbi, Rav Nosson Tzvi Finkel, taught me the secret of marriage.

And of life.

Yehi zichro baruch.

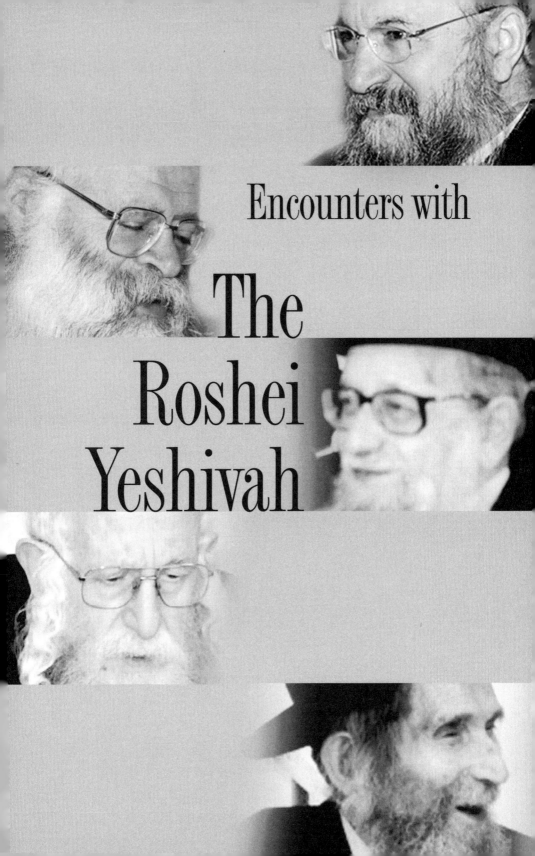

Encounters with

The
Roshei
Yeshivah

Fascinating vignettes about the rich personalities and characters of some of the kings of Israel.

These are men who have been entrusted by Shamayim with the task of education, and who fulfill their mandate with every tool, every ability, and every ounce of devotion they possess.

The Roshei Yeshivah
PART A

Rav Yaakov Hillel
Rav Yitzchak Scheiner

y first apartment — or *dirah*, as it's known to one and
all — while learning in the Mir, was located on Avodas
Yisrael Street, a few blocks from Kikar Shabbos and
just two doors down from the yeshivah of Rav Yaakov Hillel, *shlita*. The fact that my homestead was a
mere two buildings over from Yeshivas Ahavat Shalom
would give me the incredible opportunity to develop a
relationship with Rav Yaakov Hillel, one that continues
until today.

Rav Yaakov is widely considered one of the greatest
meku-balim of our generation, but I had never heard of him before
finding myself in such close proximity to his yeshivah. Here I was,
searching in every corner of Meah Shearim for the *tzaddikim* of

Yerushalayim, and Hashem in His infinite goodness sent me a next-door neighbor who certainly qualified.

It was around this time that Rav Hillel began delivering a *shiur* for *bachurim,* which I joined. Among other things, we studied *Mesilas Yesharim* together, and the *shiur* served as the kickoff point and catalyst for what would become a beautiful relationship. The fact that he was a respected kabbalist, in addition to being an acclaimed *talmid chacham*, was of major importance to me. Any time I heard about a kabbalist or "miracle worker," and was considering pursuing a connection with him, I was able to ask Rav Yaakov what he thought about making such a move. Rav Yaakov knew everyone well, and he never hesitated to warn me if he felt the individual wasn't completely trustworthy.

It was Rav Yaakov who opened my eyes to the fact that there are many so-called kabbalists who seem to be working wonders, yet who are actually con artists fleecing an unsuspecting public. Many of these people are famous; many of them are considered

Rav Yaakov Hillel and Rav Yehudah Dvir at our wedding

genuine *tzaddikim*. But there are many terrible stories where inno-
cent people searching for a miracle were betrayed after placing
their trust in those who are undeserving of it.

Rav Yaakov didn't only talk about the negative. Instead, he
provided me with the tools and the keys to discern who was
trustworthy and who was not. His *simanim* proved extremely
helpful to me and also gave me the ability to help many others
to decide whether they really wanted to trust any person who
made claims to being able to see beyond the physical world. It
wasn't long before I was eating Shabbos meals at his house and
even one memorable Purim *seudah*. If the majority of my time
was spent in the company of *gedolim* of Ashkenazi descent, Rav
Yaakov provided me with the perfect Sephardic touch to round
everything out.

◆ ◆ ◆

Rav Yaakov came to *shiur* late one day. I took one look at him
and could tell that he was beside himself. His personality was usually placid and unruffled, but on this particular day it was obvious
that something terrible must have happened. Though there was
something weighing him down, he pulled himself together and
gave the *shiur* as if all was routine.

As soon as he finished delivering the *shiur,* however, Rav Yaakov looked us in the eye and said to us, "I'm sure you all noticed
that I arrived today in a distracted mood. I was late and you could
all see that I didn't have my normal *yishuv hada'as.* There's a reason for this."

We all leaned forward expectantly, anxious to hear what it was
that had managed to upset him to such a degree.

"There's a certain key donor of mine who was just here in
Eretz Yisrael for a visit. While he was here, he called me up as he
normally does, and we had a nice conversation. Before we hung
up, I said to him, 'Since you are already here, it would be a good
idea for you to come in to the yeshivah now. You could take a
look around. Besides, you usually send me a check at this time
of year. This way you know the matter was already taken care of.'

"'I'm sorry, I can't come in to see you right now,' the man apologized, 'and I'll send you the check as soon as I fly back home.'

"I said to him, 'My friend, you're making a mistake. When it comes to these type of *tzedakah* situations, never push off writing the check, because you never know what might happen to prevent you from carrying out the mitzvah that you planned on doing!'

"Some intangible feeling inside me kept pushing me to try again and again. But the man insisted on doing things his way. There was no way he could take care of things now. It would absolutely have to wait until he returned to *chutz la'aretz*.

"I tried to convince him that he was making a mistake, but was unable to persuade him to change his mind. The man called me back a few hours later. He was beside himself with grief, choking up as he tried to get the words out.

"'What happened?' I asked him as a terrible premonition filled my heart.

"'They called me from America a few minutes ago, Rebbi—'

"'Yes?'

"'My son — my son — was just shot and killed in a holdup.'

"Terrible, wracking sobs shook his voice so hard I could barely make out what he was saying over the phone line.

"I don't know why I was so insistent with this man before," Rav Yaakov continued, "but it's clear to me that had he given me the check while he was still here, this act would have saved his son's life. Charity saves a person from death. There is not a doubt in my mind that he would have been saved!

"*Rabbosai*," Rav Yaakov concluded, his voice choking, "this man was given the power to save his son's life; he was granted the opportunity to do the specific mitzvah that could have changed everything. He chose to push it off and thereby lost his chance."

The power of giving *tzedakah* was clearly brought home to me that day by Rav Yaakov's firsthand story. But even more: seeing how Rav Yaakov took it almost for granted that the man could have completely rewritten the heavenly decree with a relatively small action on his part made a deep impression on me.

◆ ◆ ◆

Years passed. I never lost touch with Rav Yaakov. At one point I began teaching in a certain yeshivah. One of the *kollel* members there was very involved in "facilitated communication" with autistic children. This type of approach became popular back in the 90's, with many people putting great faith in the messages spelled out by these children through the "assistance" of their facilitators. This *kollel yungerman* claimed that there were many rabbis who supported this form of communication and who were very excited about the results he saw and the things the children "said."

On one occasion he decided to arrange a field trip for the entire yeshivah, including the *Rosh Yeshivah* and myself, to the home of one of these autistic children, so we could witness first-hand how amazing this method was.

We witnessed a facilitated communication from start to finish, and in all honesty I didn't find it particularly impressive or authentically persuasive.

The *Rosh Yeshivah* asked the child a question, and when he responded through the facilitator, the *Rosh Yeshivah*'s conclusion was that this couldn't be authentic, since the answer was a clear contradiction to the words of *Chazal*. Yet, though the *Rosh Yeshivah* spoke convincingly, the crowd of *bachurim* still seemed impressed.

Then I had a brainstorm.

"I have one question that I want to ask. Is that O.K.?"

The facilitator consented.

"I have a rebbi named Rav Yaakov Hillel," I told the boy, "and I want to know if I can rely on everything he tells me from a Torah standpoint. Can I trust him 100 percent?"

The child's facilitated response was a clear and unequivocal yes. Thanking them for their time, the entire yeshivah left the building in search of a public phone (this was before everyone had cell phones). We found one a block away, and I called Rav Yaakov Hillel.

"Rebbi, what is your opinion of facilitated communication with autistic children?"

"It's nonsense. *Chas v'shalom* — we don't work that way. If we start bringing proofs from these kind of things, then tomorrow it will be a rock that speaks and the next day a fish that talks. *Klal Yisrael* doesn't go this way. It's a waste of time!"

I thanked him and, after hanging up the phone, turned to the yeshivah.

"*Rabbosai*, if you believe in Rav Yaakov Hillel as a *tzaddik* and respected kabbalist, then here's your answer. And if you believe in facilitating through autistic children, they themselves attested to the fact that he is completely trustworthy and that his opinion can be relied on 100 percent. As you all heard, Rav Yaakov is not in favor of this type of thing, going so far as to call it nonsense!"

In the end, Rav Yaakov served as the perfect deciding factor.

(As an aside, when a local bookstore held a going-out-of-business sale, I purchased a whole pile of *sefarim* at very low prices. One of these was a compilation of questions that had been asked to autistic children and their facilitated responses. I happened to have been holding the book in my hands when I entered the home of Rav Nachum Eisenstein, a foremost disciple of Rav Elyashiv, for something or other. When Rav Nachum caught sight of the book, he spoke up in his typical no-nonsense way. "Rav Elyashiv says to throw that book in the garbage!")

◆ ◆ ◆

Rav Yaakov Hillel has a very developed and thorough philosophy when it comes to the subject of kabbalists. A person's mystical powers and abilities have to stem from the Torah. If you find a person who spends his days sitting and learning Torah, and he sets aside a little time to meet with people and word spreads that he gives worthy *eitzos*, we can believe that.

But if the person claiming to be a *mekubal* is not recognized by the *gedolim* as a true Torah scholar, and all we know about him is the fact that he possesses incredible "powers," that is the strongest sign that this person is not to be trusted. Universally acclaimed *mekubal* though he may be, Rav Yaakov Hillel always gave me the same answer when I asked him who people visiting from America should visit. Two names. Always the same two. Rav Nosson Tzvi Finkel and Rav Chaim Kanievsky.

I once asked Rav Yaakov about a certain famous practice that people do to remove *ayin hara* from themselves. (There are quite a few.)

His response came back at me fast and quick.

"You can do it on a cat with the same results."

Rav Refael Levin, who was considered one of the greatest experts alive when it came to the removal of *ayin hara*, told me that he himself only used practices taught him by his father. "I only do the things I have in *mesorah* from my father," was how he put it.

Rav Yaakov taught me a large amount of Torah. And he also taught me that while mysticism certainly has its place in the school and body of Jewish thought, the main thing is regular Torah learning with diligence and purity.

◆ ◆ ◆

My paternal grandfather was an "*alter Mirrer*" who filled his days with an admirable mixture of Torah, *avodas Hashem*, and *gemilas chasadim*. He managed a fund-raising office on the Lower East Side of Manhattan for the Kaminetz Yeshivah of Yerushalayim. He spent about half a day at the office, part of that time studying with a *chavrusa*, then continued his day at MTJ, where he had a daily learning session with the same *chavrusa* with whom he had studied back in Shanghai. They had been study partners for over 50 years, and as a child, when I saw the two of them learning together, they still seemed as fresh a pair of *chavrusa*s as if they'd met the week before.

In the summers I'd take the train over to Manhattan to work in the office. There, in the warm room, with a ceiling fan circling lazily overhead, I'd stuff envelopes to be sent out to the yeshivah's mailing list while listening to the sweet sound of my *zeide* learning in the other room. Good memories.

(My *zeide* told me that some 40 years before I began working for him, Rebbetzin Ruchama Shain worked at the same job. It was nice to know that I was in such august company.)

There were additional benefits to working at that office — such as the fact that I was privileged to meet the Kaminetzer *Rosh Yeshivah*, Rav Yitzchok Scheiner, *shlita*, and the yeshivah's *mashgiach*, Rav Moshe Aharon Stern, *zt"l*, on their frequent trips to the States to raise funds. When I grew up and went to learn in Eretz Yisrael, I made a priority of renewing my relationship with Rav Yitzchok Scheiner, becoming a *ben bayis* in his home.

Rav Yitzchok lives on Tzefania Street in the heart of Geulah, and I ate many, many Shabbos meals at his home. Rav Yitzchok's Shabbos table was a complete Torah experience. Here was a man entirely engrossed in his Torah learning. He'd begin the *seudah* with a *Ketzos*, follow that up by showing how it applied to the Gemara, all the while encouraging the guests sitting around the table to involve themselves in his lofty world.

The *Ketzos* he'd used to jump-start the meal would accompany us throughout the entire evening, much like a musical theme might flow in and out of a song, reappearing every few bars. We'd sing a *zemer*, and as soon as it was over, Rav Yitzchok would carry on with another fresh thought on the *Ketzos*, tying everything together in the most beautiful way imaginable. All this while his Rebbetzin sat, basking in the sight of her husband completely immersed in his Torah with an enjoyment that bordered on the sublime.

As the conversation ebbed and flowed through the hills and dales of complicated and complex Torah thought, the Rebbetzin would serve an abundant array of delicious food accompanied by her refrain of "*Ess, ess, men darf haben ko'ach tzu lernen* — Eat, eat, you need to have strength to learn Torah!" Her love of Torah was tangible — almost as if you could reach out and touch it — such was its power.

Once, while engaging in a discussion with the Rebbetzin, we touched on the subject of Rav Zundel Kroizer.

"You should know," confided the Rebbetzin, "that Rav Zundel is one of the *lamed vav tzaddikim* of our generation."

This was another example of one *tzaddik*, or in this case, two *tzaddikim*, Rav Yitzchok and his Rebbetzin, sharing a personal relationship with the other *tzaddikim* living in their world. As I mentioned previously, everyone has friends. It's part of the human condition. In most cases, a *tzaddik's* friends are similar to him. They share the same interests and are excited by the same things. This is a very important detail for a person who wants to find and become close to *tzaddikim*.

The Roshei Yeshivah
PART B

Rav Shmuel Yaakov Bornstein
Rav Chaim Sarna
Rav Yosef Lieberman
Rav Ahron Leib Shteinman

I stayed in Eretz Yisrael for Pesach two years in a row. I spent both of those Seders in the home of Rav Shmuel Yaakov Bornstein, *shlita*, who was then *Rosh Yeshivah* of Chevron Geulah and who is today *Rosh Yeshivah* of Kiryas Melech.

Being in his presence for the Seder made an indelible impression on me. I met Rav Shmuel Yaakov through my father, who had learned in Chevron Yeshivah during the same period as he. Rav Shmuel Yaakov had stayed at our home on one occasion

Rav Shmuel Yaakov Bornstein (l.) and Rav Yitzchok Nosson Kupershtok
at our wedding

during a visit to the States, so it was only natural for me to look
him up when I came to learn in Yerushalayim. From there, our
relationship blossomed and flourished.

Some *tzaddikim* serve Hashem through poverty and hardship,
while others serve Hashem through beauty and a royal approach.
The Seder in the Bornstein home epitomized *malchus,* royalty.
Both the quality of the Torah that emanated from the *Rosh Yeshivah*'s
mouth and the way the Rebbetzin set the table were worthy
of kingship. The apartment radiated elegance. The table seemed
to stretch from one end of the room to the other, and every place
was set with exquisite china and crystal.

The Seder was extremely satisfying both spiritually and materially.
Everything about Rav Shmuel Yaakov and his Rebbetzin
reflected nobility and majesty. Their home was filled with objets
d'art, and there was an abundance of elegantly presented and
delicious foods on their table.

But that was just the start, because Rav Shmuel Yaakov's Torah
was the spiritual counterpart to the *gashmiyus* in his home. It was
all part of the way they served Hashem.

Sitting at their Seder was akin to sitting before the king at a royal court. Breathtaking. Memorable. Uplifting. And when the Seder finally wound its way to the end, it was really just beginning. Because Rav Shmuel Yaakov had his *Shir HaShirim* open before him, and the conclusion of the Seder was the signal to begin reciting the deepest, most lofty Torah thoughts and ideas on Shlomo HaMelech's classic work. Not for an hour or even two. Rav Shmuel Yaakov said Torah for the rest of the night, until it was time to recite the morning *Shema*. We were tired, he was tired — we drank seltzer to stay awake (one is not allowed to eat after the Seder) — yet he wasn't fazed by the challenge of learning through the darkest hours of the night, until the sky grew crimson and streaked with the early-morning orange and pink hues of sunrise, fulfilling the Rambam's words to learn until sleep overcomes you. And all this after four cups of wine!

It was an evening of such incredible beauty. Beautiful home. *Zemiros* of beauty. Rav Shmuel Yaakov's voice rich and velvety. If I close my eyes for a second or two, I can still remember it all. That room, the drapes and paintings on the wall, the majesty, the silver and crystal and art, the shelves of *sefarim*, decanters of ruby-red wine…and at the head of it all, singing with all his heart, Rav Shmuel Yaakov, his heart opened, the Torah pouring forth like a fountain, erupting like a volcano long dormant whose power has suddenly been unleashed.

What a night it was.

◆   ◆   ◆

Once, while escorting Rav Shmuel Yaakov home from shul, I related something amazing that I had personally witnessed in the home of Rav Nosson Tzvi. Of course, Rav Shmuel Yaakov was anxious to hear the story.

"Rav Nosson Tzvi and I were learning together one day," I related, "when he had a sudden brainstorm. He decided to open up another *beis medrash* with a certain amount of seats, where they would learn a particular topic. There was a sparkle in his eye, and I knew that I was watching history in the making.

"Apologizing to me for the interruption, Rav Nosson Tzvi called his brother-in-law Rav Yisroel Glustein and asked him to please come see him right away. When Rav Glustein arrived, Rav Nosson Tzvi explained his idea: new study hall, this amount of seats, this *limud*... (If I'm not mistaken, this would eventually become the *beis medrash* known as Shalmei Simcha.)

"Rav Glustein looked at Rav Nosson Tzvi with a mixture of amusement and admiration and asked the obvious question. '*Kesef mina lan*? Where will the money come from?'

" 'That I didn't work out yet,' Rav Nosson Tzvi replied.

"Clearly the financial aspect of the operation didn't faze him in the slightest.

"Not only that," I went on, "but another time he announced that whoever finished the entire *masechta* that the yeshivah was studying that *zeman* and was tested on it with high marks would receive 1,000 shekels. With a student body like that of the Mir, this could mean raising an astronomical sum of money!"

Rav Shmuel Yaakov looked at me and said, "*Oy*, Rav Nosson Tzvi, how does he take these responsibilities on himself?"

Then, a second later, Rav Shmuel Yaakov exclaimed, "*Aderaba*, just the opposite! It's because he's willing to take such awesome responsibilities on his frail shoulders that he's successful and receives such abundant *siyatta d'Shmaya*!"

◆　◆　◆

Rav Chaim Sarna was the *Rosh Yeshivah* of Chevron Geulah. His father, Rav Yechezkel Sarna, had been the world-famous founder of the Chevron Yeshivah, and Rav Chaim was an extremely illustrious personage in his own right. My father had started developing a relationship with Rav Chaim during his stint at Chevron, and he instructed me to build a connection with him as well.

I went to see Rav Chaim at his home during my first Succos in the country. I was new in Eretz Yisrael, and everything was novel and fascinating. I had heard much talk about visiting the Kosel on Succos, and in my mind I imagined myself trekking through

Rav Chaim Sarna at our wedding

the Jewish Quarter of the Old City, *lulav* and *esrog* in hand, while surrounded by thousands of other Jews, all intent on davening together at the holy Wall.

I had been invited to Rav Chaim's home for the *seudah* that Succos day, and because I had davened at the Kosel and it had been a little difficult making it back through the crowds, I reached his home a little later than I would have otherwise.

"Where are you coming from?" he asked me.

"I davened at the Kosel."

I have to tell you, I was not expecting the vehement reaction that came my way.

"Who davens at the Kosel?"

"I don't understand," I responded. "Isn't that the most holy spot in the world?"

"Look, Binyomin," he said to me, "The only reason I'm allowing myself to take you to task like this is because I see that you're your father's son and a special *bachur*. Based on who you are, you're a *ben bayis* in my home already."

He paused, while I readied myself to hear what he had to say.

"Who davens at the Kosel on Succos? Are you a tourist? The Kosel is not a place to daven *Shacharis.* You go to the Kosel to say *Tehillim,* but davening — that you are supposed to do in yeshivah!"

Of course he was right. Davening at the Kosel on a *Yom Tov* morning means being surrounded by thousands of people and dozens of *minyanim.* The atmosphere is exciting and loud, making it very difficult to concentrate.

"Visit the Kosel as much as you want," Rav Chaim concluded, "but when it comes to davening, stay in yeshivah."

◆ ◆ ◆

I'd visit Rav Chaim Sarna at least once every few months. Every time we were together, he'd always make sure to mention how important it was to not spend too much time over a few lines of Gemara.

"This is not the way a person becomes a *talmid chacham.*"

"How then?"

"By learning entire *masechtas* and by knowing them well. By studying *Bavli* and *Yerushalmi.* You know, Binyomin," he'd reminisce in nostalgic tones, "I studied in the same class as Rav Chaim Kanievsky when we were children. While everyone else was kvetching over a *sugya,* Rav Chaim was moving rapidly through *masechta* after *masechta.* Today," he'd conclude, "all those former classmates of ours are huge *lamdanim,* but when it comes to a practical question in *hilchos Shabbos,* they wait on line to ask Rav Chaim what he thinks."

He would always use Rav Chaim Kanievsky as an example, and he made me give him my word that I'd never learn any other way. Rav Chaim Sarna's persistence was a very influential factor in my decision to study a *masechta* from start to finish. He gave me the desire to learn through *Bavli* and *Yerushalmi* and I credit him with giving me the push that I needed to turn what might have forever remained dreams into reality.

I studied the entire *Shas Yerushalmi* over a 12-year period. When I spoke at the *siyum,* I credited Rav Chaim Sarna for my achievement, stating that his continuous reiteration of the need for a Jew to study the entire Torah helped me reach my goal.

◆ ◆ ◆

Rav Yosef Lieberman, *shlita,* one of the most esteemed *poskim* in Yerushalayim today, served as another source of inspiration. Besides filling the position of rav in the Sadigura *beis medrash* on Shmuel HaNavi Street and serving as *rosh kollel* of Kollel Shomrei HaChomos, he's also the author of a vast body of halachic (11 volumes of *shailos* and *teshuvos,* at last count) and other Torah writings.

He has accomplished so much in his life, even while working as an architect in his younger years. There are quite a few larger yeshivah buildings in Yerushalayim that were designed by him.

"How were you able to accomplish so much?" I once asked him. "I mean, you've written 30 *sefarim* — *nigleh, nistar,* halachah, *aggadah* — you're a *rav* and a *rosh kollel,* and for many years you worked as a professional in the business world. How did you manage to do so, so much?"

Learning *Mishnah Berurah* with Rav Yosef Lieberman

"If you're an orderly person," he explained, "you can do anything. Even during the years when I was working as an architect, I still managed to set aside no less than eight hours a day for learning."

I still visit Rav Yosef from time to time; he is so sweet and such an extraordinary *talmid chacham* that I love spending time with him. On one occasion I happened to mention that I was currently trying to learn *Talmud Yerushalmi* on my own. He understood that I was finding it difficult. This was prior to ArtScroll's *Yerushalmi* revolution, and while everyone in the world and his brother were learning the *daf* and you could always find someone to discuss any question you had on a *sugya*, when it came to *Yerushalmi*, it was an entirely different and lonely world. You were basically on your own for the journey.

If I would have been learning it as part of a *kollel* or with a study partner, it would have been different, but since I was doing it all on my own, many were the times that I contemplated dropping out and giving up.

On every occasion that I came to visit Rav Yosef, be it on a *Chol Hamo'ed* afternoon or a *motza'ei Shabbos*, he'd always make sure to ask, "Tell me, Reb Binyomin, where are you currently holding in *Yerushalmi*?" and I always knew that the next time I came to see him, he'd be asking me the same question again. The knowledge of his expectations and pride in the goal I had undertaken gave me a boost that remained with me through a journey that felt endless at times.

There was only one time that I actually decided to close my Gemara and give up the battle. It happened while learning *maseches Kelayim*, which is one of the most difficult tractates in the *Yerushalmi*. I couldn't figure out the calculations, and I was on my own, and at some point I just said to myself, *I can't do this anymore. I'm not understanding what I'm learning and there's no point!*

I closed the Gemara, genuinely unsure whether I was going to carry on or when.

The next day everything changed.

One of my neighbors, who works for ArtScroll, "happened" to mention to me that ArtScroll had just published an edition of *Yerushalmi Kelayim*.

"Really?" I said, uncertain flutter of hope filling my heart. "You have it?"

He brought it over to my house. I opened it up to the place where I was stuck, and after learning for just a few minutes, I was able to breathe easy once again, since the ArtScroll team of outstanding *talmidei chachamim* had outdone themselves on this particular project. I was filled with newfound aspiration that I would in fact succeed in crossing the finish line after all.

◆ ◆ ◆

Right off the corner where Chazon Ish Street meets Rabbi Akiva stands an old, worn-down Bnei Brak structure typical of the style of building that was prevalent back in the country's early days. Upon ascending the ramshackle staircase and entering the building, one reaches the home of Rav Aharon Leib Shteinman, *shlita*.

The apartment is as simple a dwelling place as exists and epitomizes the Chafetz Chaim's description of one living his life as only a traveler, on his way to the World to Come. There is a *beis medrash* in the house and a kitchen that has remained unchanged for decades. I have visited Rav Aharon Leib at home on quite a few occasions, emerging inspired every time.

For a man of truly advanced age, Rav Aharon Leib still has his finger on the pulse of the nation and is visited by thousands for *berachos* or advice. One morning I was approached by an acquaintance who lives in my neighborhood, and he told me that he had a question that he wanted to ask Rav Aharon Leib. Would I be able to accompany him?

"What's going on?"

"It's like this. We lived in the States for many years, where I developed a successful business that did very well. So much so that I was able to take early retirement and move to Eretz Yisrael."

"So what happened?"

Rav Aharon Leib signing a letter of approbation

"Once we arrived in the country I began learning for half a day in one of the local *kollelim*, and I found it very enjoyable."

"Sounds good."

"It was. But after a while, I felt like I needed more. I wasn't content with half a day anymore and began feeling like I was ready to commit to a full-day *kollel* schedule."

"That's a big leap!"

"I know. That's why I want to ask Rav Aharon Leib if I should take this upon myself."

We drove to Bnei Brak, parked across the street from 5 Chazon Ish, and joined the line to see Rav Shteinman. It wasn't a long wait, and 20 minutes later I was already explaining the situation to Rav Aharon Leib.

Rav Aharon Leib listened attentively to the question of whether my neighbor should significantly expand his day of learning. Considering that Rav Shteinman is a leader of the *litvishe* Torah world, one might imagine that his immediate response to such a statement would be "Great idea! Go learn!"

That, in fact, was not the case.

Rav Shteinman looked the man up and down, taking in his demeanor and appearance.

"You're going to begin learning the whole day," he said. "How are you going to do that? Where are you going to rest when you get tired?"

"I'll put my head down on a *shtender*."

Rav Shteinman gave the man a dubious look.

"You're going to lay your head down on a *shtender*? You're coming from America, you're used to sleeping on a thick mattress, you'll be able to live like that? Are you sure about this?"

The man nodded his head emphatically.

"What are you going to eat for lunch?"

"I'll bring sandwiches with me from home."

The whole interchange between them was ironic on so many levels. Here was Rav Aharon Leib, living in a house similar to the Chafetz Chaim's abode, with no chair matching another, his bed ancient, rickety, and yet he was giving this man the third degree about his ability to live more simply, without letup or mercy!

I couldn't help but recall the story they tell about a time when a group of contractors came to see Rav Shteinman for *berachos*. They stepped into his apartment and stared in silent shock at the utter simplicity that met their eyes.

Rav Aharon Leib asked what they were staring at.

"Nothing," one of the contractors replied. "We just can't believe that this is the way the *Rosh Yeshivah* lives! We'd like to redo the *Rosh Yeshivah's* entire apartment."

"*Yesh li kol tuv.* I have everything good in the world," Rav Aharon Leib responded, seemingly unable to fathom what they wanted from him.

So on the one hand here was Rav Shteinman, a man who needs nothing, who barely eats or sleeps, but who understood exactly what sort of lifestyle his visitor was accustomed to and what he needed in order to be happy and productive!

The wealthy man remained undeterred by Rav Aharon Leib's skepticism.

"I'm ready to do everything necessary," he reassured Rav Aharon Leib. "I'll sleep on a *shtender*, eat sandwiches, and be out of the house all day. It's what I really want to do, and I'm prepared to do a little *mesirus nefesh* to further my goals."

At that point Rav Aharon Leib was ready to accept that this man was for real. He then gave him a *berachah* for much *hatzlachah* in his every endeavor.

My friend's mother passed away four years later, and he decided to commission the writing of a *sefer Torah* in her memory. Wanting to honor Rav Shteinman with the writing of a letter, we traveled to his home, *sefer Torah* in hand.

"Rosh Yeshivah," I said to Rav Aharon Leib, "I was here with this man four years ago. He came asking the Rosh Yeshivah's permission to learn full-time. The Rosh Yeshivah was apprehensive about whether he had the *kochos hanefesh* to succeed, but, *baruch Hashem*, it's four years later and he's *shteiging* away with the passion and *bren* of a young *bachur*!"

Rav Aharon Leib looked the man in the face, treated him to a warm smile, and uttered a few words: "*Anu ameilim u'mekablim sechar* — We toil in Torah and receive reward."

His smile was a thing of tremendous beauty — the pride evident on his holy visage. It was as if he were saying, "*Mein teiyere mentsch*, my dear man, you managed to do it!"

Afterword

Afterword

I n general, I have felt a sense of *siyatta d'Shmaya* at work when I accompany people to the homes of *tzaddikim* to ask for advice or *berachos*. Since most of these great men are elderly, it's not always possible to arrange the meetings in advance, especially since many of them don't even own telephones. But we'll arrive at their homes, and time after time, they'll be there waiting to see us, and we won't even have to wait.

And then there are other days, when things don't work out as planned...

♦ ♦ ♦

A religious film producer working in the secular Israeli movie world asked me to take one of her star actresses to visit various *gedolim*. The actress, who was not religious, had starred in a film about chassidim and as a result had been begun to show interest in Torah and mitzvos, and the producer felt that visits to *tzaddikim* would help bring her even closer.

The producer wanted to accompany us around the different Yerushalmi neighborhoods, but she was busy caring for her father, who was ill, and she couldn't get away. Still, she wanted the actress to check things out herself.

I spoke with the actress on the phone and was convinced that she was truly searching for something more, so I agreed to show her around, since even though her life centered around the media, you just never know...

Really wanting the visits to go smoothly, I made sure to call Rav Simcha Levin before we came to ask him what time to arrive. He was enthusiastic about the proposed visit and told me unequivocally to bring her to see him.

We arrived at Rav Simcha's home, and lo and behold, most uncharacteristically for Rav Simcha, he wasn't there, and his family had no idea when he was going to return home. We stood outside Rav Simcha's home for two hours waiting to see him, and I finally gave up when I realized that it just wasn't happening.

Clearly *Shamayim* was putting the brakes on my carefully laid plans.

I had prepared her well for the big day and told her about each and every *gadol,* and in the end we spent most of our time outside their homes. Yes, she asked me many questions in halachah and *hashkafah*, and I answered her and she learned a lot, but it was not what I'd had in mind. The conversation was productive, and yet — that's not why she had come. But clearly, that was exactly what Hashem wanted her to hear.

Out of the five people that I wanted her to meet that day, she ended up meeting a grand total of one: Rebbetzin Kupershtok.

When we arrived at the Kupershtok home, I knew that the actress was going to come dressed modestly. I had warned her before our visit of the dress code, and she passed the *tznius* test with flying colors. Truthfully, I was a little anxious and concerned whether she was ready to meet Rebbetzin Kupershtok, but this was a once-in-a-lifetime chance and sometimes you just have to go with the flow.

Trying my best to lay the groundwork for the meeting, I went so far as to call up the Rebbetzin's daughter the day before. I asked her to warn her mother that the girl I was bringing to see her was not yet religious, and that she should please go easy on her, since I doubted she was ready for a fire-and-brimstone Yerushalmi *mussar shmuess* about the evils of our times and the modern world.

The moment we entered the tiny apartment in Batei Broide and I asked the Rebbetzin where her daughter was, I knew we were in trouble.

"She went to Meron to daven."

This meant that the Rebbetzin had not been warned who she was dealing with. Not only that, since the girl had come dressed modestly, there was no way for the Rebbetzin to guess her background. At some point, when her guest picked up a piece of cake and took a bite without first making a *berachah*, Rebbetzin Kupershtok started giving it to her: "What it this? Not making a *berachah* before you eat —"

And then, "You have to marry a boy who will sit and learn Torah, not like the *chofshim* (free ones; i.e., secular Jews) —" while she had no idea that the girl sitting so demurely at her dining-room table was a "*chofshi*" actress from Tel Aviv who had no way of relating to anything she was saying!

Obviously this was what Hashem had wanted her to hear from the Rebbetzin, but how ironic this was: everything was turning out exactly the opposite of what I had planned!

◆　◆　◆

Man thinks and plans and Hashem laughs. We do what we think we are supposed to do, we try our best — and then Hashem decides what is supposed to happen. Sometimes a person comes to see a *gadol*, and it's a truly uplifting experience. At other times, the *gadol* can come down on a person like a ton of bricks and give him a *mussar shmuess* to remember for life!

At the end of the day, we should never forget that any *gadol* we visit, be it a hidden *tzaddik* or a revealed leader, is a servant of the *Ribbono shel Olam*, His messenger, merely passing on whatever we are meant to hear.

(As for the actress? The jury is still out on that case; it's taking time for her to decide what kind of life changes she's willing to make. But clearly, Hashem is the One Who decided what it was she had to hear.)

◆ ◆ ◆

On the other hand, there are other times when you see the precision and power of a visit to the *gedolim* in an undeniable fashion. There's a *yungerman* who sits alongside me at the *kollel* where I learn every morning. One day he turned to me and said, "I heard that you visit Rav Chaim on a regular basis, is that true?"

I nodded my head. "Yes."

"Is there any time in the near future when I'll be able to accompany you to see him?"

"What's the reason you want to see Rav Chaim?"

He sighed and told me that he has a 7-year-old son who was born with severe health issues. The child's legs couldn't grow properly, and this little boy had undergone many operations in his young life to try and stretch his legs and tendons and help him develop as much as possible. He was no longer an infant, but he was only able to crawl and he had the use of only one of his arms. Everything else was paralyzed. It was a heartbreaking situation, and I decided to help him see Rav Chaim as quickly as possible.

"I have to go to a *sheva berachos* in Bnei Brak this Wednesday," I told him. "I know that Rav Chaim will come to this *sheva berachos* for a short while. That's when we'll ask him for a *berachah* for you."

He thanked me profusely and the matter was decided.

I hadn't realized until we were about to leave that my friend intended on bringing his son along with us for the trip. It was no easy feat getting him into the car and settled, but the boy was scheduled for another serious operation in the coming weeks and his father wanted their *berachah* from Rav Chaim to be face-to-face.

We arrived in Bnei Brak and entered the shul where the *sheva berachos* was taking place. That was when things began to unravel. Rav Chaim was supposed to arrive at a certain time, and he was detained: a delay that turned what should have been a half-hour stay in Bnei Brak into a three-hour wait, with a 7-year-old boy in a specially designed chair who was out of his home way past his bedtime.

To complicate matters even further, word spread that Rav Chaim was going to be attending this particular *sheva berachos*, and before we knew it, hundreds of people were lined up outside the shul, waiting to see if they could ask him for a *berachah* or even just catch a glimpse of him as he entered the hall. With a crowd of this size, it was going to be almost impossible for me to get this man the attention he so desperately needed for his son.

Again, I want to point out as someone who brings people to *gedolim* on a regular basis, you try your best and hope that all goes smoothly. Sometimes it does; sometimes it doesn't.

Half an hour had become three hours.

A *sheva berachos* of 50 people had multiplied into a bona fide mob scene.

But I had promised to try, and I had no intention of giving up. When Rav Chaim finally arrived, I made sure to corner both Rav Chaim's driver and his *gabbaim*. I explained the situation, and how we had waited for three hours with a seriously ill child.

"There's no way we can possibly leave here tonight without a *berachah* from Rav Chaim," I told them urgently.

And, wonder of wonders, they agreed with me.

It was a night where no one out of the hundreds of *bachurim* crowding that street ended up receiving a *berachah*. They whisked Rav Chaim into the hall without allowing anyone to approach him and then out again and back to the car, the entire time keeping the crowd at bay.

There was, however, one exception. This man and his son. They were allowed to approach the car. The *yungerman* told Rav Chaim who he was, about his son's medical condition, and how he was scheduled for another round of surgery in the upcoming weeks. Rav Chaim listened patiently.

"*Berachah v'hatzlachah*," he said.

That was it. The audience was over.

I'm not going to deny that I was a little disappointed. I had been hoping that Rav Chaim would tell the man something out of the ordinary — something that would cheer him up and give him hope. And even though I know that a *"berachah v'hatzlachah"* from Rav Chaim is priceless, I couldn't help but wonder whether the father was disappointed.

In the end, the father thanked me for all my efforts, showing no hint of disappointment, and we went home.

That was a Wednesday night.

On Thursday the man didn't come to *kollel*, so I didn't get a chance to discuss our trip. On Sunday he arrived in the *beis medrash*, his face glowing with happiness.

"You're not going to believe this," he said to me.

I tried my best to figure out what could have occurred. His son couldn't walk, could hardly move his body, could barely talk. What could possibly have happened between the previous Wednesday and Sunday?

"You should know," he began, "that nobody had any real hopes that my son will ever walk. His disabilities are just too severe. That's not even something that we're hoping for at this point. But there's something else, another difficult challenge that faces us each and every day, and there — there, we do have some hope. I am referring to the fact that my son is 7 years old and still in diapers. You can imagine how difficult this is for our entire family.

"On Thursday," he continued, "they called me up from the school he attends every day until 3 o'clock in the afternoon to inform us that our son had just gone to the bathroom by himself! They had been working on this with him, and he wasn't responding well, but suddenly, on the very day following Rav Chaim's *berachah*, our son controlled himself and went to the bathroom — a development that will change all our lives in an unimaginable way."

You had to see the look of incredible joy that covered this father's face as he uttered these words. Almost impossible to describe, it was the look of a man who had seen a miracle and knew it.

"He did this on Shabbos, too, and so we know that it's not a one-time fluke. It's something that he is now capable of."

His eyes shone with hope and love for his son and gratefulness to the *Ribbono shel Olam* for His *chesed*, and for the messengers like Rav Chaim who have been granted the *kochos* to give *berachos* and bring about *yeshuos* to *Klal Yisrael*.

There's a point here that I want to stress. A person goes to see a *tzaddik*. He waits outside for hours, and finally, finally, manages to receive a two-word "*berachah v'hatzlachah*." Maybe he wonders, *Was it worth it?*

And then sometimes, the very next day, there's a *yeshuah*.

Because *a "berachah v'hatzlachah"* — even just a "*berachah v'hatzlachah*" — from a *gadol hador* like Rav Chaim is no simple thing. Not at all.

And you never know what will happen, in the world of the *gedolim*.

Glossary

a gute voch (Yiddish) — lit., *a good week*; traditional greeting said after Havdalah at the departure of the Sabbath.

ad meah v'esrim — lit., *till 120*; traditional blessing for long life.

aderaba (Aramaic) — to the contrary.

Afilu cherev chadah — even if a sharp sword [rests at a person's neck, he should not refrain from praying for mercy]

aggadah — homiletical, non-halachic teaching of the Sages.

agunos — lit., *chained*; women who cannot remarry because their husbands are missing or because they have not received halachic divorces.

Ah, azelecheh goldene verter fun de heiliger Rabbbeinu Yonah! (Yiddish) — Oh! Such golden words from the holy Rabbeinu Yonah!

ahavas Yisrael — love for other Jews; love of Jews.

alter Mirrer (Yiddish) — on who had studied in the Mirrer Yeshivah in pre-war Europe.

Amora'im — Sages cited in the Gemara.

Amos — cubit; a distance of 1½-2 feet.

amud — 1. lectern or podium. 2. one folio of the Talmud.

anashim achim anachnu — we are men who are brothers.

Anu ameilim u'mekablim sechar — we strive [in Torah study] and receive reward; [they strive in other pursuits and do not receive reward].

aron kodesh — holy ark in which Torah Scrolls are kept.

askan— community activist.

aveirah — sin; transgression.

avodah — 1. the service of God, whether in sacrifice, prayer, or self-refinement. 2. work, effort, service.

avodas hakodesh — holy service.

avodas Hashem — service of of Hashem.

avreich (pl. avreichim) — a young married man.

ayin hara — an evil eye.

Az mah (interrogative) — then what?; and if so?

b'chavrusa — with a study partner.

b'karov — soon.

b'lev shalem — wholeheartedly.

b'simchah — with joy and happiness.

baal (pl. baalei) chesed — one who performs acts of kindness.

baal chov — one who owes a debt.

baal ruach hakodesh — one who merits spiritual guidance.

baal teshuvah — a penitent; one who returns to mitzvah observance

baalei mussar — those who toil in the study of ethical conduct.

bachur (pl. bachurim) — young man; an unmarried young man, used to denote a student in a yeshivah.

bakar — cattle.

Barchuni L'Shalom — lit., *bless us for peace*; the third phrase of the liturgical *Shalom Aleichem* recited at the Friday night meal.

baruch Hashem — lit., *Blessed is Hashem*; an expression of appreciation of Hashem's goodness.

bas Yisrael — lit., *daughter of Israel*; a Jewish girl.

batei — the houses of ....

Bava Basra — the tractate that deals primarily with the laws of property.

Bava Kamma — the tractate that deals primarily with the laws of damages.

Bava Metzia — the tractate that deals primarily with tort law.

Bavli — lit, *Babylonian;* the Babylonian Talmud.

bayis — a house.

bedikas chametz — the search for *chametz* (leavened food) carried out on the night before Pesach.

bein hasedarim — between lectures.

beis din — a Rabbinical court.

beis din shel matah — lit., *lower court;* a Rabbinical court in this world.

beis medrash — a study hall where Torah is learned, often used as a synagogue as well.

bekius — proficiency; wide-ranging knowledge of a given subject.

ben — son.

ben bayis — a person who, though not related, is considered part of the family.

ben Torah — one who studies and observes the teachings of the Torah.

bentch (Yiddish) — 1. recite Grace after Meals. 2. to bless someone.

bentching (Yiddish) — 1. reciting Grace After Meals. 1. the text of Grace of Meals.

berachah (pl. *berachos*) — a blessing

berachah v'hatzlachah — "blessing and success."

bimah — table or platform in the synagogue from which the Torah is read.

Birkas HaTorah — blessings of the Torah, recited each morning and when one is called up during the Torah reading in the synagogue.

bitachon — lit., *trust;* trust in Hashem.

blatt — a folio page.

bli ayin hara — lit., *without the "evil eye."*

bnei Torah — those who are part of the yeshivah world.

bren — lit., *burn;* enthusiasm and fire for something.

bris (pl. *brisos*) — circumcision.

bubbe ma'aseh — nonsense; fairy tale.

chaburah — 1. a group (usually a group that studies together). 2. lecture or discourse delivered to a group.

chacham (pl. *chachamim*) — wise man.

Chachamim heim l'hara u'leheitiv lo yada'u —

"They are wise at doing evil, but know not how to do good" (*Yirmiyahu* 4:22).

chal — take effect

chalilah — heaven forbid.

chametz — leavened foods prohibited during the Passover festival.

chareidi — strictly religiously observant.

chas veshalom — Heaven forbid.

chasan — a bridegroom.

chashuve — important; prominent; renowned.

chassidishe — Hassidic.

chasunah — a wedding.

chatzos — halachic midnight.

chaveirim — devout Jews; friends.

Chavra, chavra is lei — a friend has a friend.

chavrusa — a study partner.

chavrusashaft (Yiddish) — a study partnership.

Chazal — acronym for *chachameinu zichronom livrachah,* "Our Sages of blessed memory."

cheder — school, usually an elementary school (spec. for Jewish studies)

chesed — kindness; acts of beneficence; charitable giving.

cheshbon — an accounting.

chevrah — a group.

chevrah kaddisha — burial society.

chiddush (pl. *chiddushim*) — Talmudic or halachic novellae.

chillul Shabbos — desecration of the Sabbath.

chinuch — Jewish education; the obligation for a parent to train a child to perform mitzvos.

chisaron — a failing; a flaw.

chizuk — encouragement.

Chol Hamo'ed — the intermediate days between the first and last days of Pesach and Succos.

chov — a debt.

Chovos HaLevavos — *Duties of the Heart,* a classic work of Jewish thought written by Rabbi Bachya ibn Pekudahin the 11th century.

Chumash — one of the Five Books of the Torah; the Five Books collectively.

chuppah — 1. wedding canopy. 2. the marriage ceremony.

chutz la'aretz — outside of the Land of Israel.

da'as — knowledge; full moral comprehension.

da'as Torah — Torah viewpoint; one who assesses situations solely through the perspective of Torah.

Da'as Zekeinim MiBa'alei HaTosafos — a Torah commentary by the authors of Tosafos (see Tosafos).

daf (pl. *dafim*; *dapim*) — lit., *page*; one folio of the Gemara.

daf yomi — daily study of one folio of the Gemara.

dag — a fish

dalet — a letter of the Hebrew alphabet.

dapim — see *daf*.

davka — 1. specifically. 2. spitefully.

dayan — halachic decisor or judge.

der bachur darf essen (Yiddish) — the boy needs to eat.

derashah — a Torah lecture; sermon or Torah discourse.

derech — 1. path. 2. method. 3. a way.

derech haTorah — lit., *the path of Torah*; right-eousness.

derush — homiletic interpretation.

devarim beteilim — an activity or discussion that is frivolous or unimportant.

dikduk — Hebrew grammar.

din — (Jewish) law

dirah — an apartment.

divrei Torah — short speeches on Torah topics.

dos gefelt mir nisht (Yiddish) — this doesn't please me.

dos is in ayer zechus (Yiddish) — this is in your merit.

ehrliche Yid (Yiddish) — an upright, honest Jew.

ehrlichkeit (Yiddish) — honesty.

ein adam koneh Torah ela balailah — a person cannot acquire Torah knowledge except [by learning] at night.

Eishes Chayil — *Mishlei* 31:10-31, traditionally recited before the Friday-night Shabbos meal.

eitzah (pl. *eitzos*) — advice.

eizeh matanah yafah! — what a beautiful gift!

el zeh abit el ani u'nicheih ruach v'chareid al devari — "but it is to this that I look: to the poor and broken-spirited person, who is zealous regarding My word" (*Yeshaya* 66:2).

emunah — faith.

emunah peshutah — simple, total faith in Hashem.

emunas chachamim — belief in the advice of Torah scholars.

erev Pesach — Passover eve.

erev Shabbos — the eve of the Sabbath; Friday.

erev Yom Tov — the eve of a holiday.

esrog — citron, one of the Four Species taken in hand during the Succos Festival.

Ess, ess, men darf haben ko'ach tzu lernen (Yiddish) — eat, eat; one must have strength to learn.

farher (Yiddish) — test or examination, generally oral, often a prerequisite for admission to a yeshivah.

frum (Yiddish) — religious; Torah observant.

gabbai (pl. *gabbaim*) (Yiddish) — synagogue sexton; personal attendant; person responsible for the proper functioning of a synagogue or other communal body.

gadol (pl. *gedolim*) — lit., *great*; a great Torah scholar; a term used to refer to a person of great stature.

gadol hador (pl. *gedolei hador*) — spiritual leader of the generation.

galus — exile; (cap.) the Diaspora.

gashmiyus — materialism; something physical.

gedolei Yisrael — outstanding Torah scholars.

geirus — conversion (to Judaism).

gemach — a free-loan society; a service providing help to those in need.

Gemara — (cap.) the Talmud. (l.c.) a volume of the Talmud.

gemilas chasadim — acts of loving-kindness.

geven (Yiddish) — had been.

gezel akum — stealing from a non-Jew.

gimmel — a letter of the Hebrew alphabet/

goral — lottery; throwing of lots.

gut Shabbos (Yiddish) — Sabbath greeting: "have a good Sabbath."

hachnasas kallah — sponsoring a bride with items or money she needs in order to marry.

hachnasas sefer Torah — the joyous ceremony in which a new Torah Scroll is first brought to a synagogue.

hadras panim — a shining countenance.

hagaon hagadol — the great sage.

Hakadosh Baruch Hu — The Holy One, Blessed Is He (i.e., Hashem).

hakaras hatov — gratitude; expressing gratitude.

hakodesh — the holy.

HaMapil — a prayer said just before going to sleep.

hanefesh — the soul.

hanhagos — customs; manners of behavior.

Hashem — lit., *the Name*; a respectful way to refer to G-d.

Hashem menas chelki v'chosi attah tomich gorali — "Hashem is my allotted portion and my share, You guide my destiny" (*Tehillim* 16:5).

Hashem ya'azor — Hashem will help.

hashgachah — (l.c.) rabbinic supervision; (cap.) Divine Providence.

hashgachah pratis — Divine Providence.

hashkafah — outlook; ideology; worldview; perspective.

haskamah — agreement; written approbation for a Torah work.

hasmadah — diligence in learning

hatov v'hameitiv — Who is good and Who does good (Hashem); a blessing recited upon learning of good tidings.

hatzlachah — success.

he'aros — comments.

heilige (Yiddish) — holy.

heilige Bashefer (Yiddish) — the holy Creator.

hertz zich ein (Yiddish) — listen; pay attention.

hesped — a eulogy.

hester — literally, *hidden;* referring to when God hides His countenance

heterim — permissions; questionable halachic leniencies.

hilchos — the laws of ....

hishtadlus — one's own efforts.

hodayah — thanksgiving.

Iggeres — a letter.

Iggeres HaRamban — "The Letter of the Ramban," a letter containing moral advice, written by the Ramban.

kabbalah — (u.c.) the body of Jewish mystical teachings. (l.c.) lit., *acceptance*; the

act of taking on a specific action to elevate oneself spiritually; an obligation taken upon oneself.

kabbalas haTorah — receiving the Torah at Mount Sinai.

Kabbalas Shabbos — the traditional prayer recited at the beginning of the Sabbath service on Friday evening.

Kal va'chomer — logical deduction; an *a fortiori* argument; one of the thirteen principles of Biblical hermeneutics.

kallah — a bride; an engaged girl.

kapote — a frock.

kasha — a question.

Kavata itim laTorah — "Did you set aside times for Torah study?" the second question one who has passed away is asked by the Heavenly tribunal.

kavod — honor; respect.

kavod haTorah — the honor and respect due to the Torah.

kedushah — holiness

kehillah — a congregation; a community.

Kelayim — the tractate that deals with the laws of forbidden mixtures of seeds, animals, and cloths.

Kesef mina lan — from where will we get the money?; a play on the words of a Talmudic question

kesher — a connection; a bond.

Kesubos — the tractate dealing primarily with marriage obligations and the marriage contract.

Ketzos, Ketzos Hachoshen — a commentary on *Shulchan Aruch Choshen Mishpat,* the section of the Code of Jewish Law dealing with financial matters.

kever (pl. *kevarim*) — a grave.

kevius — set schedule; permanence.

kiddush — the blessing over wine recited at the evening and morning meals on Shabbos and Yom Tov; a reception after Sabbath morning prayers at which *Kiddush* is recited and refreshments are served.

kiddushin — part of the marriage ceremony.

kinderlach (Yiddish) — an affectionate term for children.

kisufa (Aramaic) — embarrassment.

kivrei — the graves of ....

Klal Yisrael — the Jewish nation.

kochos — strengths; abilities.

kodesh hakodashim — Holy of Holies; the inner chamber of the Sanctuary.

Koheles — *Ecclesiastes.*

kollel (pl. *kollelim*) — an academy of higher Jewish study, usually for married men.

krias hashem — the honor of calling out the baby's name during the *bris* ceremony.

kuntras — a pamphlet.

kvitlach — written petitions for help or spiritual guidance.

l'ilui nishmas; l'iluy nishmaso — to provide merit to the soul of ....

lamdanim — analytic Talmudic scholars.

Lamed vav tzaddik (pl. *tzaddikim*) — one of the thirty-six righteous persons upon whose merit the world exists.

lashon hara — lit., *evil speech*; derogatory speech; slander; gossip; harmful speech.

leidah kalah — an easy birth.

leishev ba'succah — lit., *to sit in the succah*; the blessing recited upon fulfilling the mitzvah of succah.

levayah — a funeral.

limud — Torah learning; subject.

litvish — lit., *Lithuanian*; adjective describing non-chassidic Jews of Eastern European extraction; yeshivos that follow the traditions of the Lithuanian yeshivos of pre-war Europe.

litvishe — following the litvish tradition.

Lo karah klum — "nothing happened."

lulav (pl. *lulavim*) — a palm branch, one of the Four Species taken in hand on Succos.

Ma'ariv — the evening prayer service

ma'asim b'chol yom — daily occurrences.

machleket yoldot — maternity ward

maftir — the last segment of the Torah reading on Shabbos and Yom Tov; the honor of being called to the Torah for the reading of that portion.

maggid — speaker or lecturer who uses stories to teach moral lessons.

maggid shiur (pl. *maggidei shiur*) — a lecturer.

makpid — exacting; stringent; punctilious.

malchus — kingship; royalty.

mamesh — literally.

marbitz Torah — one who disseminates Torah

Masechta, maseches — tractate of Mishnah or Talmud.

mashal (pl. *meshalim*) — a parable.

mashgiach (pl. *mashgichim*) — 1. (cap.) dean of students in a yeshiva who oversees students' spiritual and ethical development. 2. kashrut supervisor.

masmid (pl. *masmidim*) — an exceptionally diligent person.

matanos l'evyonim — gifts to the poor mandated to be given on Purim.

matzliach — successful.

mazel — good fortune.

mechallel Shabbos — one who desecrates the Sabbath.

mechanech (pl. *mechanchim*) — an educator.

mechazeik — to strengthen; to encourage.

mechilah — forgiveness.

mechutan — one's child's father-in-law; a relative through marriage

mefurishe — something that is clearly stated in ....

mehudar — beautiful, of higher halachic quality.

mekabel tumah — subject to being contaminated by tumah (ritual impurity).

mekubal (pl. *mekubalim*) — a Kabbalist.

melamed — a teacher, esp. of young children.

mem — a letter of the Hebrew alphabet.

Men darf teshuvah tun — we must already repent.

Men darf unton de kapote — we must don our frock.

menachem aveil — to comfort a mourner; to pay a condolence call

Menachos — the tractate that deals with the laws of offerings of flour and other produce.

mentsch (Yiddish) — lit., *man*; connotes a person who exemplifies integrity, respect, and kindness.

mesader kiddushin — the one who officiates at the marriage ceremony.

Mesilas Yesharim — *The Way of the Upright,* a classic work of Jewish thought and ethics, authored by Rabbi Moshe Chaim Luzzatto in the 18th century.

mesiras nefesh — self-sacrifice; total and unlimited devotion.

mesirus — devotion.

mesivta — yeshivah high school.

mesorah — Jewish heritage; the received tradition; tradition.

mevatel — to nullify oneself.

mezonos — sustenance; the blessing made on certain foods made of grain.

Mi Shebeirach — a prayer invoking Heavenly blessings.

middos harachamim — Hashem's various attributes of mercy.

midrashim — homiletic teachings of the Sages.

mikveh — ritual bath.

mili dikedushah — holy words.

min haShamayim — (decreed) from Heaven.

Minchah — the afternoon prayer service

Minchas Chinuch — a classic, complex work analyzing the 613 commandments. It was authored by Rabbo Yosef Babad in the 19th century.

minhag (pl. *minhagim*) — custom.

minyan (pl. *minyanim*) — quorum of ten men necessary for conducting a prayer service.

mishnah (pl. *mishnayos*) — paragraph of the Mishnah; (cap.) teachings of the Tannaim that form the basis of the Talmud, the Oral Torah.

mishpachah — family

mochel — to forgive.

Modeh Ani — "I admit in front of You"; prayer upon awakening in the morning, expressing gratitude for life.

moradige — awe-inspiring.

motza'ei Shabbos — Saturday night; the time of the departure of the Sabbath.

muktzeh — an object that may not be handled on Shabbos.

mussar — ethical teachings geared toward self-refinement; reproof.

mussar seder — a time set aside for the study of ethical teachings.

mussar shmuess — lecture on self-refinement.

Nedarim — the tractate that deals with the laws of vows.

nefesh — the soul; the spirit.

nein (Yiddish) — no.

neitz — sunrise, the most preferable time to recite *Shemoneh Esrei* during the morning prayer service.

ner tamid — a candle or light that is kept burning permanently, especially in a shul.

nes galui — an open miracle.

neshamah (pl. *neshamos*) — the soul.

niftar (m.) *nifteres* (f.) — (n.) a person who has died. (v.) died.

niggun (pl. *niggunim*) — tune; Jewish tunes or melodies, often sung during special occasions.

nigleh — revealed; the portions of the Torah studied by all.

nistar — hidden; the esoteric portions of the Torah.

nisyonos — tests, esp. spiritual tests.

Nu (interjection) — well?

nusach —1. style of prayer service. 2. melody used during a prayer service.

Olam HaEmes — lit., *the World of Truth;* i.e., the World to Come.

olei regalim — those who, when the Temple stood, make the pilgrimage to Jerusalem to celebrate Passover, Shavuos, and Succos.

Orach Chaim — the section of the Code of Jewish Law that addresses the laws that apply every day, on Shabbos, and on Yom Tov.

otzer hasefarim — a library; esp. one housing Torah works.

oveid Hashem (pl. *ovdei Hashem*) — a servant of G-d.

panim — face; faces.

parashah (pl. *parashiyos*) — the weekly Torah portion; parchment inscribed with Torah paragraphs and inserted into *tefillin;* the parchment scroll of a *mezuzah.*

parnassah — livelihood.

pashut — simple; obvious.

pasken — (n.) a halachic ruling; (v.) to render a halachic ruling.

pasuk (pl. *pesukim*) — Scriptural verses.

pasul — invalid; inadequate.

patch (Yiddish) — a slap.

perek (pl. *perakim*) — a chapter.

peritzus — immodesty.

petirah — lit., *departure;* death; the moment of death.

peyos — sideburns or side curls, worn by Orthodox Jewish males.

Pitum HaKetores — a passage from the Mishnah, recited in the daily prayers, describing the components of the Temple's Incense Offering

posek (pl. *poskim*) — a halachic authority.

posek hador — the supreme halachic authority of a generation.

psak — a halachic ruling.

*punktlach (*Yiddish) — exactly.

pushka (Yiddish) — a charity collection box.

ra'ayah she'ein aleha teshuvah — irrefutable proof.

Rabban shel Kol Bnei HaGolah — lit., *the teacher of all those in the Diaspora*; an honorific title referring to the leader of the generation.

rabbanim — rabbis.

Rabbanit — Rebbetzin; wife of the Rabbi.

Rabbosai — lit., *gentlemen*, a polite term of address.

rachamim — mercy; pity.

Rachmaneh litzlan — G-d forbid.

Ramban — Nachmanides

rasha — an evil-doer; a wicked individual.

Rashi — acronym for Rabbi Shlomo Yitzchaki, 11th-century scholar who wrote the basic commentaries on the Bible and Talmud.

Rashkebahag — acronym for *Rabban shel Kol Bnei HaGolah* (see above).

rav (pl. *rabbanim*) — rabbi; a spiritual leader.

rebbe (pl. *rebbeim*) — a rav; a rabbi or teacher.

rega — a moment.

regel — lit, *foot*; one of the three Pilgrimage Festivals.

Ribbono shel Olam — lit., *Master of the World*; i.e., Hashem.

Rishon (pl. *Rishonim*) — early commentators on the Talmud, 11th-15th centuries.

rosh kollel — the dean of a kollel.

rosh yeshivah (pl. *roshei hayeshivah*) — the dean of a yeshivah; senior lecturer in a yeshivah.

roshei teivos — initial letters, often forming an acronym; abbreviation

ruach — spirit; enthusiasm.

ruach hakodesh — Divine inspiration.

S'iz duh a mezuzah! (Yiddish) — there is a *mezuzah* here!

Sach hakol — after all (is said and done).

sakanah — danger.

sandak — person who holds the baby while the *bris* is performed.

seder (pl. *sedarim*) — 1. study period. 2. study session. 3. (u.c.) Pesach-night ritual during which the Haggadah is recited. 4. set time, usually for learning. 5. any of the six Orders of the Mishnah.

seder limud — curriculum.

sefer (pl. *sefarim*) — a book, specifically a book on holy subjects or a learned topic.

Sefer Tehillim — the Book of *Psalms*.

sefer Torah (pl. *Sifrei Torah*)— a Torah Scroll.

segulah — a spiritual remedy.

sereifas chametz — burning of the chametz on the eve of Passover.

seudah (pl. *seudos*) — a meal; esp. a meal served on Shabbos or Yom Tov.

seudas hodayah — lit., *meal of thanksgiving*; a festive meal served on the occasion when one wants to give thanks to Hashem.

sha'ar — a gate.

Shabbos; Shabbos Kodesh — the Sabbath; the holy Sabbath.

Shacharis — the morning prayer service

shadchan — a matchmaker.

shadchanus — money or gift given to the shadchan.

shalom aleichem — lit., *peace be on you*; traditional greeting; (cap.) Friday evening song of welcome to the ministering angels.

shamash — attendant; sexton, personal assistant.

Shamayim — Heaven; the Heavens.

Shas — the Talmud.

Shas Bavli — the Babylonian Talmud.

Shas Yerushalmi — the Jerusalem Talmud.

she'eilah (pl. *she'eilos*) — question, esp. a question asked of a rabbinical authority regarding a halachic issue

she'eino yodei'a lishol — lit., *one who does not know how to ask;* one of the Four Sons mentioned in the Passover Haggadah.

Shechinah — Divine Presence; the spirit of the Omnipresent manifested on earth.

Shema Yisrael —"Hear O Israel"; this prayer, recited twice daily, expresses the essence of Jewish faith.

shemiras einayim — guarding oneself against improper sights.

shemiras halashon — guarding against improper speech, such as gossip, slander, and other forms of forbidden speech.

shemiras Shabbos — Sabbath observance.

Shemoneh Esrei — lit., *18*; the prayer, originally eighteen blessings but now nineteen, that forms the central core of each weekday prayer service

sheva berachos — 1. the seven blessings recited at a wedding. 2. the week-long festivities following a wedding. 3. festive meals, celebrated during the week after a wedding, at which the seven blessings are recited. 4. the seven blessings recited under the *chuppah*.

shidduch (pl. *shidduchim*) — 1. match, esp. a marriage match. 2. a proposed marriage match.

shiluach hakein — the mitzvah of sending away the mother bird before taking her eggs.

Shir HaShirim — *Song of Songs*.

shiur (pl. *shiurim*) — 1. a Torah lecture. 2. the required amount (e.g., of eating forbidden food to be considered a punishable act). 3. halachic amount.

shiur klali — a "general" lecture; i.e, one attended by students of various levels (not just one grade level) in a yeshivah.

shivah — lit., *seven*; the seven-day mourning period immediately following the death of a close relative.

Shivisi Hashem — "I place Hashem [before me always]" *(Tehillim* 16:8); the imperative to always feel that one is standing before Hashem.

Shivisi Yidden — Jews who are always cognizant that they are in the presence of Hashem.

shlita — acronym for (Hebrew) "May he live a long and good life."

shmuess (Yiddish) — discussion; mussar discourse

shomer Shabbos — one who observes the laws of Shabbos.

shteig (Yiddish) — to advance in learning.

shtender (Yiddish) — a lectern.

shtickel Torah (Yiddish) — a "piece" of Torah; a Torah thought.

shtiebel (Yiddish) — lit., *room*; a small synagogue, often situated in a house; small synagogue, used mainly by Chassidim.

shtreimel — a fur hat commonly worn by Hassidic men on the Sabbath and holidays.

shuk — marketplace.

Shulchan Aruch — Code of Jewish Law

shver — a father-in-law

siddur kiddushin — officiating at a wedding, which is considered the most prominent honor

Sifrei Torah — Torah Scrolls.

simanim — symbols; foods traditionally eaten on Rosh Hashanah because of their symbolic implications; chapters in a legal code

simchah (pl. *simchas*) — happiness, joy; a joyous occasion; a happy occasion; celebration.

simchas hachaim — joie de vivre; joy of life

siyatta d'Shmaya — Heavenly assistance; help from Hashem.

siyum (pl. *siyumim*) — celebration marking the completion of a course of Torah or Talmud study.

sofer — a religious scribe; scribe who writes religious materials such as a Torah Scroll, a *mezuzah, tefillin*, etc.

succah — the booth in which Jews are commanded to dwell during Succos.

sugya (pl. *sugyos*) (Aramaic) — a topic; conceptual unit in Talmud study; topic in Talmud.

talmid (pl. *talmidim*) — a student.

talmid chacham (pl. *talmidei chachamim*) — lit., *the student of a wise person*; a Torah scholar.

Talmud Bavli — the Babylonian Talmud.

Talmud Yerushalmi — the Jerusalem Talmud.

tam — taste; flavor.

Tanach — acronym for *Torah, Neviim, Kesuvim*; the written Torah, including the Five Books of Moses, the eight books of Prophets, and eleven books of Writings.

Tanna'im — the Sages of the Mishnah.

tefillah (pl. *tefillos*) — Jewish prayer

tefillas shav — a prayer that is in vain.

Tehillim — 1. the Book of *Psalms*. 2. (lower case) psalms.

teshuvah (pl. *teshuvot*) — 1. answer. 2. repentance. 3. rediscovery of Torah Judaism. 4. an response to a halachic query.

tikkun — rectification.

Tikkun Chatzos — prayer mourning the destruction of the Holy Temple, recited at midnight.

tisch (Yiddish) — lit., *table*; a chassidic gathering around a Hassidic Rebbe.

to'eles — *purpose.*

Tosafos — 1. critical and explanatory notes on the Talmud by French and German scholars of the 12th–14th centuries. 2. The authors of those notes, collectively.

tza'ar ba'alei chaim — the sin of causing pain to a living being.

tzaddik (pl. *tzaddikim)* — a righteous person.

tzaros — problems; difficult, painful situations.

tzedakah — charity.

tzidkus — righteousness.

tznius — modesty standard in speech, behavior, and dress.

vasikin — 1. the Shacharis service performed at the earliest possible time. 2. those who pray Shacharis at the earliest possible time.

vort — 1. a Torah thought. 2. an engagement celebration.

yachid b'doro — one who is unique in his generation.

yahrtzeit (Yiddish) — the anniversary of a death.

yasher ko'ach — idiom expressing gratitude.

Yedid Nefesh — lit., *beloved of the soul*; a liturgical song that begins with these words.

Yehi Ratzon — May it be His will.

yehi zichro baruch — may his memory be for a blessing

Yerushalayim shel Ma'alah — the Heavenly Jerusalem.

yeshivah (pl. yeshivos) — a school of Jewish studies a Torah academy.

yeshivah bachur — a boy who attends a yeshivah.

yeshivah ketanah — an elementary school.

yeshuah — help; rescue; remedy.

yetzer hara — evil inclination; the negative impulse to behave contrary to the Torah's commandments

Yevamos — the tractate that deals with the laws of levirate marriage.

Yiddishkeit (Yiddish) — Judaism; the Jewish way of life.

yiheyeh b'seder — it will all work out.

Yiras Shamayim — lit., *fear of Heaven*; connotes reverence for G-d, an all-pervasive attitude of piety.

yishuv hada'as — calmness.

yissurim — pains; suffering.

Yom Tov — a Jewish holiday; a Festival

yud — a letter of the Hebrew alphabet.

yungerman (pl. *yungerleit*) (Yiddish) — young married man, usually referring to one studying in a yeshivah or kollel.

zechus — merit; merit; privilege.

zeide (Yiddish) — grandfather.

zeman (pl. *zemanim*) — time; period; semester.

zemer (pl. *zemiros*) — song, esp. one sung at Shabbos and festive meals.

zerizus — enthusiasm; urgency.

Zevachim — the tractate that deals with the laws of animal offerings.

zimun — lit., *invitation*; the brief introduction to Grace After Meals recited when at least 3 adult males are present.

zt"l — acronym for *zecher tzaddik l'verachah*, may the righteous person be remembered as a blessing.